Engineering Autonomous Vehicles and Robots

Engineering Autonomous Vehicles and Robots

The DragonFly Modular-based Approach

Shaoshan Liu
PerceptIn
Fremont, CA
USA

Registered Offices
John Wiley & Sons, Inc., 111 River Street, Hoboken, NJ 07030, USA
John Wiley & Sons Ltd, The Atrium, Southern Gate, Chichester, West Sussex, PO19 8SQ, UK

Editorial Office
The Atrium, Southern Gate, Chichester, West Sussex, PO19 8SQ, UK

For details of our global editorial offices, customer services, and more information about Wiley products visit us at www.wiley.com.

Wiley also publishes its books in a variety of electronic formats and by print-on-demand. Some content that appears in standard print versions of this book may not be available in other formats.

Library of Congress Cataloging-in-Publication Data

Names: Liu, Shaoshan, author.
Title: Engineering autonomous vehicles and robots : the DragonFly
   modular-based approach / Shaoshan Liu.
Description: First edition. | Hoboken : Wiley-IEEE Press, 2020. | Includes
   bibliographical references and index.
Identifiers: LCCN 2019058288 (print) | LCCN 2019058289 (ebook) | ISBN
   9781119570561 (hardback) | ISBN 9781119570554 (adobe pdf) | ISBN
   9781119570547 (epub)
Subjects: LCSH: Automated vehicles. | Mobile robots.
Classification: LCC TL152.8 .L585 2020 (print) | LCC TL152.8 (ebook) |
   DDC 629.04/6–dc23
LC record available at https://lccn.loc.gov/2019058288
LC ebook record available at https://lccn.loc.gov/2019058289

Cover Design: Wiley
Cover Images: Courtesy of Shaoshan Liu; Background © Chainarong Prasertthai/Getty Images

Set in 9.5/12.5pt STIXTwoText by SPi Global, Chennai, India

Printed and bound by CPI Group (UK) Ltd, Croydon, CR0 4YY

10 9 8 7 6 5 4 3 2 1

Contents

1

Affordable and Reliable Autonomous Driving Through Modular Design

1.1 Introduction

In recent years, autonomous driving has become quite a popular topic in the research community as well as in industry, and even in the press, but besides the fact that it is exciting and revolutionary, why should we deploy autonomous vehicles? One reason is that ridesharing using clean-energy autonomous vehicles will completely revolutionize the transportation industry by reducing pollution and traffic problems, by improving safety, and by making our economy more efficient.

More specifically and starting with pollution reduction: there are about 260 million cars in the US today. If we were to convert all cars to clean-energy cars, we would reduce annual carbon emissions by 800 million tons, which would account for 13.3% of the US commitment to the Paris Agreement [1]. Also, with near-perfect scheduling, if ridesharing autonomous vehicles could be deployed, the number of cars could be reduced by 75% [2]. Consequently, these two changes combined have the potential to yield an annual reduction of 1 billion tons in carbon emission, an amount roughly equivalent to 20% of the US Commitment to the Paris Agreement.

As for safety improvement, human drivers have a crash rate of 4.2 accidents per million miles (PMM), while the current autonomous vehicle crash rate is 3.2 crashes PMM [3]. Yet, as the safety of autonomous vehicles continues to improve, if the autonomous vehicle crash rate PMM can be made to drop below 1, a whopping 30 000 lives could be saved annually in the US alone [4].

Lastly, consider the impact on the economy. Each ton of carbon emission has around a $220 impact on the US GDP. This means that $220 B could be saved annually by converting all vehicles to ride-sharing clean-energy autonomous vehicles [5]. Also, since the average cost per crash is about $30 000 in the US, by dropping the autonomous vehicle crash rate PMM to below 1, we could achieve another annual cost reduction of $300 B [6]. Therefore, in the US alone, the universal adoption of ride-sharing clean-energy autonomous vehicles could save as much as $520 B annually, which almost ties with the GDP of Sweden, one of the world's largest economies.

Nonetheless, the large-scale adoption of autonomous driving vehicles is now meeting with several barriers, including reliability, ethical and legal considerations, and, not least of

Engineering Autonomous Vehicles and Robots: The DragonFly Modular-based Approach,
First Edition. Shaoshan Liu.
© 2020 John Wiley & Sons Ltd. Published 2020 by John Wiley & Sons Ltd.

which, affordability. What are the problems behind the building and deploying of autonomous vehicles and how can we solve them? Answering these questions demands that we first look at the underlying design.

1.2 High Cost of Autonomous Driving Technologies

In this section we break down the costs of existing autonomous driving systems, and demonstrate that the high costs of sensors, computing systems, and High-Definition (HD) maps are the major barriers of autonomous driving deployment [7] (Figure 1.1).

1.2.1 Sensing

The typical sensors used in autonomous driving include Global Navigation Satellite System (GNSS), Light Detection and Ranging (LiDAR), cameras, radar and sonar: *GNSS receivers*, especially those with real-time kinematic (RTK) capabilities, help autonomous vehicles localize themselves by updating global positions with at least meter-level accuracy. A high-end GNSS receiver for autonomous driving could cost well over $10 000.

LiDAR is normally used for the creation of HD maps, real-time localization, as well as obstacle avoidance. LiDAR works by bouncing a laser beam off of surfaces and measuring the reflection time to determine distance. LiDAR units suffer from two problems: first, they are extremely expensive (an autonomous driving grade LiDAR could cost over $80 000); secondly, they may not provide accurate measurements under bad weather conditions, such as heavy rain or fog.

Cameras are mostly used for object recognition and tracking tasks, such as lane detection, traffic light detection, and pedestrian detection. Existing implementations usually mount multiple cameras around the vehicle to detect, recognize, and track objects. However, an important drawback of camera sensors is that the data they provide may not be reliable

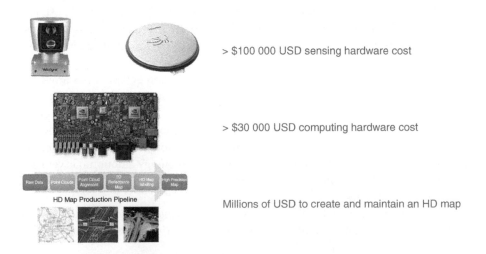

Figure 1.1 Cost breakdown of existing autonomous driving solutions.

under bad weather conditions and that their sheer amount creates high computational demands. Note that these cameras usually run at 60 Hz, and, when combined, can generate over 1 GB of raw data per second.

Radar and sonar: The radar and sonar subsystems are used as the last line of defense in obstacle avoidance. The data generated by radar and sonar show the distance from the nearest object in front of the vehicle's path. Note that a major advantage of radar is that it works under all weather conditions. Sonar usually covers a range of 0–10 m whereas radar covers a range of 3–150 m. Combined, these sensors cost less than $5000.

1.2.2 HD Map Creation and Maintenance

Traditional digital maps are usually generated from satellite imagery and have meter-level accuracy. Although this accuracy is sufficient for human drivers, autonomous vehicles demand maps with higher accuracy for lane-level information. Therefore, HD maps are needed for autonomous driving.

Just as with traditional digital maps, HD maps have many layers of information. At the bottom layer, instead of using satellite imagery, a grid map is generated by raw LiDAR data, with a grid granularity of about 5 cm by 5 cm. This grid basically records elevation and reflection information of the environment in each cell. As the autonomous vehicles are moving and collecting new LiDAR scans, they perform self-localization by performing a real time comparison of the new LiDAR scans against the grid map with initial position estimates provided by GNSS [8].

On top of the grid layer, there are several layers of semantic information. For instance, lane information is added to the grid map to allow autonomous vehicles to determine whether they are on the correct lane when moving. On top of the lane information, traffic sign labels are added to notify the autonomous vehicles of the local speed limit, whether traffic lights are nearby, etc. This gives an additional layer of protection in case the sensors on the autonomous vehicles fail to catch the signs.

Traditional digital maps have a refresh cycle of 6–12 months. However, to make sure the HD maps contain the most up-to-date information, the refresh cycle for HD maps should be shortened to no more than one week. As a result, operating, generating, and maintaining HD maps can cost upwards of millions of dollars per year for a mid-size city.

1.2.3 Computing Systems

The planning and control algorithms and the object recognition and tracking algorithms have very different behavioral characteristics which call for different kinds of processors. HD maps, on the other hand, stress the memory [9]. Therefore, it is imperative to design a computing hardware system which addresses these demands, all within limited computing resources and power budget. For instance, as indicated in [9], an early design of an autonomous driving computing system was equipped with an Intel® Xeon E5 processor and four to eight Nvidia® K80 graphics processing unit (GPU) accelerators, connected with a Peripheral Component Interconnect-E (PCI-E) bus. At its peak, the whole system, while capable of delivering 64.5 Tera Operations Per Second (TOPS), consumed about 3000 W, consequently generating an enormous amount of heat. Also, at a cost of $30 000, the whole solution would be unaffordable (and unacceptable) to the average consumer.

1.3 Achieving Affordability and Reliability

Many major autonomous driving companies, such as Waymo, Baidu, and Uber, and several others are engaged in a competition to design and deploy the ultimate ubiquitous autonomous vehicle which can operate reliably and affordably, even in the most extreme environments. Yet, we have just seen that the cost for all sensors could be over $100 000, with the cost for the computing system another $30 000, resulting in an extremely high cost for each vehicle: a demo autonomous vehicle can easily cost over $800 000 [10]. Further, beyond the unit cost, it is still unclear how the operational costs for HD map creation and maintenance will be covered.

In addition, even with the most advanced sensors, having autonomous vehicles coexist with human-driven vehicles in complex traffic conditions remains a dicey proposition. As a result, unless we can significantly drop the costs of sensors, computing systems, and HD maps, as well as dramatically improve localization, perception, and decision-making algorithms in the next few years, autonomous driving will not be universally adopted.

Addressing these problems, a reliable autonomous vehicle has been developed by us and for low-speed scenarios, such as university campuses, industrial parks, and areas with limited traffic [11,12]. This approach starts with low speed to ensure safety, thus allowing immediate deployment. Then, with technology improvements and with the benefit of accumulated experience, high-speed scenarios will be envisioned, ultimately having the vehicle's performance equal that of a human driver in any driving scenario. The keys to enable affordability and reliability include using sensor fusion, modular design, and high-precision visual maps (HPVMs).

1.3.1 Sensor Fusion

Using LiDAR for localization or perception is extremely expensive and may not be reliable. To achieve affordability and reliability, multiple affordable sensors (cameras, GNSS receivers, wheel encoders, radars, and sonars) can be used to synergistically fuse their data. Not only do these sensors each have their own characteristics, drawbacks, and advantages but they complement each other such that when one fails or otherwise malfunctions, others can immediately take over to ensure system reliability. With this sensor fusion approach, sensor costs are limited to under $2000.

The localization subsystem relies on GNSS receivers to provide an initial localization with sub-meter-level accuracy. Visual odometry can further improve the localization accuracy down to the decimeter level. In addition, wheel encoders can be used to track the vehicles' movements in case of GNSS receiver and camera failures. Note that visual odometry deduces position changes by examining the overlaps between two frames. However, when a sudden motion is applied to the vehicle, such as a sharp turn, it is possible that visual odometry will fail to maintain localization due to the lack of overlapping regions between two consecutive frames.

The active perception subsystem seeks to assist the vehicle in understanding its environment. Based on this understanding and a combination of computer vision and of millimeter wave (mmWave) radars to detect and track static or moving objects within a 50 m range, the vehicle can make action decisions to ensure a smooth and safe trip. With stereo vision, not only can objects including pedestrians and moving vehicles be easily recognized but the distance to these detected objects can be accurately pinpointed as well. In addition, mmWave radars can also detect and track fast-moving objects and their distances under all weather conditions.

The passive perception subsystem aims to detect any immediate danger and acts as the last line of defense of the vehicle. It covers the near field, i.e. a range of 0–5 m around the vehicle. This is achieved by a combination of mmWave radars and sonars. Radars are very good moving object detectors and sonars are very good static object detectors. Depending on the current vehicle speed, when something is detected within the near field, different policies are put into place to ensure the safety of the vehicle.

1.3.2 Modular Design

In the recent past, designs of autonomous driving computing systems have tended to be costly but affordable computing solutions are possible [9]. This has been made possible by the application of modular design principles which push computing to the sensor end so as to reduce the computing demands on the main computing units. Indeed, a quad-camera module such as the DragonFly sensor module [11] alone can generate image data at a rate of 400 Mbps. If all the sensor data were transferred to the main computing unit, it would require this computing unit to be extremely complex, with many consequences in terms of reliability, power, cost, etc.

Our approach is more practical: it entails breaking the functional units into modules and having each module perform as much computing as possible. This makes for a reduction in the burden on the main computing system and a simplification in its design, with consequently higher reliability. More specifically, a GPU SoM (System on Module) is embedded into the DragonFly module to extract features from the raw images. Then, only the extracted features are sent to the main computing unit, reducing the data transfer rate a 1000-fold. Applying the same design principles to the GNSS receiver subsystem and the radar subsystem reduces the cost of the whole computing system to less than $2000.

1.3.3 Extending Existing Digital Maps

Creating and maintaining HD maps is another important component of deployment costs. Crowd-sourcing the data for creating HD maps has been proposed. However, this would require vehicles with LiDAR units, and we have already seen that LiDARs are extremely expensive and thus not ready for large-scale deployment. On the other hand, crowd-sourcing visual data is a very practical solution as many cars today are already equipped with cameras.

Hence, instead of building HD maps from scratch, our philosophy is to enhance existing digital maps with visual information to achieve decimeter-level accuracy. These are called HPVMs. To effectively help with vehicle localization, HPVMs consists of multiple layers:

1. The bottom layer can be any of the existing digital maps, such as Open Street Map; this bottom layer has a resolution of about 1 m.
2. The second layer is the ground feature layer. It records the visual features from the road surfaces to improve mapping resolution to the decimeter level. The ground feature layer is particularly useful when in crowded city environments where the surroundings are filled with other vehicles and pedestrians.
3. The third layer is the spatial feature layer, which records the visual features from the environments; this provides more visual features compared with the ground feature layer. It also has a mapping resolution at the decimeter level. The spatial feature layer is particularly useful in less-crowded open environments such as the countryside.
4. The fourth layer is the semantic layer, which contains lane labels, traffic light and traffic sign labels, etc. The semantic layer aids vehicles in making planning decisions such as routing.

1.4 Modular Design

Before we go into the details of the rest of this book, let us briefly go over the modular design methodology and introduce each module. Hopefully with this introduction, readers will be able to easily follow the contents of this book.

Figure 1.2 shows a DragonFly Pod [13], a low-speed autonomous passenger pod built utilizing the modular design methodology described in this book. This vehicle consists of multiple components, a RTK GNSS module for localization, a DragonFly computer vision module for localization (using visual inertial odometry technology) and active perception,

Figure 1.2 Modular design of a DragonFly Pod.

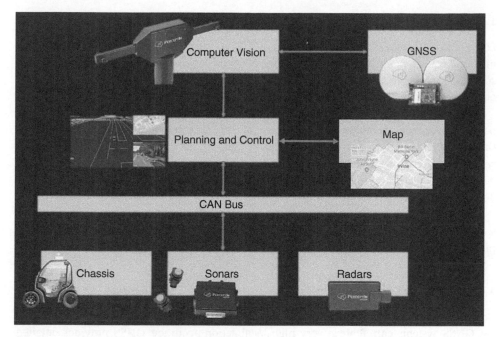

Figure 1.3 Modular design architecture.

a mmWave radar and a sonar for passive perception, a planning and control module for real-time planning, and a chassis module. Figure 1.3 shows the architecture diagram of this design and shows how the modules interact with each other.

1.4.1 Communication System

First, to connect different modules to form a working system, a reliable communication system is needed. The Controller Area Network (CAN) bus is the most widely used in-vehicle communication network today due to its simplicity, and it can be used to connect Electronic Control Units (ECUs), sensors, and other components to enable communication with each other. Before going into the details of other components, readers should first understand how the CAN bus works.

1.4.2 Chassis

The traditional vehicle chassis utilizes mechanical control, such as mechanical cables, hydraulic pressure, and other ways of providing a driver with direct, physical control over the speed or direction of a vehicle.

However, for autonomous driving to work, we need a drive-by-wire-ready chassis such that the chassis can apply electronic controls to activate the brakes, control the steering, and operate other mechanical systems. Specifically, the chassis module provides the basic application program interfaces for the planning and control module, such that the planning and control module can perform steer, throttle, and brake actions to make sure that the vehicle travels on the planned trajectory.

1.4.3   mmWave Radar and Sonar for Passive Perception

For mid-range obstacle detection, we can apply 77 GHz mmWave radar such that the planning and control module can make decisions when obstacles are detected. Similarly, sonars cover near-range obstacles and act as the very last line of defense; once sonars detect an obstacle, they directly signal the chassis to stop to minimize risks of an accident.

mmWave radar and sonar sensors can be combined and used for passive perception. By passive perception, we mean that when obstacles are detected, the raw data are not fed to the planning and control module for decision making. Instead, the raw data are directly sent to the chassis through the CAN bus for quick decision making. In this case, a simple decision module is implemented in the chassis to stop the vehicle when an obstacle is detected within a short range.

The main reason for this design is that when obstacles are detected in close range, we want to stop the vehicle as soon as possible instead of going through the complete decision pipeline. This is the best way to guarantee the safety of passengers as well as pedestrians.

1.4.4   GNSS for Localization

The GNSS system is a natural choice for vehicle localization, especially with RTK capability, GNSS systems can achieve very high localization accuracy. GNSS provides detailed localization information such as latitude, longitude, altitude, as well as vehicle heading. Nonetheless, GNSS accuracy suffers when there are buildings and trees blocking an open sky, leading to multipath problems. Hence, we cannot solely rely on GNSS for localization.

1.4.5   Computer Vision for Active Perception and Localization

Computer vision can be utilized for both localization and active perception. For localization, we can rely on visual simultaneous localization and mapping (VSLAM) technologies to achieve accurate real-time vehicle locations. However, VSLAM usually suffers from cumulative errors such that the longer the distance the vehicle travels, the higher the localization error. Fortunately, by fusing VSLAM and GNSS localizations, we can achieve high accuracy under different conditions, because GNSS can be used as the group-truth data when it is not blocked, and VSLAM can provide high accuracy when GNSS is blocked.

In addition, computer vision can be used for active perception as well. Using stereo vision, we can extract spatial or depth information of different objects; using deep learning techniques, we can extract semantic information of different objects. By fusing spatial and semantic information, we can detect objects of interest, such as pedestrians and cars, as well as getting their distance to the current vehicle.

1.4.6   Planning and Control

The planning and control module receives inputs from perception and localization modules, and generates decisions in real time. Usually, different behaviors are defined for a planning and control module and under different conditions, one behavior is chosen.

A typical planning and control system has the following architecture: first, as the user enters the destination, the *routing module* checks the map for road network information and generates a route. Then the route is fed to the *behavioral planning module*, which checks the traffic rules to generate motion specifications. Next, the generated route along with motion specifications are passed down to the *motion planner*, which combines real-time perception and localization information to generate trajectories. Finally, the generated trajectories are passed down to the *control system*, which reactively corrects errors in the execution of the planned motions.

1.4.7 Mapping

A mapping module provides essential geographical information, such as lane configurations and static obstacle information, to the planning and control module. In order to generate real-time motion plans, the planning and control module can combine perception inputs, which detect dynamic obstacles in real time, localization inputs, which generate real-time vehicle poses, and mapping inputs, which capture road geometry and static obstacles.

Currently, fully autonomous vehicles use high definition 3D maps. Such high precision maps are extremely complex and contain a trillion bytes of data to represent not only lanes and roads but also semantic and locations of 3D landmarks in the real world. With HD maps, autonomous vehicles are able to localize themselves and navigate in the mapped area.

1.5 The Rest of the Book

In the previous sections we have introduced the proposed modular design approach for building autonomous vehicles and robots. In the rest of the book, we will delve into these topics, and present the details of each module as well as how to integrate these modules to enable a fully functioning autonomous vehicle or robot.

The first part of the book consists of Chapters 2–8, in which we introduce each module, including communication systems, chassis technologies, passive perception technologies, localization with RTK GNSS, computer vision for perception and localization, planning and control, as well as mapping technologies.

- Chapter 2: In-Vehicle Communication Systems
- Chapter 3: Chassis Technologies for Autonomous Robots and Vehicles
- Chapter 4: Passive Perception with Sonar and mmWave Radar
- Chapter 5: Localization with RTK GNSS
- Chapter 6: Computer Vision for Perception and Localization
- Chapter 7: Planning and Control
- Chapter 8: Mapping

The second part of the book consists of Chapters 9 and 10, in which we present two interesting case studies: the first one is about applying the modular design to build low-speed autonomous vehicles; and the second one is about how NASA builds its space robotic explorer using a modular design approach.

- Chapter 9: Building the DragonFly Pod and Bus
- Chapter 10: Enabling Commercial Autonomous Space Robotic Explorers

From our practical experiences, the capabilities of autonomous vehicles and robots are often constrained by limited onboard computing power. Therefore, in the final part of the book, we delve into state-of-the-art approaches in building edge computing systems for autonomous vehicles and robots. We will cover onboard edge computing design, vehicle-to-everything infrastructure, as well as autonomous vehicle security.

- Chapter 11: Edge Computing for Autonomous Vehicles
- Chapter 12: Innovations on the Vehicle-to-Everything Infrastructure
- Chapter 13: Vehicular Edge Security

1.6 Open Source Projects Used in this Book

As you can see, an autonomous driving system is a highly complex system that integrates many technology pieces and modules. Hence, it is infeasible and inefficient to build everything from scratch. Hence, we have referred to many open source projects throughout the book to help readers to build their own autonomous driving systems. Also, throughout the book we have used PerceptIn's autonomous driving software stack to demonstrate the idea of modular design. The open source projects used in this book are listed below:

- *CANopenNode* [14]: This is free and open source CANopen Stack is for CAN bus communication.
- *Open Source Car Control* [15]: This is an assemblage of software and hardware designs that enable computer control of modern cars in order to facilitate the development of autonomous vehicle technology. It is a modular and stable way of using software to interface with a vehicle's communications network and control systems.
- *OpenCaret* [16]: This is an open source Level-3 Highway autopilot system for Kia Soul EV.
- *NtripCaster* [17]: A GNSS NTRIP (Networked Transport of RTCM via Internet Protocol) Caster takes GNSS data from one or more data stream sources (Base Stations referred to as NTRIP Servers) and provides these data to one or more end users (often called rovers), the NTRIP Clients. If you need to send data to more than one client at a time, or have more than one data stream, you will need a Caster.
- GPSD *(GPS Daemon)* [18]: This is a service daemon that monitors one or more GNSS receivers attached to a host computer through serial or USB ports, making all data on the location/course/velocity of the sensors available to be queried on Transmission Control Protocol port 2947 of the host computer. With GPSD, multiple location-aware client applications can share access to supported sensors without contention or loss of data. Also, GPSD responds to queries with a format that is substantially easier to parse than the NMEA 0183 emitted by most GNSS receivers.

- *Kalibr* [19]: This is a toolbox that solves the following calibration problems:
  - – Multiple camera calibration: intrinsic and extrinsic calibration of a camera system with non-globally shared overlapping fields of view.
  - – Visual-inertial calibration (camera-IMU): spatial and temporal calibration of an IMU with respect to a camera system.
  - – Rolling shutter camera calibration: full intrinsic calibration (projection, distortion, and shutter parameters) of rolling shutter cameras.

- *OpenCV* [20]: OpenCV (Open Source Computer Vision Library) is an open source computer vision and machine learning software library. OpenCV was built to provide a common infrastructure for computer vision applications and to accelerate the use of machine perception in the commercial products.
- *ORB-SLAM2* [21]: This is a real-time SLAM library for Monocular, Stereo and RGB-D cameras that computes the camera trajectory and a sparse 3D reconstruction. It is able to detect loops and relocalize the camera in real time.
- *libELAS* [22]: This is a cross-platform C++ library with MATLAB wrappers for computing disparity maps of large images. Input is a rectified grayscale stereo image pair of the same size. Output is the corresponding disparity maps.
- *Mask R-CNN* [23]: This is a deep learning model for object detection and instance segmentation on Keras and TensorFlow.
- *Baidu Apollo* [24]: Apollo is a high performance, flexible architecture which accelerates the development, testing, and deployment of autonomous vehicles.
- *OpenStreetMap* [25]: This is a collaborative project to create a free editable map of the world. The geodata underlying the map are considered the primary output of the project. The creation and growth of OpenStreetMap has been motivated by restrictions on use or availability of map data across much of the world, and the advent of inexpensive portable satellite navigation devices.

References

1 U.S. Department of Energy (2017). Emissions from Hybrid and Plug-In Electric Vehicles. https://www.afdc.energy.gov/vehicles/electric_emissions.php (accessed 1 December 2017).

2 MIT CSAIL (2016). Study: carpooling apps could reduce taxi traffic 75%. https://www.csail.mit.edu/news/study-carpooling-apps-could-reduce-taxi-traffic-75 (accessed 1 December 2017).

3 VirginiaTech (2017). Automated vehicle crash rate comparison using naturalistic data. https://www.vtti.vt.edu/featured/?p=422 (accessed 1 December 2017).

4 U.S. Department of Transportation (2016). U.S. Driving Tops 3.1 Trillion Miles in 2015. https://www.fhwa.dot.gov/pressroom/fhwa1607.cfm (accessed 1 December 2017).

5 Moore, F.C. and Diaz, D.B. (2015). Temperature impacts on economic growth warrant stringent mitigation policy. *Nature Climate Change* 5 (2): 127–131.

6 New York State Department of Transportation (2016). Average Accident Costs. https://www.dot.ny.gov/divisions/operating/osss/highway-repository/39D1F023EC4400C6E0530A3DFC0700C6 (accessed 1 December 2017).

7 Liu, S., Li, L., Tang, J. et al. (2017). *Creating Autonomous Vehicle Systems*, Synthesis Lectures on Computer Science, vol. 6, 1–186. Morgan & Claypool Publishers.

8 Liu, S., Tang, J., Wang, C. et al. (2017). A unified cloud platform for autonomous driving. *Computer* (12): 42–49.

9 Liu, S., Tang, J., Zhang, Z., and Gaudiot, J.-L. (2017). Computer architectures for autonomous driving. *Computer* 50 (8): 18–25.

10 AutonomousStuff (2017). Lincoln MKZ Platform. https://autonomoustuff.com/product/lincoln-mkz (accessed 1 October 2018).

11 YouTube (2018). PerceptIn DragonFly Sensor Module https://www.youtube.com/watch?v=WQUGB-IqbgQ&feature=youtu.be (accessed 1 October 2018).

12 Vega, P. (2018). UC Irvine grad works to make a self-driving car costing under $10,000. *Los Angeles Times*. http://www.latimes.com/socal/daily-pilot/news/tn-dpt-me-driverless-cars-20180105-story.html (accessed 8 January 2018).

13 PerceptIn (2017). PerceptIn DragonFly Pod. https://www.perceptin.io/products (accessed 1 October 2019).

14 GitHub (2019). CANopenNode. https://github.com/CANopenNode/CANopenNode (accessed 1 October 2019).

15 GitHub (2019). Open Source Car Control. https://github.com/PolySync/oscc (accessed 1 October 2019).

16 GitHub (2019). OpenCaret. October 2019, https://github.com/frk2/opencaret (accessed 1 October 2019).

17 GitHub (2019). NtripCaster. https://github.com/nunojpg/ntripcaster (accessed 1 October 2019).

18 gpsd (2019). gpsd – a GPS sevice daemon. https://gpsd.gitlab.io/gpsd/index.html (accessed 1 October 2019).

19 GitHub (2019). Kalibr. https://github.com/ethz-asl/kalibr (accessed 1 October 2019).

20 OpenCV (2019). OpenCV. https://opencv.org (accessed 1 October 2019).

21 GitHub (2019). ORB-SLAM2. https://github.com/raulmur/ORB_SLAM2 (accessed 1 October 2019).

22 Geiger, A. (2019). libELAS. http://www.cvlibs.net/software/libelas (accessed 1 October 2019).

23 GitHub (2019). Mask R-CNN. https://github.com/matterport/Mask_RCNN (accessed 1 October 2019).

24 GitHub (2019). Baidu Apollo. https://github.com/ApolloAuto/apollo (accessed 1 October 2019).

25 GitHub (2019). OpenStreetMap. https://github.com/openstreetmap (accessed 1 October 2019).

2

In-Vehicle Communication Systems

2.1 Introduction

As shown in Figure 2.1, one key component in the modular design architecture is the in-vehicle communication network, which allows Electronic Control Units (ECUs), sensors, and other components to communicate with each other. Note, the Controller Area Network (CAN) bus is the most widely used in-vehicle communication network today due to its simplicity.

In this chapter, we introduce in-vehicle communication systems. We first introduce CAN bus, which is a high-integrity serial bus system for networking intelligent devices. Also, we introduce FlexRay, a deterministic, fault-tolerant, and high-speed bus system developed in conjunction with automobile manufacturers and leading suppliers; FlexRay is meant to gradually replace CAN as the default in-vehicle communication network. In addition, we introduce CANopen, a communication protocol and device profile specification for embedded systems used in automation, as well as CANopenNode, a free and open source CANopen Stack written in ANSI C in an object-oriented way. We believe this chapter will provide sufficient background for readers to understand in-vehicle communication networks.

2.2 CAN

A CAN bus is a high-integrity serial bus system for networking intelligent devices. CAN buses and devices are common components in automotive and industrial systems. Using a CAN interface device, applications can be developed to communicate with a CAN network [1,2].

In the past few decades, the need for improvements in automotive technology caused increased usage of electronic control systems for functions such as engine timing, anti-lock brake systems, and distributor-less ignition. Originally, point-to-point wiring systems connected electronic devices in vehicles. As more and more electronics in vehicles resulted in bulky wire harnesses that were heavy and expensive, point-to-point wiring was no longer scalable.

To eliminate point-to-point wiring, automotive manufacturers replaced dedicated wiring with in-vehicle networks, which reduced wiring cost, complexity, and weight. In 1985, Bosch developed the CAN, which has emerged as the standard in-vehicle network.

Engineering Autonomous Vehicles and Robots: The DragonFly Modular-based Approach, First Edition. Shaoshan Liu.
© 2020 John Wiley & Sons Ltd. Published 2020 by John Wiley & Sons Ltd.

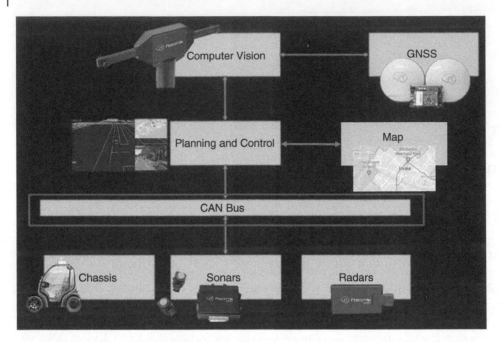

Figure 2.1 Modular design architecture.

CAN provides a cheap, durable network that allows the devices to communicate through the ECUs. CAN allows the ECUs to have one CAN interface rather than analog inputs to every device in the system. This decreases overall cost and weight in automobiles. Each of the devices on the network has a CAN controller chip and is therefore intelligent. All transmitted messages are seen by all devices on the network. Each device can decide if the message is relevant or if it can be filtered.

As CAN implementations increased in the automotive industry, CAN (high speed) was standardized internationally as ISO 11898. Later, low-speed CAN was introduced for car body electronics. Finally, single-wire CAN was introduced for some body and comfort devices. Major semiconductor manufacturers, such as Intel, Motorola, and Philips, developed CAN chips. By the mid-1990s, CAN was the basis of many industrial device networking protocols, including DeviceNet and CANOpen.

As shown in Figure 2.2, CAN specifies the media access control (MAC) and physical layer signaling (PLS) as it applies to layers 1 and 2 of the OSI model. MAC is accomplished using a technique called nondestructive bit-wise arbitration. As stations apply their unique identifiers to the network, they observe if their data are being faithfully produced.

If it is not, the station assumes that a higher priority message is being sent and, therefore, halts transmission and reverts to receiving mode. The highest priority message gets through and the lower priority messages are resent at another time. The advantage of this approach is that collisions on the network do not destroy data and eventually all stations gain access to the network. The problem with this approach is that the arbitration is done on a bit-by-bit basis requiring all stations to hear one another within a bit time (actually less than a bit time).

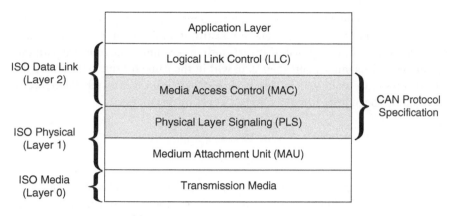

Figure 2.2 CAN protocol layers.

At a 500 kbps bit rate, a bit time is 2000 ns which does not allow much time for transceiver and cable delays. The result is that CAN networks are usually quite short and frequently less than 100 m at higher speeds. To increase this distance either the data rate is decreased or additional equipment is required.

CAN transmissions operate using the producer/consumer model. When data are transmitted by a CAN device, no other devices are addressed. Instead, the content of the message is designated by an identifier field. This identifier field, which must be unique within the network, not only provides content but the priority of the message as well. All other CAN devices listen to the sender and accept only those messages of interest.

This filtering of the data is accomplished using an acceptance filter which is an integral component of the CAN controller chip. Messages which fail the acceptance criteria are rejected. Therefore, receiving devices consume only the messages of interest from the producer. As Figure 2.3 shows, a CAN frame consists mainly of an identifier field, a control field, and a data field. The control field is 6 bits long, the data field is 0–8 bytes long and the identifier field is 11 bits long for standard frames (CAN specification 2.0A) or 29 bits long for extended frames (CAN specification 2.0B). Source and destination node addresses have no meaning using the CAN data link layer protocol.

Bus arbitration is accomplished using a nondestructive bit-wise arbitration scheme. It is possible that more than one device may begin transmitting a message at the same time. Using a "wired AND" mechanism, a dominant state (logic 0) overwrites the recessive state (logic 1). As the various transmitters send their data out on the bus, they simultaneously listen for the faithful transmission of their data on a bit-by-bit basis until it is discovered that someone's dominant bit overwrote their recessive bit. This indicates that a device with a higher priority message, one with an identifier of lower binary value, is present and the

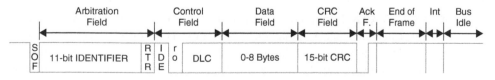

Figure 2.3 CAN message format.

loser of the arbitration immediately reverts to receiving mode and completes the reception of the message. With this approach no data are destroyed and, therefore, throughput is enhanced. The losers simply try again during their next opportunity. The problem with this scheme is that all devices must assert their data within the same bit time and before the sampling point otherwise data will be falsely received or even destroyed. Therefore, a timing constraint has been introduced that impacts cabling distance.

2.3 FlexRay

The FlexRay bus is a deterministic, fault-tolerant, and high-speed bus system developed in conjunction with automobile manufacturers and leading suppliers [3]. FlexRay delivers the error tolerance and time-determinism performance requirements for drive-by-wire applications.

Many aspects of FlexRay are designed to keep costs down while delivering top performance in a rugged environment. FlexRay uses unshielded twisted pair cabling to connect nodes together. FlexRay supports single- and dual-channel configurations which consist of one or two pairs of wires, respectively. Differential signaling on each pair of wires reduces the effects of external noise on the network without expensive shielding. Most FlexRay nodes typically also have power and ground wires available to power transceivers and microprocessors. Dual-channel configurations offer enhanced fault tolerance and/or increased bandwidth.

Most first-generation FlexRay networks only utilize one channel to keep wiring costs down but as applications increase in complexity and safety requirements, future networks will use both channels. FlexRay buses require termination at the ends, in the form of a resistor connected between the pair of signal wires. Only the end nodes on a multi-drop bus need termination. Too much or too little termination can break a FlexRay network. While specific network implementations vary, typical FlexRay networks have a cabling impedance between 80 Ω and 110Ω, and the end nodes are terminated to match this impedance. Termination is one of the most frequent causes of frustration when connecting a FlexRay node to a test setup. Modern PC-based FlexRay interfaces may contain onboard termination resistors to simplify wiring.

2.3.1 FlexRay Topology

Unlike CAN, FlexRay supports multiple topologies, including simple multi-drop passive connections as well as active star connections for more complex networks. Depending on a vehicle's layout and level of FlexRay usage, selecting the right topology helps designers optimize cost, performance, and reliability for a given design.

- *Multi-drop bus*: FlexRay is commonly used in a simple multi-drop bus topology that features a single network cable run that connects multiple ECUs together. This is the same topology used by CAN and is familiar to OEMs, making it a popular topology in first-generation FlexRay vehicles. In this topology, each ECU can "branch" up to a small distance from the core "trunk" of the bus. The ends of the network have termination resistors installed that eliminate problems with signal reflections. Because FlexRay operates at high frequencies, up to 10 Mbps compared with CAN's 1 Mbit, FlexRay designers must take care to correctly terminate and lay out networks to avoid signal integrity problems. The multi-drop format also fits nicely with vehicle harnesses that commonly share a similar type of layout, simplifying installation and reducing wiring throughout the vehicle.

- *Star network*: The FlexRay standard supports "star" configurations which consist of individual links that connect to a central active node. This node is functionally similar to a hub found in PC ethernet networks. The active star configuration makes it possible to run FlexRay networks over longer distances or to segment the network in such a way that makes it more reliable should a portion of the network fail. If one of the branches of the star is cut or shorted, the other legs continue functioning. Since long runs of wires tend to conduct more environmental noise, such as electromagnetic emissions from large electric motors, using multiple legs reduces the amount of exposed wire for a segment and can help increase noise immunity.
- *Hybrid network*: The bus and star topologies can be combined to form a hybrid topology. Future FlexRay networks will likely consist of hybrid networks to take advantage of the ease-of-use and cost advantages of the bus topology while applying the performance and reliability of star networks where needed in a vehicle.

2.3.2 The FlexRay Communication Protocol

The FlexRay communication protocol is a time-triggered protocol that provides options for deterministic data that arrive in a predictable time frame (down to the microsecond) as well as CAN-like dynamic event-driven data to handle a large variety of frames. FlexRay accomplishes this hybrid of core static frames and dynamic frames with a pre-set communication cycle that provides a predefined space for static and dynamic data. This space is configured with the network by the network designer.

While CAN nodes only need to know the correct baud rate to communicate, nodes on a FlexRay network must know how all the pieces of the network are configured in order to communicate. As with any multi-drop bus, only one node can electrically write data to the bus at a time. If two nodes were to write at the same time, you end up with contention on the bus and data become corrupt. There are a variety of schemes used to prevent contention on a bus. CAN, for example, used an arbitration scheme where nodes will yield to other nodes if they see a message with higher priority being sent on a bus. While flexible and easy to expand, this technique does not allow for very high data rates and cannot guarantee timely delivery of data.

FlexRay manages multiple nodes with a Time Division Multiple Access (TDMA) scheme. Every FlexRay node is synchronized to the same clock, and each node waits for its turn to write on the bus. Because the timing is consistent in a TDMA scheme, FlexRay is able to guarantee determinism or the consistency of data delivery to nodes on the network. This provides many advantages for systems that depend on up-to-date data between nodes. Embedded networks are different from PC-based networks in that they have a closed configuration and do not change once they are assembled in the production product. This eliminates the need for additional mechanisms to automatically discover and configure devices at run time.

Table 2.1 Comparisons between CAN and FlexRay.

	CAN	FlexRay
Bandwidth	1 Mbps	10 Mbps
Number of channels	1	2
Frame data length	0~8	0~254
Communication	Dynamic arbitration	TDMA
Complexity	Low	High
Composability	No	Yes
Flexibility	One topology	Many different topologies

By designing network configurations ahead of time, network designers save significant cost and increase reliability of the network. For a TDMA network such as FlexRay to work correctly, all nodes must be configured correctly. The FlexRay standard is adaptable to many different types of networks and allows network designers to make tradeoffs between network update speeds, deterministic data volume, and dynamic data volume among other parameters. Every FlexRay network may be different, so each node must be programmed with correct network parameters before it can participate on the bus.

Table 2.1 provides a summary of comparisons between CAN and FlexRay [4]. For the rest of this chapter, we will focus on CAN as this is still the most popular protocol today and it is simple to use.

2.4 CANopen

CANopen is a communication protocol and device profile specification for embedded systems used in automation. In terms of the OSI model (shown in Figure 2.1), CANopen implements the layers above and including the network layer. The CANopen standard consists of an addressing scheme, several small communication protocols, and an application layer defined by a device profile [5].

The CANopen communication protocol has support for network management (NMT), device monitoring, and communication between nodes, including a simple transport layer for message segmentation and desegmentation. The lower level protocol implementing the data link and physical layers is usually CAN, although devices using some other means of communication (such as Ethernet Powerlink, EtherCAT) can also implement the CANopen device profile.

The basic CANopen device and communication profiles are given in the CiA 301 specification released by CAN in Automation. Profiles for more specialized devices are built on top of this basic profile, and are specified in numerous other standards released by CAN in Automation, such as CiA 401 for I/O modules and CiA 402 for motion control.

Every CANopen device has to implement certain standard features in its controlling software. A communication unit implements the protocols for messaging with the other nodes in the network. Starting and resetting the device is controlled via a state machine. It must contain the states Initialization, Pre-operational, Operational, and Stopped.

The transitions between states are made by issuing a NMT communication object to the device. The object dictionary is an array of variables with a 16-bit index. Additionally, each variable can have an 8-bit subindex. The variables can be used to configure the device and reflect its environment, i.e. contain measurement data.

The application part of the device actually performs the desired function of the device, after the state machine is set to the operational state. The application is configured by variables in the object dictionary and the data are sent and received through the communication layer.

2.4.1 Object Dictionary

CANopen devices must maintain an object dictionary, which is used for configuration and communication with the device. An entry in the object dictionary is defined by:

- Index, the 16-bit address of the object in the dictionary.
- Object name (Object Type/Size), a symbolic type of the object in the entry, such as an array, record, or simple variable.
- Name, a string describing the entry.
- Type, this gives the datatype of the variable (or the datatype of all variables of an array).
- Attribute, which gives information on the access rights for this entry, this can be read/write, read-only, or write-only.
- The Mandatory/Optional field (M/O) defines whether a device conforming to the device specification has to implement this object or not.

The basic data types for object dictionary values such as Boolean, integers, and floats are defined in the standard (their size in bits is optionally stored in the related type definition, index range 0x0001–0x001F), as well as composite data types such as strings, arrays, and records (defined in index range 0x0040–0x025F). The composite data types can be subindexed with an 8-bit index; the value in subindex 0 of an array or record indicates the number of elements in the data structure, and is of type UNSIGNED8.

2.4.2 Profile Family

CANopen defines a standardized application for distributed industrial automation systems based on CAN. The CANopen profile family is based on a "Communication Profile," which specifies the basic communication mechanisms and on a standardized form for describing the functionality of devices.

The most important device types such as digital and analog I/O modules, drives, operating devices, sensors, or programmable controllers are described by so-called "Device Profiles." In the device profiles the functionality, parameters, and data of standard devices of the corresponding types are specified. Based on the standardized profiles, devices of different manufacturers can be accessed via the bus in exactly the same manner. Therefore devices of different manufacturers are interoperable and exchangeable.

The key element of the CANopen standard is the description of the device functionality by means of an "Object Dictionary" (OD). The object dictionary is divided into two sections. The first section contains general device information such as device identification, manufacturer name, and so on, as well as communication parameters. The second section describes the specific device functionality. A 16-bit index and an 8-bit subindex identify an entry ("object") in the object dictionary. The entries in the object dictionary provide the standardized access to the "Application Objects" of a device, such as input and output signals, device parameters, device functions, or network variables.

You can describe the functionality and characteristics of a CANopen device by means of an "Electronic Data Sheet" (EDS) using an ASCII format. An EDS must be understood as a kind of template for describing all the data and features of device as accessible from the network. The actual device settings are described by the so-called "Device Configuration File" (DCF). The EDS and DCF can be provided in the form of a data file, which can be downloaded from the Internet or stored inside the device.

2.4.3 Data Transmission and Network Management

Similar to other field bus systems, CANopen distinguishes two basic data transmission mechanisms: the access to entries of the object dictionary through "Service Data Objects" (SDOs) The exchange of process data through "Process Data Objects" (PDOs). PDOs are transmitted according to the producer–consumer principle in the form of broadcast messages and can be event-triggered, cyclically transmitted, or requested by a node without any additional protocol overhead. A PDO can be used for the transmission of a maximum of 8 data bytes.

In connection with a synchronization message ("Synchronous PDO"), the transmission as well as the acceptance of PDOs can be synchronized across the network. The mapping of application objects into the data field of a PDO is configurable through a data structure called "PDO Mapping" which is stored in the object dictionary. This allows the dynamic configuration of a device according to the specific requirements of an application.

The transmission of data via an SDO channel is performed in the form of a client–server relationship between two nodes. The addressing of an object dictionary entry is accomplished by providing the index and the subindex of the entry. Transmitted messages can be of very large length. The transmission of SDO messages of more than 8 bytes involves an additional fragmentation protocol overhead. Standardized event-triggered "Emergency Messages" of high priority are reserved to report device malfunctions. A common system time can be provided through a system time message.

NMT functions such as controlling and monitoring the communication status of the nodes are accomplished by a NMT facility. This is organized according to a logical master–slave relationship. Two mechanisms for node monitoring ("node-guarding" and "heartbeat-messaging") are provided alternatively. The assignment of CAN message identifiers to PDOs and SDOs is possible by direct modifications of identifiers in the data structure of the object dictionary or, for simple system structures, through the use of predefined identifiers. Besides device profiles, a variety of application specific profiles developed by several specific interest groups are currently available and a wide variety of manufacturers support CANopen by means of CANopen-based devices, tools for configuration, and testing as well as certified CANopen protocol stacks.

2.4.4 Communication Models

CAN bus, the data link layer of CANopen, can only transmit short packages consisting of an 11-bit identifier, a remote transmission request (RTR) bit and 0–8 bytes of data. The CANopen standard divides the 11-bit CAN frame identifier into a 4-bit function code and 7-bit CANopen node ID. This limits the number of devices in a CANopen network to 127 (0 being reserved for broadcast). An extension to the CAN bus standard (CAN 2.0 B) allows extended frame identifiers of 29 bits but in practice CANopen networks big enough to need the extended identifier range are rarely seen. In CANopen the 11-bit identifier of a CAN-frame is known as a communication object identifier, or COB-ID. In the case of a transmission collision, the bus arbitration used in the CAN bus allows the frame with the smallest identifier to be transmitted first and without a delay. Using a low code number for time critical functions ensures the lowest possible delay.

Different kinds of communication models are used in the messaging between CANopen nodes. In a master–slave relationship, one CANopen node is designated as the master, which sends or requests data from the slaves. The NMT protocol is an example of a master–slave communication model. A client–server relationship is implemented in the SDO protocol, where the SDO client sends data (the object dictionary index and subindex) to an SDO server, which replies with one or more SDO packages containing the requested data (the contents of the object dictionary at the given index). A producer–consumer model is used in the Heartbeat and Node Guarding protocols. In the push model of producer–consumer, the producer sends data to the consumer without a specific request, whereas in the pull model, the consumer has to request the data from the producer.

2.4.5 CANopenNode

CANopenNode is free and open source CANopen Stack is written in ANSI C in an object-oriented way [6]. It runs on different microcontrollers, as a standalone application, or with a real-time operating system. Stack includes master functionalities.

CANopenNode implements the following CANopen features:

- NMT slave to start, stop, reset device. Simple NMT master.
- Heartbeat producer–consumer error control.
- PDO linking and dynamic mapping for fast exchange of process variables.
- SDO expedited, segmented and block transfer for service access to all parameters.
- SDO master.
- Emergency message.
- Sync producer–consumer.
- Non-volatile storage.

CANopenNode itself does not have complete working code for any microcontroller. It is only the library with the stack and drivers for different microcontrollers. CANopenNode contains sample codes, which should compile on any system with a template driver, which actually does not access CAN hardware. CANopenNode should be used as a git submodule included in a project with specific hardware and specific application.

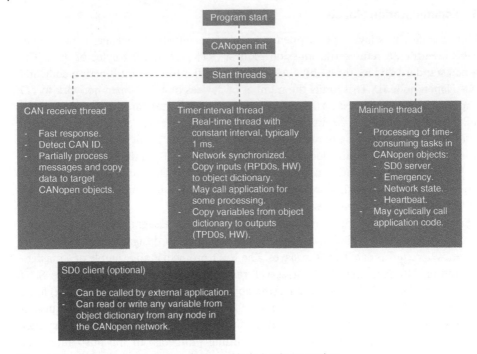

Figure 2.4 Flowchart of a typical CANopenNode implementation.

Figure 2.4 shows the flowchart of a typical CANopenNode implementation: when the program starts, it calls CANopen init, and spawns multiple threads. The CAN receive thread listens for any CAN messages and provides fast responses by processing messages and copying data to target CANopen objects. The timer interval thread is a real-time thread that wakes up every millisecond to deal with inputs to and outputs from the object dictionary. The mainline thread handles the processing of time-consuming tasks by calling the corresponding application code.

References

1 National Instruments (2017). Controller Area Network (CAN) Tutorial. http://download. ni.com/pub/devzone/tut/can_tutorial.pdf (accessed 1 October 2018).

2 Contemporary Controls (2017). CAN Tutorial. https://www.ccontrols.com/pdf/CANtutorial. pdf (accessed 1 October 2018).

3 National Instruments (2017). FlexRay Automotive Communication Bus Overview. http://www.ni.com/white-paper/3352/en (accessed 1 October 2018).

4 Forsberg, A. and Hedberg, J. (2012). Comparison of FlexRay and CAN-bus for real-time communication. *IEEE Transactions on Industrial Electronics* 58 (3).

5 CAN in Automation (2017). CANopen. https://www.can-cia.org/canopen (accessed 1 October 2019).

6 GitHub (2019). CANopenNode. https://github.com/CANopenNode/CANopenNode (accessed 1 October 2019).

3

Chassis Technologies for Autonomous Robots and Vehicles

3.1 Introduction

As shown in Figure 3.1, a chassis executes commands issued by the planning and control module, and is the "physical body" of an autonomous vehicle or robot. In this chapter we introduce chassis technologies for autonomous robots and vehicles. This chapter is divided into three parts: first, we briefly introduce the basic chassis technologies, especially drive-by-wire, required for building autonomous vehicles and robots. Drive-by-wire refers to electronic systems that replace traditional mechanical controls [1]. Instead of using cables, hydraulic pressure, and other ways of providing a driver with direct, physical control over the speed or direction of a vehicle, drive-by-wire technology uses electronic controls to activate the brakes, control the steering, and operate other mechanical systems. There are three main vehicle control systems that are commonly replaced with electronic controls: electronic throttle control, brake-by-wire, and steer-by-wire.

Secondly, we introduce two open source projects, the Open Source Car Control (OSCC) and OpenCaret [2,3]. OSCC is an assemblage of software and hardware designs that enable computer control of modern cars in order to facilitate the development of autonomous vehicle technology. It is a modular and stable way of using software to interface with a vehicle's communications network and control systems. OpenCaret builds on top of OSCC to enable a L3 highway autopilot system for modern cars. Especially, this project contains detailed information of converting a Kia Soul EV into an autonomous vehicle chassis.

Finally, we introduce a detailed case study, the PerceptIn Chassis Software Adaptation Layer, which provides a layer of abstraction for different chassis, so that chassis manufacturers can easily integrate PerceptIn's autonomous driving technology stack to convert their chassis into autonomous vehicles.

3.2 Throttle-by-Wire

Unlike traditional throttle controls that couple the gas pedal to the throttle with a mechanical cable, these systems use a series of electronic sensors and actuators. As shown in Figure 3.2,

Engineering Autonomous Vehicles and Robots: The DragonFly Modular-based Approach, First Edition. Shaoshan Liu.

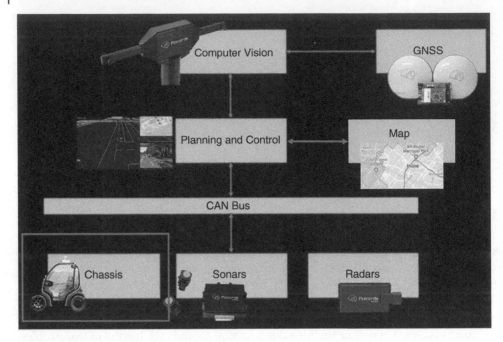

Figure 3.1 Modular design architecture.

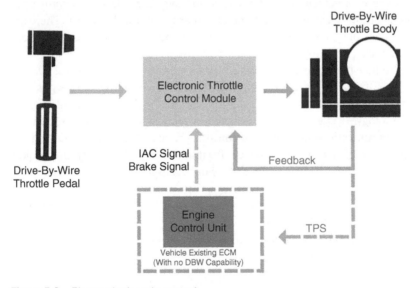

Figure 3.2 Electronic throttle control.

in vehicles that use true electronic throttle control (ETC), the gas pedal sends a signal that causes an electromechanical actuator to open the throttle.

A typical ETC system consists of an accelerator pedal module, a throttle valve that can be opened and closed by an electronic throttle body (ETB), and a powertrain control module or engine control module (PCM or ECM). The ECM is a type of electronic control unit

(ECU), which is an embedded system that employs software to determine the required throttle position by calculations from data measured by other sensors, including the accelerator pedal position sensors, engine speed sensor, vehicle speed sensor, and cruise control switches. The electric motor is then used to open the throttle valve to the desired angle via a closed-loop control algorithm within the ECM. The throttle valve is a part of the ETB. On the vehicles equipped with the throttle controller sensor, the throttle opening is determined based on how far the gas pedal was pressed.

3.3   Brake-by-Wire

A brake-by-wire system consists of a spectrum of technologies that range from electrohydraulic to electromechanical, and both can be designed with fail-safes in mind. Traditional hydraulic brakes make use of a master cylinder and several slave cylinders. When the driver pushes down on the brake pedal, it physically applies pressure to the master cylinder. In most cases, that pressure is amplified by a vacuum or hydraulic brake booster. The pressure is then transmitted via brake lines to the brake calipers or wheel cylinders.

Anti-lock brake systems were early precursors of modern brake-by-wire technologies, in that they allowed the brakes of a vehicle to be pulled automatically with no driver input. This is accomplished by an electronic actuator that activates the existing hydraulic brakes, and a number of other safety technologies have been built on this foundation.

Electronic stability control, traction control, and automatic braking systems all depend on an anti-lock braking system and are peripherally related to brake-by-wire technology. In vehicles that use electro-hydraulic brake-by-wire technology, the calipers located in each wheel are still hydraulically activated. However, they are not directly coupled to a master cylinder that is activated by pushing on the brake pedal. Instead, pushing on the brake pedal activates a sensor or series of sensors.

The control unit then determines how much braking force is required at each wheel and activates the hydraulic calipers as needed. In electromechanical brake systems, there is no hydraulic component at all. These true brake-by-wire systems still use sensors to determine how much brake force is required, but that force is not transmitted via hydraulics. Instead, electromechanical actuators are used to activate the brakes located in each wheel.

3.4   Steer-by-Wire

Most vehicles use a rack and pinion unit or worm and sector steering gear that is physically connected to the steering wheel. When the steering wheel is rotated, the rack and pinion unit or steering box also turns. A rack and pinion unit can then apply torque to the ball joints via tie rods, and a steering box will typically move the steering linkage via a pitman's arm.

In vehicles that are equipped with steer-by-wire technology, there is no physical connection between the steering wheel and the tires. In fact, steer-by-wire systems do not technically need to use steering wheels at all. When a steering wheel is used, some type of steering feel emulator is typically used to provide the driver with feedback. The control of the wheels' direction will be established through electric motors which are actuated by ECUs monitoring the steering wheel inputs from the driver.

3.5 Open Source Car Control

To learn more about drive-by-wire technologies for autonomous robots and vehicles, OSCC is a good starting point [2]. OSCC is an assemblage of software and hardware designs that enable computer control of modern cars in order to facilitate the development of autonomous vehicle technology. It is a modular and stable way of using software to interface with a vehicle's communications network and control systems.

OSCC enables developers to send control commands to the vehicle, read control messages from the vehicle's OBD-II Controller Area Network (CAN) network, and forward reports for current vehicle control state, such as steering angle and wheel speeds. Control commands are issued to the vehicle component ECUs via the steering wheel torque sensor, throttle position sensor, and brake position sensor.

This low-level interface means that OSCC offers full-range control of the vehicle without altering the factory safety-case, spoofing CAN messages, or hacking advanced driver-assistance systems features. Although OSCC currently supports only the 2014 or later Kia Soul (petrol and EV), the application program interface (API) and firmware have been designed to make it easy to add new vehicle support.

3.5.1 OSCC APIs

Open and close CAN channel to OSCC Control CAN.

```
oscc_result_t oscc_open( uint channel );
oscc_result_t oscc_close( uint channel );
```

These methods are the start and end points of using the OSCC. oscc_open will open a socket connection on the specified CAN channel, enabling it to quickly receive reports from and send commands to the firmware modules. oscc_close can terminate the connection.

Enable and disable all OSCC modules.

```
oscc_result_t oscc_enable( void );
oscc_result_t oscc_disable( void );
```

After you have initialized your CAN connection to the firmware modules, these methods can be used to enable or disable the system. This allows your application to choose when to enable sending commands to the firmware. Although you can only send commands when the system is enabled, you can receive reports at any time.

Publish control command to the corresponding module.

```
oscc_result_t publish_brake_position( double normalized_position );

oscc_result_t publish_steering_torque( double normalized_torque );

oscc_result_t publish_throttle_position( double normalized_position );
```

These commands will forward a double value to the specified firmware module. The double values are [0.0, 1.0] for brake and throttle, and [−1.0, 1.0] for steering where −1.0 is counterclockwise and 1.0 is clockwise. The API will construct the appropriate values to send as spoofed voltages to the vehicle to achieve the desired state. The API also contains safety checks to ensure no voltages outside of the vehicle's expected range are sent.

Register callback function to handle OSCC report and on-board diagnostics (OBD) messages.

```
oscc_result_t subscribe_to_brake_reports( void(*callback)(oscc_brake_report_s
*report) );

oscc_result_t
subscribe_to_steering_reports( void(*callback)(oscc_steering_report_s
*report) );

oscc_result_t
subscribe_to_throttle_reports( void(*callback)(oscc_throttle_report_s
*report) );

oscc_result_t subscribe_to_fault_reports( void(*callback)(oscc_fault_report_s
*report) );

oscc_result_t subscribe_to_obd_messages( void(*callback)(struct can_frame
*frame) );
```

In order to receive reports from the modules, your application will need to register a callback handler with the OSCC API. When the appropriate report for your callback function is received from the API's socket connection, it will then forward the report to your software.

3.5.2 Hardware

OSCC is based on the 2014 Kia Soul, which ships with steering-by-wire and throttle-by-wire. Hence the actuators of these two systems can be controlled electronically and these systems can be exploited in order to gain full control of the actuators.

However, this vehicle does not have electronically controlled brakes, and a brake-by-wire system has to be integrated. The actuators can be added in-line to the Kia brake system in order to control brake pressure. To achieve lateral and longitudinal control of the Kia Soul it is necessary to control three separate automotive systems, interface with the existing Vehicle CAN bus, and power the additional microprocessors and actuators. Each of the control modules introduced into the vehicle are built around Arduino controllers.

Hardware gateway: The Kia Soul has a handful of different CAN buses on board. The OBD-II CAN network has vehicle state information such as steering wheel angle, wheel speeds, and brake pressure. This information is useful for algorithms such as proportional–integral–derivative (PID) control and path planning. Rather than sharing the vehicle's OBD-II bus and possibly interfering with the vehicle's native messages, OSCC has its own CAN bus called Control CAN where commands and reports are sent and received. The CAN Gateway acts as a bridge between the vehicle's native OBD-II bus and Control CAN, forwarding relevant OBD-II messages from the OBD-II bus to the Control CAN bus, which can be consumed by applications subscribing to the OBD messages. The CAN gateway sits on both the Control CAN bus and the OBD-II CAN bus but only publishes CAN messages in one direction: toward the Control CAN bus from the OBD-II CAN bus.

Hardware steering: The steering system of the Kia Soul is an Electric Power Assisted Steering (EPAS) system. The steering column contains a high current DC motor, as well as a torque sensor. The torque sensor measures the direction and amount of force on the steering wheel and outputs an analog signal to the EPAS microprocessor. The microprocessor then controls the motor to "assist" the vehicle steering.

Hardware throttle: The throttle system of the Kia Soul is an ETC system. Instead of a mechanical cable linkage between the throttle body and the accelerator pedal, there is a position sensor on the accelerator pedal and a motorized throttle body. The ETC system can be controlled by removing the accelerator position sensor (APS) input to the ETC microprocessor and injecting spoofed position values. The pedal position sensor uses redundant position sensors that both output analog signals.

Hardware brake: Unfortunately, braking in the Kia Soul is a traditional mechanical system, the factory standard Soul has no ability to control braking electronically. There are a number of models of vehicles with electronically controlled brake systems, notably the 2004–2009 Prius. This model Prius uses an electronically controlled actuator with no microprocessor; it is controlled from the Prius ECU. There are 7 pressure sensors on the device, 10 proportional solenoids, an accumulator, a pump, diagnostics components, and a pressure relief valve. This unit can be sourced from auto salvage yards and installed into the existing Kia brake system without adversely affecting the stock brake system and adding by-wire control.

3.5.3 Firmware

The brake firmware is responsible for reading values from the brake pedal sensor, sending reports on its state, and receiving brake commands and fault reports from the control CAN. When the brake firmware receives a brake command message, it will then output the commanded high and low spoof signals onto its connection to the ECU, sending it brake requests. Receiving a fault report will cause the brake module to disable.

The steering firmware is responsible for reading values from the torque sensor, sending reports on its state, and receiving steering commands and fault reports from the control CAN. When the steering firmware receives a steering command message, it will then output the commanded high and low spoof signals onto its connection to the EPAS ECU, sending it torque requests. Receiving a fault report will cause the steering module to disable.

The throttle firmware is responsible for reading values from the APS, sending reports on its state, and receiving throttle commands and fault reports from the control CAN. When the throttle firmware receives a throttle command message, it will then output the commanded high and low spoof signals onto its connection to the ECU, sending it throttle requests. Receiving a fault report will cause the throttle module to disable.

3.6   OpenCaret

OpenCaret builds on top of OSCC to enable a L3 highway autopilot system for modern cars [3]. Especially, this project contains detailed information of converting a Kia Soul EV into a drive-by-wire chassis, which we will introduce in this section.

3.6.1   OSCC Throttle

The pedal position sensor uses redundant position sensors that both output analog signals. The full range of sensor position values correlate to the full range of throttle from "closed throttle" to "wide open throttle." By injecting the two spoofed position sensor values the throttle can be controlled. The Kia ECU implements fault detection on the accelerator pedal position sensor by detecting discontinuities in the analog signals coming from the sensors. If any discontinuities appear the car will go into a fault state, with the symptom of having the mapping of the accelerator pedal greatly reduced. To overcome this the new throttle microprocessor will interpolate between the sensor position values and the spoofed values before sensing spoofed positions. A relay is used to switch the input of the ETC microprocessor from the stock pedal position sensor and the spoofed positions:

- Step 1: Locate the accelerator pedal position sensor.
- Step 2: Disconnect the pedal position sensor and connect the throttle cabling.
- Step 3: Connect the power unit with the emergency stop power bus.
- Step 4: Wire the module to the gateway module control CAN bus.

3.6.2   OSCC Brake

The brake module for the Kia Soul EV brake consists of two parts. The first part is the signals spoof and the second part is the brake light switch. To modify the brake pedal, we need to disconnect (i) the brake pedal stroke sensor and (ii) the stop light switch

Installation: The Vehicle Control Module (VCM) controls the open and closing stroke sensor for the braking as well with Normally Open (NO) and Normally Closed (NC) relays for the brake light switch.

- Step 1: Remove the brake pedal stroke sensor and stop light switch.
- Step 2: Install the VCM connector for the pedal stroke and stop light switch.

3.6.3   OSCC Steering

The EPAS motor can be controlled by removing the torque sensor input to the EPAS microprocessor and injecting spoofed torques. The Kia ECU implements fault detection on the torque sensor by detecting discontinuities in the analog signals coming from the sensors. If any discontinuities appear the car will go into a fault state, with the symptom of disabling the power steering. To overcome this, the new torque spoofing microprocessor will interpolate between the torque sensor values and the spoofed values before sensing spoofed signals. A relay is used to switch the input of the EPAS microprocessor from the stock torque sensors and the spoofed torques. A Kia Soul drive-by-wire steering system is shown in Figure 3.3.

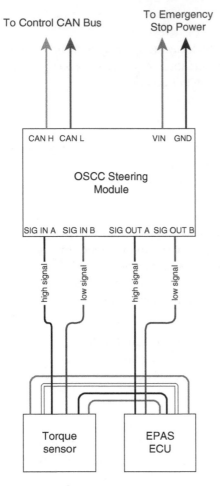

Final Steering Module Wiring

Figure 3.3 Kia Soul drive-by-wire steering.

3.7 PerceptIn Chassis Software Adaptation Layer

In this section, we provide an example of PerceptIn's chassis software adaptation layer and delve into the details of how PerceptIn manages and interacts with different vehicle chassis [4]. Figure 3.4 provides the architecture of PerceptIn's chassis software adaptation layer. Note that the Planning and Control module generates control commands and sends them down to the chassis module for execution. Also, the perception sensors, such as sonars and radars [5, 6], interact with both the chassis module for passive perception and the perception module for active perception.

The core of the chassis module consists of three parts:

- *VehicleControlUnit*: This interface provides abstraction for different chassis platforms such that the developers do not have to fully understand the details of the CAN

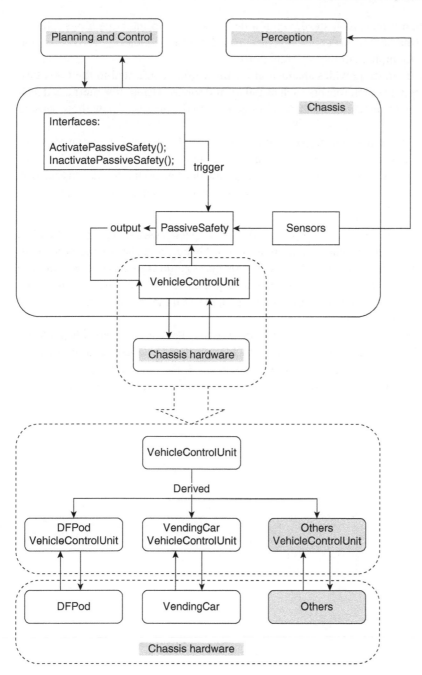

Figure 3.4 Perceptln chassis interface.

communication protocols. Instead, when a developer tries to integrate a new chassis platform, he/she only needs to derive a new class from the VehicleControlUnit virtual interface and to implement the core functions.

- *Sensors*: This interface provides abstraction for the sensors connected to the CAN bus, mostly passive perception sensors such as radars and sonars. Using this interface, developers can easily get perception data without going into the details of how these sensors work.
- *PassiveSafety*: Developers can implement and adjust their passive perception logics in this interface. For instance, a developer can decide to stop the vehicle when radar or sonar detects an obstacle 2 m ahead. In this case, the developer should take passive perception sensor data from the *Sensors* interface and implement this logic in the *PassiveSafety* interface.

Figure 3.5 shows the hardware setup diagram. For simplicity, we can use a two CAN bus setup, such that the chassis platform occupies one CAN bus, and the passive perception sensors occupy the other CAN bus. Then both CAN buses connect to the control computer through a CAN card. Of course, it is acceptable to put all sensors and the chassis on the same CAN bus as well, then in this case we have to agree with the chassis provider on what CAN ID to use for the chassis.

Figure 3.6 shows the DragonFly Pod software interface. For each new chassis platform, we need to implement the virtual interface VehicleControlUnit and its essential functions including SetSpeed, SetBrake, SetAngle, GetSpeed, GetBrake, and GetAngle. Note that these functions are required for the Planning and Control module to interact with the chassis.

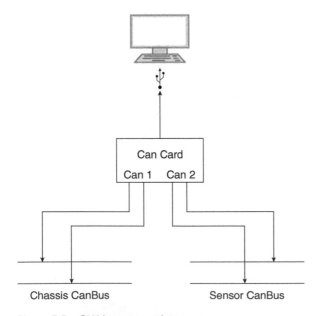

Figure 3.5 CAN bus connection setup.

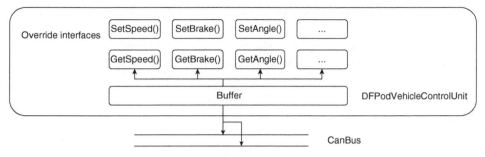

Figure 3.6 DragonFly Pod software interface.

The software interface definitions are:

```
// error code definitions
enum ErrCode {
  OK = 1,
  CAN_ERR = -1,
  BOUND_ERR = -2,
  TIME_OUT =-3
}

ErrCode SetSpeed (float val)
// this function sets the current speed of the chassis

ErrCode SetBrake (float val)
// this function sets the brake value, ranging from 0 to 100, with 100
being the strongest brake.

ErrCode SetSteeringAngle (float val)
// this function sets the steering angle, with positive being left,
and negative being right.

float GetSpeed ()
// this function gets the current speed of the chassis.

float GetBrake ()
// this function gets the current brake value

float GetSteeringAngle ()
// this function gets the current steering angle

// the following data structure defines how we store chassis status
ChassisData {
  float speed;
  float angle;
  float brake;
}
```

```
boost::signal2::connection SubscribeToChassisData(void(ChassisData&)
call_back)
// this function subscribes chassis data so that every time there is
an update from the chassis, the subscriber will receive a notification
```

References

1 YouTube (2012). Nissan drive by wire. https://www.youtube.com/watch?v=
MH7e5aUDWYY&feature=youtu.be (accessed 1 November 2018).
2 GitHub (2017). Open Source Car Control. https://github.com/PolySync/oscc (accessed
1 October 2018).
3 GitHub (2018). Drive by Wire Installation. https://github.com/frk2/opencaret/wiki/
Drive-by-wire-Installation (accessed 1 October 2018).
4 PerceptIn (2017). PerceptIn DragonFly Pod. https://www.perceptin.io/products (accessed
1 November 2018).
5 YouTube (2018). DragonFly 77 GHz millimeter Wave Radar. https://www.youtube.com/
watch?v=ZLOgcc7GUiQ (accessed 1 December 2018).
6 YouTube (2018). DragonFly Sonar. https://www.youtube.com/watch?v=-H3YdC-xSgQ
(accessed 1 December 2018).

4

Passive Perception with Sonar and Millimeter Wave Radar

4.1 Introduction

In an autonomous driving system, there are usually two different perception systems: *active* and *passive*. By active perception, we mean that the detected obstacles are sent to the planning and control module to aid decision making, and then the planning and control module will generate a list of commands based on the perceived environment. By passive perception, we mean that when obstacles are detected, the raw data are not fed to the planning and control module for decision making. Instead, the raw data are directly sent to the chassis through the Controller Area Network (CAN) bus for quick decision making. In this case, a simple decision module is implemented in the chassis to stop the vehicle when an obstacle is detected within a short range. The main reason for this design is that when obstacles are detected in close range, we want to stop the vehicle as soon as possible instead of going through the complete decision pipeline. This is the best way to guarantee the safety of passengers as well as pedestrians.

Hence, in our modular design architecture, there are three layers of protection: computer vision (active perception) for long-range obstacle detection; millimeter wave (mmWave) radar for mid-range obstacle detection; and sonar for short-range obstacle detection. Note that depending on how you design your perception system, mmWave radar can aid active perception as well. As shown in Figure 4.1, mmWave radar and sonar sensors can be used for passive perception. In this chapter, we first introduce the fundamentals of mmWave radar technologies, and then explain how we can deploy mmWave radar as well as sonar for passive perception.

4.2 The Fundamentals of mmWave Radar

mmWave is a special class of radar technology that uses short-wavelength electromagnetic waves [1]. In this section we introduce the fundamentals of mmWave radar; for a more complete and thorough review, please refer to [2].

Radar systems transmit electromagnetic wave signals that objects in their path then reflect. By capturing the reflected signal, a radar system can determine the *range*, *velocity*, and *angle* of the objects.

Engineering Autonomous Vehicles and Robots: The DragonFly Modular-based Approach,
First Edition. Shaoshan Liu.

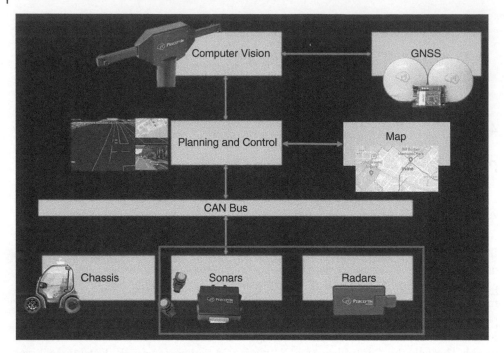

Figure 4.1 Modular design architecture.

mmWave radars transmit signals with a wavelength that is in the millimeter range, which is considered a short wavelength in the electromagnetic spectrum and is one of the advantages of this technology. As a result, one advantage of applying short wavelength is that the size of system components, such as the antennas required to process mmWave signals, is small. Another advantage is the high accuracy. A mmWave system operating at 76–81 GHz, with a corresponding wavelength of about 4 mm, will have the ability to detect movements that are as small as a fraction of a millimeter.

A complete mmWave radar system includes transmit (TX) and receive (RX) radio frequency (RF) components; analog components such as clocking; and digital components such as analog-to-digital converters (ADCs), microcontroller units (MCUs), and digital signal processors (DSPs).

A special class of mmWave technology is called frequency-modulated continuous wave (FMCW). As the name implies, FMCW radars transmit a frequency-modulated signal continuously in order to measure range as well as angle and velocity [3].

4.2.1 Range Measurement

The fundamental concept in a radar system is the transmission of an electromagnetic signal that objects reflect in its path. In the signal used in an FMCW radar, the frequency increases linearly with time. This type of signal is called a *chirp*.

An FMCW radar system transmits a chirp signal and captures the signals reflected by objects in its path. Figure 4.2 represents a simplified block diagram of the main RF components of an FMCW radar. The radar operates as follows:

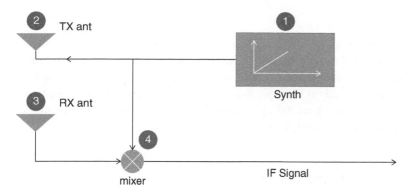

Figure 4.2 FMCW radar block diagram: 1, synthesizer; 2, TX antenna; 3, RX antenna; and 4, mixer.

- A synthesizer (synth) generates a chirp.
- The chirp is transmitted by a transmit antenna (TX ant).
- The reflection of the chirp by an object generates a reflected chirp captured by the receive antenna (RX ant).
- A "mixer" combines the RX and TX signals to produce an intermediate frequency (IF) signal. Note that a frequency mixer is an electronic component that combines two signals to create a new signal with a new frequency.

The output of the mixer has an instantaneous frequency equal to the difference of the instantaneous frequencies of the TX chirp and the RX chirp. Especially, the phase of the output is equal to the difference of the phases of the TX chirp and the RX chirp. Hence, the initial phase of the output of the mixer is the difference between the phase of the TX chirp and the phase of the RX chirp at the time instant corresponding to when the chirp was emitted. From the phase of the output of the mixer, we can then derive the distance of the detected object.

4.2.2 Velocity Measurement

In order to measure velocity, an FMCW radar transmits two chirps separated by t_c. Each reflected chirp is processed through FFT (Fast Fourier transform) to detect the range of the object; this technique is called range-FFT. The range-FFT corresponding to each chirp has peaks in the same location but with a different phase. Hence, the measured phase difference can be used to calculate the velocity of the detected object, v_c.

The two-chirp velocity measurement method does not work if multiple moving objects with different velocities are, at the time of measurement, at the same distance from the radar. Since these objects are at the same distance, they will generate reflective chirps with identical IF frequencies. As a consequence, the range-FFT will result in a single peak, which represents the combined signal from all of these objects at the same distance. In this case, in order to measure the speed, the radar system must transmit more than two chirps. It transmits a set of N equally spaced chirps. This set of chirps is called a *chirp frame*.

4.2.3 Angle Detection

An FMCW radar system can estimate the angle of a reflected signal with the horizontal plane. Angular estimation is based on the observation that a small change in the distance of an object results in a phase change in the peak of the range-FFT. This result is used to perform angular estimation, using at least two RX antennas. The differential distance from the object to each of the antennas results in a phase change in the FFT peak. The phase change enables us to estimate the angle of a reflected signal.

4.3 mmWave Radar Deployment

Figure 4.3 shows a sample configuration of how mmWave radar sensors can be installed on a vehicle. In this case, we place the radar device in the middle of the front of the vehicle for it to capture a 15–20 m range in front of the vehicle (Figure 4.4). In the case of an object entering the detection range, the radar sensor can easily detect the object and send the detection either to the chassis directly for passive perception, or to the main computing unit for active perception. Note that for most low-speed autonomous vehicles, the braking distance is less than 1 m; this allows the use of a detection range of 5 m out for active perception, and a detection range of within 5 m for passive perception. This threshold can be easily configured using our software interface.

Figure 4.5 shows the hardware test set to enable radar. Since by default the radar is connected to the CAN bus, we need a USB CAN card to attach the radar to a USB

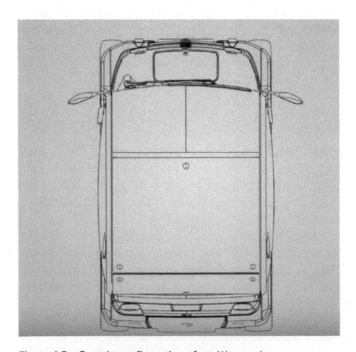

Figure 4.3 Sample configuration of mmWave radar.

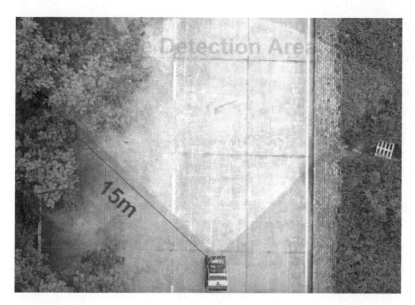

Figure 4.4   Detection range of mmWave radar.

Figure 4.5   Hardware set.

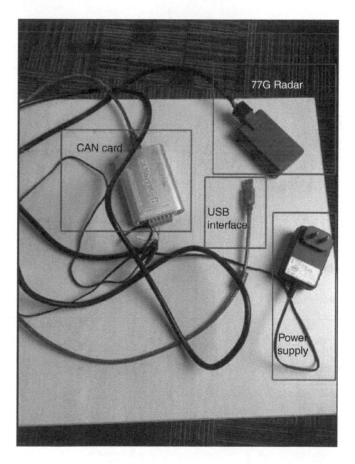

device. We also need a power supply to power the radar sensor. Once the radar sensor gets connected to the CAN card, the CAN card can be connected to your computer through USB and start reading detection data. It should be a very smooth five-minute setup.

Figure 4.6 shows the very easy-to-understand user interface (UI) of the mmWave radar, which projects any detected objects with a bird's eye view, and on the UI we show the distance as well as the orientation of the detected obstacles. These passive perception results are what the planning and control module requires to make intelligent motion decisions. A demo video of our mmWave radar in action can be found in [4]. Figure 4.7 shows the hardware specifications of this device [5].

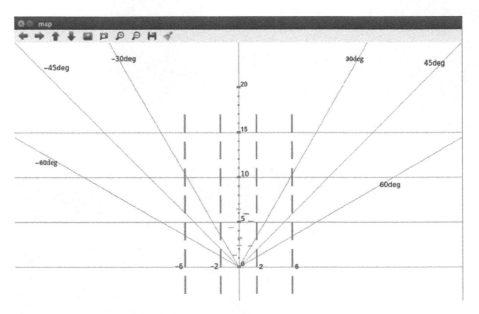

Figure 4.6   Radar detection UI.

Figure 4.7   Radar hardware specifications.

- Coverage	
Horizontal Angle [deg]:	120 (±60)
Vertical Angle [deg]:	10 (±5)
Maximum Range [m]:	30
Update Interval [ms]:	50
Maximum Tracking Targets:	64
- Accuracy	
Range [m]:	± 5%
Angle Resolution [deg]:	± 1
- Others	
DC Voltage [V]:	9~36
DC Power [W]:	< 3
Size [mm]:	102.5 × 52 × 28.5
Output Interface:	CAN (500 Kbps)

The following code snippet shows the simple data structure for radar data, which contains the object index; the range, or distance, of the object; the radial velocity of the object; the radial acceleration of the object; the Azimuth angle; and the signal strength or power. We also provide a very simple software application program interface (API) to capture radar data for you to build your own passive or active perception logics.

```
struct MWR_Data {

  int index; // object index (range: 0 - 63)

  float Range; // usually the range is within 30 meters.

  float RadialVelocity; // radial velocity

  float RadialAcc; // radial acceleration

  float Azimuth;  // azimuth angle with clockwise direction.

  float Power;  // detection signal strength

  MWR_Data(int i, float Rg, float RV, float RA, float Az, float Pw)
      : index(i), Range(Rg), RadialVelocity(RV), RadialAcc(RA), Azimuth(Az),
        Power(Pw) {}
};

MWRadar mwr_radar;
std::vector<MWR_Data> data;  // data means the radar's data

// Read the latest 10 frame.
mwr_radar.Read(data,10)

// Read the latest frame
mwr_radar.Read(data,1)
```

4.4 Sonar Deployment

Sonar sensors emit sound waves at a high frequency (that humans cannot hear), then wait for the sound to be reflected back, and calculate the distance based on the time required. This is similar to how radar measures the time it takes a radio wave to return after hitting an object.

Sonars can detect certain objects that radar and Light Detection and Ranging (LiDAR) may not be able to detect. For instance, radar, or even light-based sensors, have a difficult time correctly processing clear plastic; sonar sensors have no problem with this. Also, sonar sensors are unaffected by the color of the material they are sensing. On the other hand, if an object is made out of a material that absorbs sound or is shaped in such a way that it reflects the sound waves away from the receiver, readings will be unreliable.

Specifically, in our usage scenario, we use sonar sensors for the very last line of defense, guarding a 3 m range around the car to make sure the chassis can handle any immediate dangers.

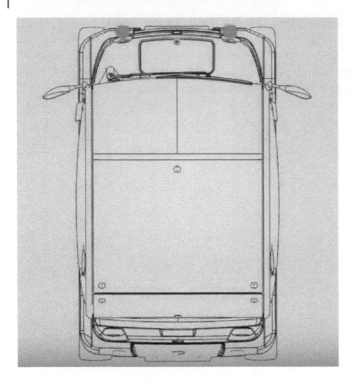

Figure 4.8 Sample configuration of sonar.

Figure 4.8 shows a sample configuration of how sonar can be installed on a vehicle. In this case, we place the sonar device in the middle of the front of the vehicle for it to capture a 3–5 m range in front of the vehicle (Figure 4.9). In the case of an object entering

Figure 4.9 Detection range of sonar.

the detection range, the sonar sensor can easily detect the object for passive perception. A demo video of our mmWave sonar in action can be found in [6].

Figure 4.10 shows the hardware test set to enable sonar. Since by default the sonar sensor is connected to the CAN bus, we need a USB CAN card to attach the sonar to the USB device. Also, we need a power supply to power the sonar sensor. Once the sonar sensor gets connected to the CAN card, the CAN card can be connected to your computer through USB and start reading detection data. It should be a very smooth five-minute setup.

Figure 4.11 shows the very easy-to-understand UI of the sonar. With two detection units, the UI projects any detected objects with a bird's eye view, and on the UI we show the distances of the detected obstacles. Figure 4.12 shows the hardware specifications of this device [5].

The following code snippet shows the simple data structure for sonar data, which contains two detection distances (one for the left detection unit and the other for the right detection unit). We also provide a very simple software API to capture sonar data for you to build your own passive perception logics.

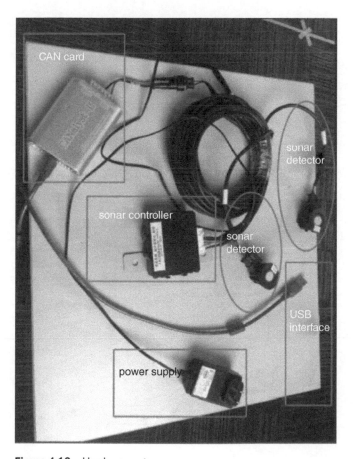

Figure 4.10 Hardware set.

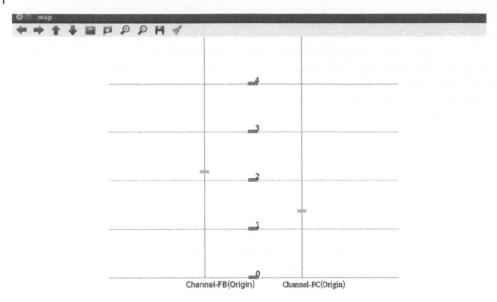

Figure 4.11 Sonar detection UI.

- Probe Beam Angle	
Horizontal Direction:	85°
Vertical Direction:	30°
Ultrasonic Frequency:	58 ± 1 kHz
Waterproof Level:	IPx9
Detection Distance:	< 3 m
Blind Zone:	< 30 cm
Operating Voltage:	12 V
Communication Type:	CAN (500 Kbps)

Figure 4.12 Sonar sensor specifications.

```
struct USR_Data {

  unsigned short left_front; // object range detected by "FB" channel,
unit in millimeter.
  unsigned short right_front; // object range detected by "FC" channel,
unit in millimeter.
};

  USR sonar;
  USR_Data usr_data;
  sonar.Read(usr_data);
```

References

1 Hasch, J., Topak, E., Schnabel, R. et al. (2012). Millimeter-wave technology for automotive radar sensors in the 77 GHz frequency band. IEEE Transactions on Microwave Theory and Techniques 60 (3): 845–860.

2 Iovescu, C. and Rao, S. (2017). The fundamentals of millimeter wave sensors. http://www.ti.com/lit/wp/spyy005/spyy005.pdf (accessed 1 February 2019).

3 Hymans, A.J. and Lait, J. (1960). Analysis of a frequency-modulated continuous-wave ranging system. Proceedings of the IEE-Part B: Electronic and Communication Engineering 107 (34): 365–372.

4 YouTube (2018). DragonFly 77 GHz millimeter Wave Radar. https://www.youtube.com/watch?v=ZLOgcc7GUiQ (accessed 1 September 2019).

5 PerceptIn (2018). Products. https://www.perceptin.io/products (accessed 1 September 2019).

6 YouTube (2018). DragonFly Sonar. https://www.youtube.com/watch?v=-H3YdC-xSgQ (accessed 1 September 2019).

5

Localization with Real-Time Kinematic Global Navigation Satellite System

5.1 Introduction

Commercial Global Positioning System (GPS) receivers, such as the ones in cell phones, usually can provide meter-level accuracy in the best case. However, this is not enough for autonomous vehicles, which require centimeter-level localization. One technology to achieve centimeter accuracy is the real-time kinematic (RTK) Global Navigation Satellite System (GNSS). As shown in Figure 5.1, we introduce localization with RTK GNSS and its role in an autonomous driving technology stack in this chapter. We provide an overview of GNSS technologies, and then present a step-to-step detailed guide on setting up your own RTK GNSS system for high-precision localization (<30 cm). Note that RTK is a technique that uses carrier-based ranging and provides ranges (and therefore positions) that are orders of magnitude more precise than those available through code-based positioning.

In the rest of the chapter, we first introduce the GNSS technologies in Section 5.2; then we discuss RTK-GNSS architecture in Section 5.3; in Sections 5.4, 5.5, and 5.6, we demonstrate how to setup a cloud server to broadcast base station correction signal, or the Radio Technical Commission for Maritime Services (RTCM) signal. When a cloud server is not a good option, we also demonstrate how to set up FreeWave radio to broadcast RTCM signals.

5.2 GNSS Technology Overview

The GNSS consist of several satellite systems: GPS, GLONASS (GLObal NAvigation Satellite System), Galileo, and BeiDou. Here we use GPS as an example to provide an overview of GNSS. GPS provides coded satellite signals that can be processed in a GPS receiver, allowing the receiver to estimate position, velocity, and time [1]. For this to work, GPS requires four satellite signals to compute positions in three dimensions and the time offset in the receiver clock. The deployment of these GPS satellites is dispersed in six orbital planes on almost circular orbits with an altitude of about 20 200 km above the surface of the Earth, inclined by 55° with respect to the equator and with orbital periods of approximately 11 h 58 min.

Engineering Autonomous Vehicles and Robots: The DragonFly Modular-based Approach,
First Edition. Shaoshan Liu.
© 2020 John Wiley & Sons Ltd. Published 2020 by John Wiley & Sons Ltd.

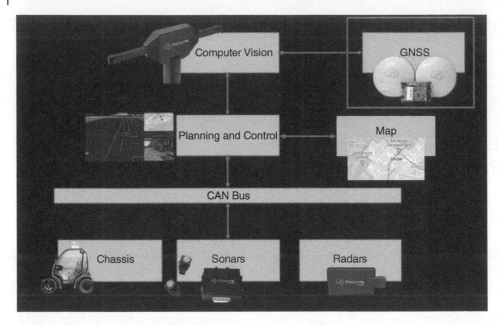

Figure 5.1 Modular design architecture.

The generated signals on board the satellites are derived from generation of a fundamental frequency $f_o = 10.23$ MHz [1]. The signal is time stamped with atomic clocks with inaccuracy in the range of only 10^{-13} s over a day. Two carrier signals in the L-band, denoted L1 and L2, are generated by integer multiplications of f_o. The carriers L1 and L2 are bi-phase modulated by codes to provide satellite clock readings to the receiver and transmit information such as the orbital parameters. The codes consist of a sequence with the states $+1$ or -1, corresponding to the binary values 0 or 1. The bi-phase modulation is performed by a $180°$ shift in the carrier phase whenever a change in the code state occurs. The satellite signals contain information on the satellite orbits, orbit perturbations, GPS time, satellite clock, ionospheric parameters, and system status messages, etc. The navigation message consists of 25 frames with each frame containing 1500 bits and each frame is subdivided into 5 subframes with 300 bits.

The next critical piece of the GNSS system is the definition of the reference coordinate system, which is crucial for the description of satellite motion, the modeling of observable satellites, and the interpretation of results. For GNSS to work, two reference systems are required: (i) space-fixed, an inertial reference system for the description of satellite motion; and (ii) earth-fixed, a terrestrial reference system for the positions of the observation stations and for the description of results from satellite geodesy. The two systems are used and the transformation parameters between the space fixed and earth fixed are well known and used directly in the GNSS receiver and post processing software to compute the position of the receivers in the earth-fixed system. The terrestrial reference system is defined by convention with three axes, where the Z-axis coincides with the earth rotation axis as defined by the Conventional International Origin. The X-axis is associated with the mean Greenwich meridian, and the Y-axis is orthogonal to both the Z and X axes and it completes the right-handed coordinate system. GPS has used WGS84 as a reference system and with WGS84 associated a geocentric equipotential ellipsoid of revolution [2].

In recent years, the emergence of GNSS receivers supporting multiple constellations has kept steady pace with the increasing number of GNSS satellites in the sky. With advancements in newer GNSS constellations, almost 100% of all new devices are expected to support multiple constellations. The benefits of supporting multiple constellations include increased availability, particularly in areas with shadowing; increased accuracy, more satellites in view improves accuracy; and improved robustness, as independent systems are harder to spoof.

Ideally, with GNSS, we can get perfect localization results with no error at all. However, there are multiple places where error can be introduced in GNSS. Here we review these potential error contributors:

- *Satellite clocks*: Any tiny amount of inaccuracy of the atomic clocks in the GNSS satellites can result in a significant error in the position calculated by the receiver. Roughly, 10 ns of clock error results in 3 m of position error.
- *Orbit errors*: GNSS satellites travel in very precise, well known orbits. However, like the satellite clock, the orbits do vary a small amount. When the satellite orbit changes, the ground control system sends a correction to the satellites and the satellite ephemeris is updated. Even with the corrections from the GNSS ground control system, there are still small errors in the orbit that can result in up to ±2.5 m of position error.
- *Ionospheric delay*: The ionosphere is the layer of atmosphere between 80 km and 600 km above the earth. This layer contains electrically charged particles called ions. These ions delay the satellite signals and can cause a significant amount of satellite position error (typically ±5 m). Ionospheric delay varies with solar activity, time of year, season, time of day, and location. This makes it very difficult to predict how much ionospheric delay is impacting the calculated position. Ionospheric delay also varies based on the radio frequency of the signal passing through the ionosphere.
- *Tropospheric delay*: The troposphere is the layer of atmosphere closest to the surface of the Earth. Variations in tropospheric delay are caused by the changing humidity, temperature, and atmospheric pressure in the troposphere. Since tropospheric conditions are very similar within a local area, the base station and rover receivers experience very similar tropospheric delay. This allows RTK GNSS to compensate for tropospheric delay, which will be discussed in the next section.
- *Multipath*: Multipath occurs when a GNSS signal is reflected off an object, such as the wall of a building, to the GNSS antenna. Because the reflected signal travels farther to reach the antenna, the reflected signal arrives at the receiver slightly delayed. This delayed signal can cause the receiver to calculate an incorrect position.

For a more detailed discussion of these errors, please refer to [3–6].

5.3 RTK GNSS

Based on our experiences, most commercially available multi-constellation GNSS systems provide a localization accuracy no better than a 2-m radius. While this may be enough for human drivers, in order for an autonomous vehicle to follow a road, it needs to know where the road is. To stay in a specific lane, it needs to know where the lane is. For an autonomous vehicle to stay in a lane, the localization requirements are in the order of decimeters.

Fortunately, RTK and Differential GNSS does provide decimeter level localization accuracy. In this subsection, we study how RTK and Differential GNSS works.

The basic concept of RTK is to reduce and remove errors common to a base station and rover pair, as illustrated in Figure 5.2. RTK GNSS achieves high accuracy by reducing errors in satellite clocks, imperfect orbits, ionospheric delays, and tropospheric delays. Figure 5.1 shows the basic concept behind RTK GNSS. A good way to correct these GNSS errors is to set up a GNSS receiver on a station whose position is known exactly, a base station. The base station receiver calculates its position from satellite data and compares that position with its actual known position, and identifies the difference. The resulting error corrections can then be communicated from the base to the vehicle.

In detail, RTK uses carrier-based ranging and provides ranges (and therefore positions) that are orders of magnitude more precise than those available through code-based positioning. Code-based positioning is one processing technique that gathers data via a coarse acquisition code receiver, which uses the information contained in the satellite pseudo-random code to calculate positions. After differential correction, this processing technique results in 5 m accuracy. Carrier-based ranging is another processing technique that gathers data via a carrier phase receiver, which uses the radio carrier signal to calculate positions. The carrier signal, which has a much higher frequency than the pseudo-random code, is more accurate than using the pseudo-random code alone. The pseudo-random code narrows the reference, and then the carrier code narrows the reference even more. After differential correction, this processing technique results in sub-meter accuracy. Under carrier-based ranging, the range is calculated by determining the number of carrier cycles between the satellite and the vehicle, and then multiplying this number by the carrier wavelength. The calculated ranges still include errors from sources such as satellite clock

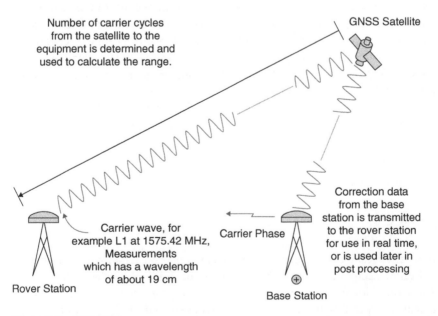

Figure 5.2 RTK GNSS.

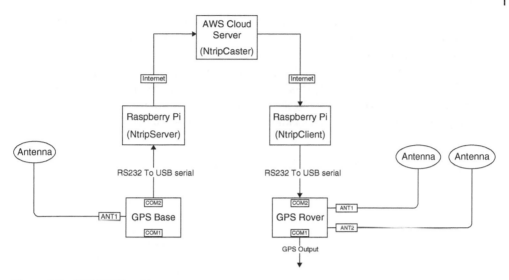

Figure 5.3 RTK GNSS architecture.

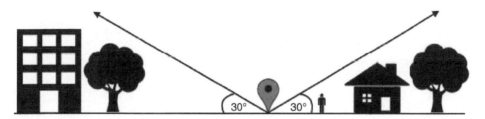

Figure 5.4 GPS antenna installation requirements.

and ephemerides, and ionospheric and tropospheric delays. To eliminate these errors and to take advantage of the precision of carrier-based measurements, RTK performance requires measurements to be transmitted from the base station to the vehicle.

With RTK GNSS, vehicles determine their position using algorithms that incorporate ambiguity resolution and differential correction. The position accuracy achievable by the vehicle depends on its distance from the base station and the accuracy of the differential corrections. Corrections are as accurate as the known location of the base station and the quality of the base station's satellite observations. Therefore, site selection is critical for minimizing environmental effects such as interference and multipath, and so is the quality of the base station and vehicle receivers and antennas.

A RTK-GNSS system uses the satellite positioning measurement method of RTK carrier phase difference technology to obtain high-precision positioning. Figure 5.3 shows how we set up our RTK GNSS system:

- First, the antenna of the base station (GPS Base) receiver is installed at a fixed position. The installation requirements are shown in Figure 5.4.
- Secondly, setting the base station receiver fixed coordinates by calculating the average of the self-positioning over a period of time.

- Thirdly, connecting the base station receiver to the Raspberry Pi (NtripServer) through a serial cable, and transmitting the location coordinates of the base station and the received satellite information to the cloud server (NtripCaster) in real time.
- Fourthly, the rover station (GPS Rover) connects the Raspberry Pi (NtripClient) by the serial port COM2 to receive the differential correction data from the cloud server, and simultaneously receives the satellite signal to solve RTK positioning.
- Finally, the rover station outputs positioning data by the serial port COM1.

5.4 RTK-GNSS NtripCaster Setup Steps

We assume you are going to set up a NtripCaster on AWS (Amazon Web Services). You can use openssh to log in your AWS instance. A sample command is:

```
sudo ssh -i /path/my-key-pair.pem ec2-user@instance-
name.compute-1.amazonaws.com
```

5.4.1 Set up NtripCaster

First, we need to install a NtripCaster using the following commands:

```
ubuntu@ip-instance:~$ git clone https://github.com/roice/ntripcaster
ubuntu@ip-instance:~$ sudo apt-get install gcc
ubuntu@ip-instance:~$ cd ntripcaster/
ubuntu@ip-instance:~/ntripcaster$ cd ntripcaster0.1.5/
ubuntu@ip-
instance:~/ntripcaster/ntripcaster0.1.5$ sudo ./configure
ubuntu@ip-instance:~/ntripcaster/ntripcaster0.1.5$ sudo apt-get
install make
ubuntu@ip-instance:~/ntripcaster/ntripcaster0.1.5$ make
ubuntu@ip-instance:~/ntripcaster/ntripcaster0.1.5$sudo make
install
```

Once it is installed, we need to set up the NtripCaster using the following commands:

```
ubuntu@ip-instance:~/ntripcaster/ntripcaster0.1.5$ cd /usr/local
ubuntu@ip-instance:/usr/local$ cd ntripcaster/
ubuntu@ip-instance:/usr/local/ntripcaster$ cd conf/
ubuntu@ip-instance:/usr/local/ntripcaster/conf$ ls
ubuntu@ip-instance:/usr/local/ntripcaster/conf$ sudo mv
ntripcaster.conf.dist ntripcaster.conf
ubuntu@ip-instance:/usr/local/ntripcaster/conf$ sudo mv
sourcetable.dat.dist sourcetable.dat
```

Next we need to modify the config file with the following commands:

```
ubuntu@ip-instance:/usr/local/ntripcaster/conf$ sudo vi
ntripcaster.conf
```

Then set the following items:

- location, rp_email, and server_url
- encoder_password

- server_name and port
- logdir path and logfile name
- Add mount point. The format is:

example: /mount:user0:123456,user1:123456

mountpoint name	user0 name	user0 password	user1 name	user1 password	more users
mount	user0	123456	user1	123456	...

```
ubuntu@ip-10-0-0-191:/usr/local/ntripcaster/conf$ more ntripcaster.conf
###################################
# NtripCaster configuration file #
################################################################################

################# Server Location and Resposible Person #########################
# Server meta info with no fuctionality.

location China-SZ
rp_email support@perceptin.io        (1)
server_url https://www.perceptin.io

############################# Server Limits #####################################
# Maximum number of simultaneous connections.

max_clients 100
max_clients_per_source 100
max_sources 40

########################### Server passwords ####################################
# The "encoder_password" is used from the sources to log in.

encoder_password ######        (2)

##################### Server IP/port configuration ##############################
# The server_name specifies the hostname of the server and must not be set to
# an IP-adress. It is very important that server_name resolves to the IP-adress
# the server is running at.
# For every port, the server should listen to, a new port line can be added.

server_name PI_NtripServer
#port 80         (3)
port 2101

######################### Main Server Logfile ###################################
# logfile contains information about connections, warnings, errors etc.

logdir /usr/local/ntripcaster/logs
logfile ntripcaster.log        (4)

####################### Access Control ###########################
# Here you specify which users have access to which mountpoints,
# one line per mount.
#
# Syntax: /<MOUNTPOINT>:<USER1>:<PASSWORD1>,<USER2>:<PASSWORD2>,....,<USERn>:<PASSWORDn>
#
# /<MOUNTPOINT>: name of the mountpoint. Must start with a slash.
# <USERi>: name of the user that has access to <MOUNTPOINT>.
# <PASSWORDi>: password of <USERi>.
#
# example:
#/mount0:user0:pass0,user1:pass1,user2:pass2
/mount : user0 : 123456, user1 : 123456        (5)
```

```
ubuntu@ip-instance:/usr/local/ntripcaster/conf$ sudo vi
sourcetable.dat
```

At the end of the sourcetable.dat file add new source data in the following format; the mount point and the network must be consistent with ntripcaster.conf file's mount point name and user0 name.

In the sourcetable.dat, one row represents a mount point. Each line is separated by a semicolon, the meaning of which is shown in the following table:

Number	Name	Description
1	STR	type:STR/CAS/NET
2	mount	Mountpoint
3	Shen Zhen	identifier
4	RTCM 3.2	Differential data format
5	1004,1008	format-details
6	1	Carrier phase data: 0 – none 1 – Single frequency 2 – Dual frequency
7	GPS	Navigation System, e.g. GPS, GPS + GLONASS
8	PI	network
9	CHN	country
10	22.58	latitude
11	113.93	longitude
12	0	Need to send NMEA: 0 – no need 1 – need
13	0	Base station type: 0 – Single base station 1 – network
14	PI	The name of the software that generated this data stream
15	none	Compression algorithm
16	B	Access protection: N – None B – Basic D – Digest
17	N	Y/N
18	115200	baud rate

5.4.2   Start NtripCaster

Once you are done with the steps above, we can start the NtripCaster:

```
ubuntu@ip-instance:~$ cd /usr/local/ntripcaster/bin
ubuntu@ip-
instance:/usr/local/ntripcaster/bin$ sudo ./ntripcaster
```

Log in to the NtripCaster server and check the server status using the following command:

```
ubuntu@ip-instance:~$ ps -aux | grep ntrip
```

Start the Ntripcaster command:

```
ubuntu@ip-instance:~$ cd /usr/local/ntripcaster/bin
ubuntu@ip-
instance:/usr/local/ntripcaster/bin$ sudo ./ntripcaster
```

We can then use the following nohup command to have a NtripCaster process running in the background:

```
ubuntu@ip-instance:~$ cd /usr/local/ntripcaster/bin
ubuntu@ip-
instance:/usr/local/ntripcaster/bin$ nohup ./ntripcaster
```

5.5 Setting Up NtripServer and NtripClient on Raspberry Pi

5.5.1 Install the Raspberry Pi System

Figure 5.5 shows the Raspberry Pi setup procedure. Raspberry Pi hardware version: Raspberry Pi 3 Model B+

- Download the Raspberry Pi system under Windows system: https://www.raspberrypi .org/downloads/raspbian/. Choose Raspbian Stretch with desktop and recommended software, and click Download ZIP to obtain the system image file.

Figure 5.5 Raspberry Pi setup.

Figure 5.6 SD card setup.

- Figure 5.6 shows the SD/TF (TransFlash) card setup procedure. Download and install the TF card formatting tool under Windows system: SD card formatter. Format the Raspberry Pi TF card in FAT32 format.
- Download and install the system image file writing tool under Windows system: win32diskimager. Write the Raspberry Pi system image to the TF card.
- After writing the system image file, open the TF card and create a new txt file in the root directory, and rename it ssh without the suffix. This file is for opening the ssh function.
- Insert the TF card into the Raspberry Pi, then connect the monitor, keyboard, mouse, and power on. Set the Raspberry Pi password and connect to WiFi in the boot setup wizard. (You can also connect to the network through a network cable).
- After completing the boot setup wizard, install RTKLIB and create a Raspberry Pi access point.
- Install and compile RTKLIB, open a terminal and run the following command:
  git clone https://github.com/tomojitakasu/RTKLIB.git

  cd /RTKLIB/app/str2str/gcc
  make //Compile and generate the str2str executable file

- Create a Raspberry Pi access point and run the following command in the terminal:
  sudo apt-get install vim

  git clone https://github.com/oblique/create_ap
  cd create_ap
  sudo make install

sudo apt-get install util-linux procps hostapd iproute2 iw haveged dnsmasq
sudo create_ap wlan0 eth0 access-point-name password//Create a WiFi access point

Note:

(a) When the Raspberry Pi creates a WiFi access point, it must first disconnect its WiFi connection, otherwise the command runs incorrectly and prompts: your adapter cannot be a station an access point at the same time.
(b) Add (sudo create_ap wlan0 eth0 access-point-name password &) to the /etc/rc.local file, and set the Raspberry Pi to automatically create a WiFi access point when it starts. The setting example is:

```
#!/bin/sh -e
#
# rc.local
#
# This script is executed at the end of each multiuser runlevel.
# Make sure that the script will "exit 0" on success or any other
# value on error.
#
# In order to enable or disable this script just change the execution
# bits.
#
# By default this script does nothing.

# Print the IP address
_IP=$(hostname -I) || true
if [ "$_IP" ]; then
  printf "My IP address is %s\n" "$_IP"
fi

nohup /home/pi/RTKLIB/app/str2str/gcc/str2str -in serial://ttyUSB0:115200:8:n:1 -out ntrips://:password@IP:port/mountpoint > /dev/null &
sudo create_ap wlan0 eth0 wifi-name password &
exit 0
```

- After setting up the WiFi access point successfully, you can use your laptop to connect the Raspberry Pi WiFi, and then log in to the Raspberry Pi via ssh pi@192.168.12.1.

5.5.2 Run RTKLIB-str2str on the Raspberry Pi

5.5.2.1 Running NtripServer on the Base Station Side

Figure 5.7 shows the circuit connection diagram of the base station. The role of the Raspberry Pi is to connect 4G terminals and transmit differential signals over the network to the NTRIP caster.

After the Raspberry Pi is plugged in the 4G terminal and can access the Internet, run the str2str program to send differential signals to the NTRIP caster. The command is as follows:

```
sudo home/pi/RTKLIB/app/str2str/gcc/str2str -in
serial://ttyUSB0:115200:8:n:1   \
-out ntrips://:password@IP:port/mountpoint
```

The result is as follows after successful execution:

```
2018/06/05 07:34:45 [CC---]    338527 B    3680 bps (0) 60.205.8.49/RTCM32_GGB
2018/06/05 07:34:50 [CC---]    340894 B    3916 bps (0) 60.205.8.49/RTCM32_GGB
2018/06/05 07:34:55 [CC---]    343199 B    3688 bps (0) 60.205.8.49/RTCM32_GGB
2018/06/05 07:35:00 [CC---]    345566 B    3924 bps (0) 60.205.8.49/RTCM32_GGB
2018/06/05 07:35:05 [CC---]    347871 B    3675 bps (0) 60.205.8.49/RTCM32_GGB
2018/06/05 07:35:10 [CC---]    350238 B    3934 bps (0) 60.205.8.49/RTCM32_GGB
2018/06/05 07:35:15 [CC---]    352543 B    3684 bps (0) 60.205.8.49/RTCM32_GGB
2018/06/05 07:35:20 [CC---]    354910 B    3918 bps (0) 60.205.8.49/RTCM32_GGB
2018/06/05 07:35:25 [CC---]    357215 B    3676 bps (0) 60.205.8.49/RTCM32_GGB
2018/06/05 07:35:30 [CC---]    359582 B    3936 bps (0) 60.205.8.49/RTCM32_GGB
2018/06/05 07:35:35 [CC---]    361887 B    3680 bps (0) 60.205.8.49/RTCM32_GGB
2018/06/05 07:35:40 [CC---]    364254 B    3916 bps (0) 60.205.8.49/RTCM32_GGB
2018/06/05 07:35:45 [CC---]    366559 B    3678 bps (0) 60.205.8.49/RTCM32_GGB
```

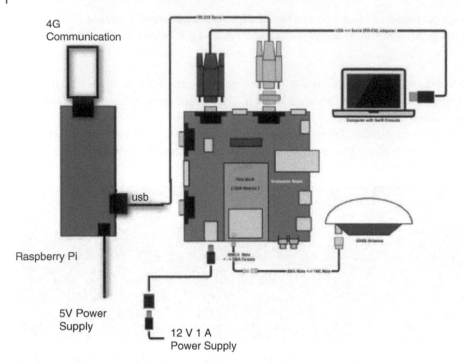

Figure 5.7 Connecting Raspberry Pi to the GNSS station.

Then write the following command to the Raspberry Pi's/etc/rc.local file to set the Raspberry Pi to run NTRIP server automatically when starting. The setting example is:

```
nohup /home/pi/RTKLIB/app/str2str/gcc/str2str -in
serial://ttyUSB0:115200:8:n:1 \
-out ntrips://:password@IP:port/mountpoint > /dev/null &
```

```
#!/bin/sh -e
#
# rc.local
#
# This script is executed at the end of each multiuser runlevel.
# Make sure that the script will "exit 0" on success or any other
# value on error.
#
# In order to enable or disable this script just change the execution
# bits.
#
# By default this script does nothing.

# Print the IP address
_IP=$(hostname -I) || true
if [ "$_IP" ]; then
  printf "my IP address is %s\n" "$_IP"
fi

nohup /home/pi/RTKLIB/app/str2str/gcc/str2str -in serial://ttyUSB0:115200:8:n:1 -out ntrips://:password@IP:port/mountpoint > /dev/null &

sudo create_ap wlan0 eth0 wifi-name password &

exit 0
```

5.5.2.2 Running NtripClient on the GNSS Rover

The role of the Raspberry Pi is to connect 4G terminals and receive differential signals over the network from the NTRIP caster. After the Raspberry Pi is plugged in the 4G terminal and can access the Internet, run the str2str program to receive differential signals from the NTRIP caster. The command is as follows:

```
sudo /home/pi/RTKLIB/app/str2str/gcc/str2str -in \
ntrip://user:password:@IP:port/mountpoint -out
serial://ttyUSB0:115200:8:n:1
```

Then write the following command to the Raspberry Pi's/etc/rc.local file to set the Raspberry Pi to run NTRIP client automatically when starting. The setting format is:

```
nohup /home/pi/RTKLIB/app/str2str/gcc/str2str -in \
ntrip://user:password@IP:port/mountpoint -out
serial://ttyUSB0:115200:8:n:1 >/dev/null &
```

5.6 Setting Up a Base Station and a GNSS Rover

5.6.1 Base Station Hardware Setup

Figure 5.8 shows the base station setup architecture; Figure 5.9 shows the components required for the base station setup; Figure 5.10 shows the base station setup steps; Figure 5.11 shows how to connect your base station receiver to a PC; and Figure 5.12 shows the proper way to place a base station antenna (in a place with open sky, for example on a roof top).

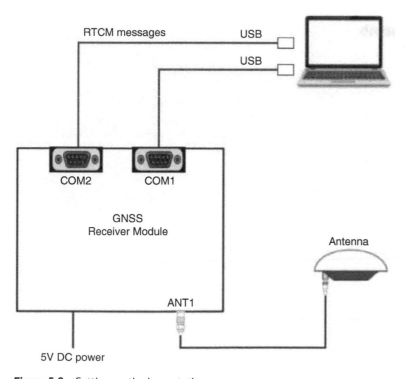

Figure 5.8 Setting up the base station.

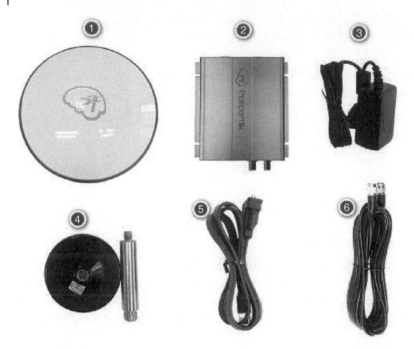

Figure 5.9 Components: 1, antenna; 2, GNSS receiver module; 3, power supply (5 V); 4, magnetic foundation plate; 5, serial to USB connector; and 6, antenna cable (TNC male to TNC male).

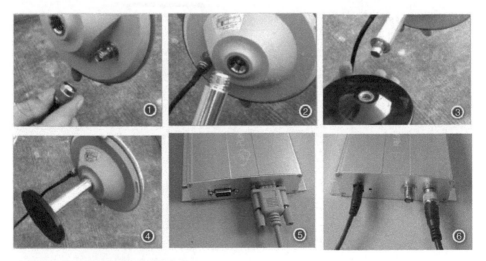

Figure 5.10 Setup steps.

5.6.2 Base Station Software Setup

First enter the following commands:

```
sudo apt-get install cutecom
sudo cutecom
```

Figure 5.11 Connection to PC.

Figure 5.12 Placement of a GNSS base station antenna.

Then check the COM1 serial device number on PC (/dev/ttyUSB0) as shown below, then click Open device. Figure 5.13 shows the device setup interface.

Next set the base antenna position.

Input "freset" in the command line and press the "Enter" button. Figure 5.14 shows how to input the freset command.

Figure 5.15 shows what will be seen if the "freset" command is executed successfully.

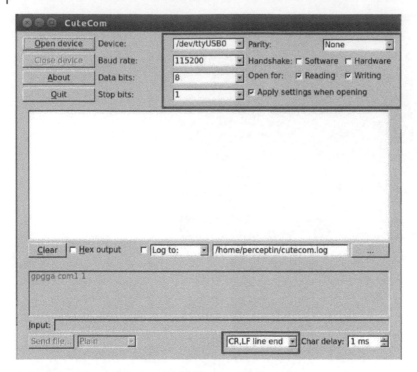

Figure 5.13 Device setup interface.

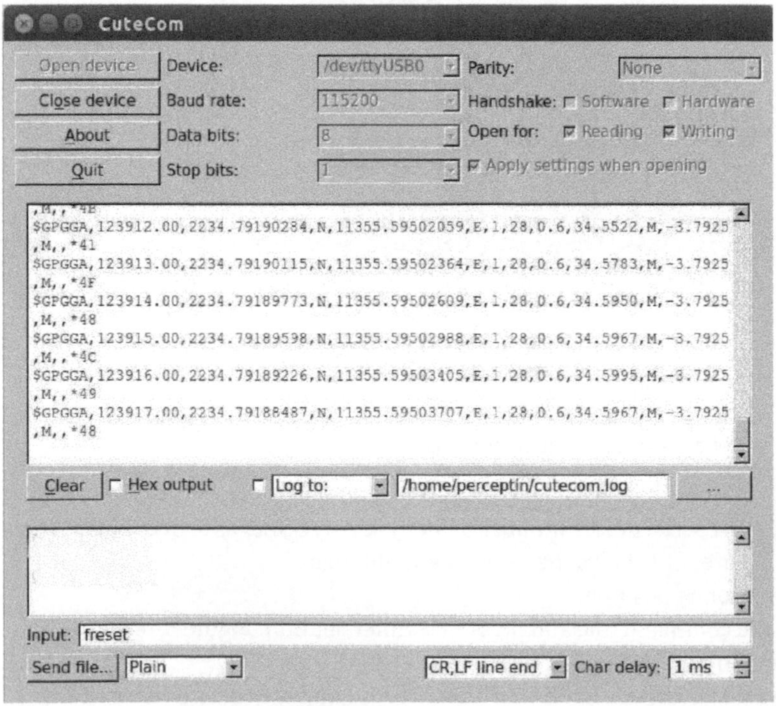

Figure 5.14 Input of the freset command.

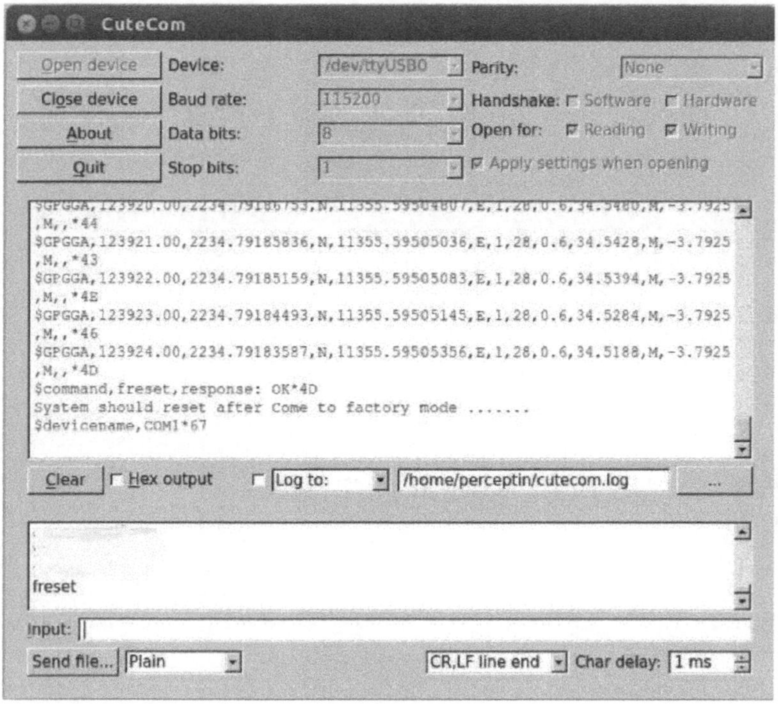

Figure 5.15 Freset command successful.

Enter the following command: gpgga com1 1

//set the output GPGGA frequency 1 Hz. If executed successfully, you will see "$command,gpgga com1 1,response: OK * 49" and the GPGGA message [7]. Figure 5.16 illustrates this.

Enter the following command: mode base time 60 1.5 2.5

//If executed this command successfully will display "$command,mode base time 60 1.5 2.5, response OK * 78". Then we need to wait 60 s when the GPGGA fix status is 7, base station set ok.

Figure 5.17 shows the "command successful" screenshot and Figure 5.18 shows the proper GPGGA fix status.

$GPGGA,045526.002234.79008586,N,11355.59480467,E,7,25,0.6,34.7453,M,-3.7924,M,,*43

Enter the following command: rtcm1006 com2 10

//If successful you will see "$command,rtcm1006 com2 10, response OK * 03"

Enter the following command: rtcm1033 com2 10

//If successful you will see "$command,rtcm1033 com2 10, response OK * 05"

Enter the following command: rtcm1074 com2 1

//If successful you will see "$command,rtcm1074 com2 1, response OK * 36"

Enter the following command: rtcm1124 com2 1

//Set BDS correction message, if command successful you will see "$command,rtcm1124 com2 1, response OK * 32"

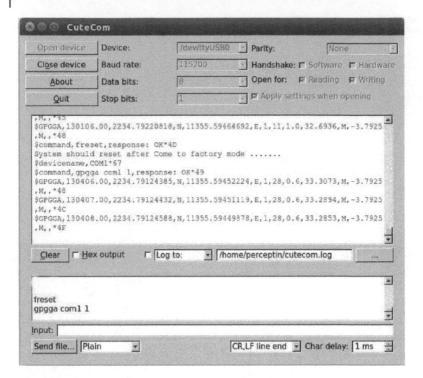

Figure 5.16 "gpgga com1 1" command successful.

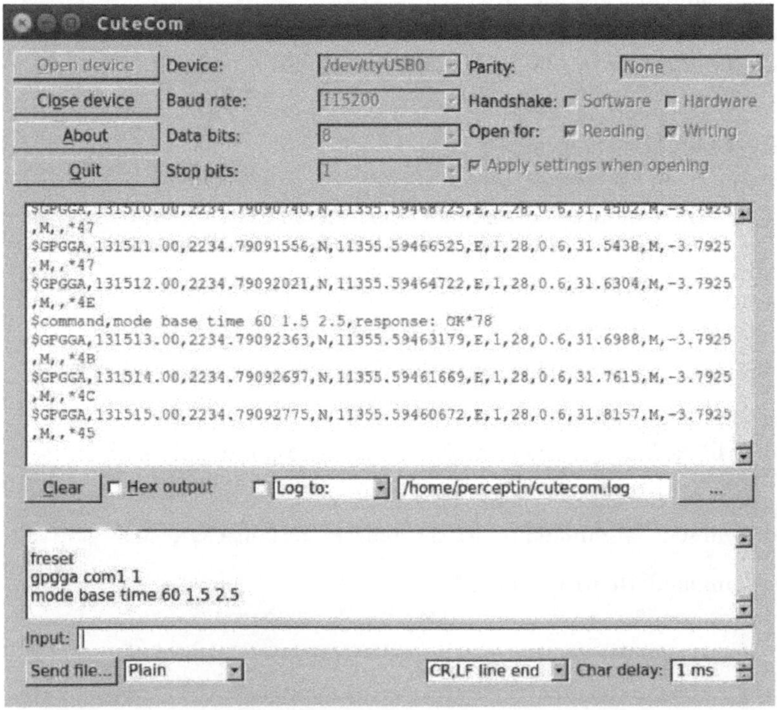

Figure 5.17 "mode base time 60 1.5 2.5" command successful.

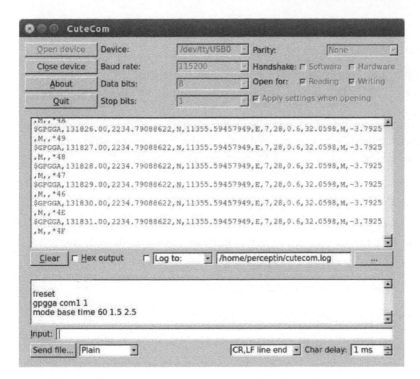

Figure 5.18 GPGGA flx status.

Enter the following command: rtcm1084 com2 1

//Set GLONASS correction message, if command successful you will see "$command, rtcm1084 com2 1, response OK * 39"

Enter the following command: rtcm1094 com2 1

//Set Galileo correction message, if command successful you will see "$command, rtcm1094 com2 1, response OK * 38"

Enter the following command: saveconfig

//save config, if command successful you will see "$command,saveconfig, response OK * 55"

Note:

If we want to get a more accurate base station signal, a long base time shall be set. For example:

mode base time 7200 1.5 2.5. Usually we want to set the base time to be at least two hours to get a highly stable base station signal.

If we want to set the base antenna position manually, we could execute the following command:

mode base latitude longitude altitude

Example:

mode base 22.5798755945 113.926580413 34.1254713577

//the base station position is latitude = 22.5798755945, longitude = 113.926580413, altitude = 34.1254713577. The units of latitude and longitude are degree, the unit of altitude is meter.

If we want to skip the waiting time (mode base time 7200 1.5 2.5) when restarting the base station after configured first time, we need to set the base antenna position manually after we have obtained the averages of the GPS positions. For example:

By the GPGGA message:
\$GPGGA,045526.002234.79008586, N,11355.59480467,E, 7,25,0.6,34.7453,M,-3.7924,M,,*43

In the GPGGA message the format of latitude is ddmm.mm and the format of longitude is dddmm.mm. We need to transform the format of latitude and longitude to degree, calculated as follows:

$$\text{Latitude} = 22 + (34.79008586 / 60) = 22.579834764$$

$$\text{Longitude} = 113 + (55.59480467 / 60) = 113.926580078$$

And then execute the following command:

mode base 22.579834764 113.926580108 34.7453
saveconfig

Connecting to the NtripCaster in Linux:
The str2str module of RTKLIB is used to set up the NtripServer and NtripClient.

Steps to set up NtripServer in Linux:
Compile RTKLIB

```
git clone https://github.com/tomojitakasu/RTKLIB.git
cd /RTKLIB/app/str2str/gcc
make
```

```
perceptin@perceptin-TM1704:~/RTKLIB/RTKLIB-master/app/str2str/gcc$ ls
binex.o      javad.o     preceph.o    rtcm3e.o   sbas.o       str2str      ublox.o
crescent.o   makefile    rcvraw.o     rtcm3.o    skytraq.o    str2str.o
geoid.o      novatel.o   rt17.o       rtcm.o     solution.o   stream.o
gw10.o       nvs.o       rtcm2.o      rtkcmn.o   ss2.o        streamsvr.o
```

Test base station COM2 output to NtripCaster

Check the COM2 serial device number on PC (/dev/ttyUSB1), then execute the following command:

```
sudo /home/perceptin/RTKLIB/RTKLIB-
master/app/str2str/gcc/str2str   -in  \
serial://ttyUSB1:115200:8:n:1   -out
ntrips://:password@IP:PORT/Mountpoint
```

If data connected to NtripCaster, you will see:

```
2018/06/05 07:34:45 [CC---]    338527 B    3680 bps (0) 60.205.8.49/RTCM32_GGB
2018/06/05 07:34:50 [CC---]    340894 B    3916 bps (0) 60.205.8.49/RTCM32_GGB
2018/06/05 07:34:55 [CC---]    343199 B    3688 bps (0) 60.205.8.49/RTCM32_GGB
2018/06/05 07:35:00 [CC---]    345566 B    3924 bps (0) 60.205.8.49/RTCM32_GGB
2018/06/05 07:35:05 [CC---]    347871 B    3675 bps (0) 60.205.8.49/RTCM32_GGB
2018/06/05 07:35:10 [CC---]    350238 B    3934 bps (0) 60.205.8.49/RTCM32_GGB
2018/06/05 07:35:15 [CC---]    352543 B    3684 bps (0) 60.205.8.49/RTCM32_GGB
2018/06/05 07:35:20 [CC---]    354910 B    3918 bps (0) 60.205.8.49/RTCM32_GGB
2018/06/05 07:35:25 [CC---]    357215 B    3676 bps (0) 60.205.8.49/RTCM32_GGB
2018/06/05 07:35:30 [CC---]    359582 B    3936 bps (0) 60.205.8.49/RTCM32_GGB
2018/06/05 07:35:35 [CC---]    361887 B    3680 bps (0) 60.205.8.49/RTCM32_GGB
2018/06/05 07:35:40 [CC---]    364254 B    3916 bps (0) 60.205.8.49/RTCM32_GGB
2018/06/05 07:35:45 [CC---]    366559 B    3678 bps (0) 60.205.8.49/RTCM32_GGB
```

If base station COM2 output to NtripCaster is successful, we need to plug the COM2 USB into the base station Raspberry Pi.

5.6.3   GNSS Rover Setup

5.6.3.1   Rover Hardware Setup

A rover station is composed of two GNSS antenna, which output the position and vehicle heading. Figure 5.19 shows the rover hardware setup architecture; Figure 5.20 shows the components needed for the rover; Figure 5.21 shows the proper way to set up the antennas on a rover; and Figure 5.22 shows the proper cable connection.

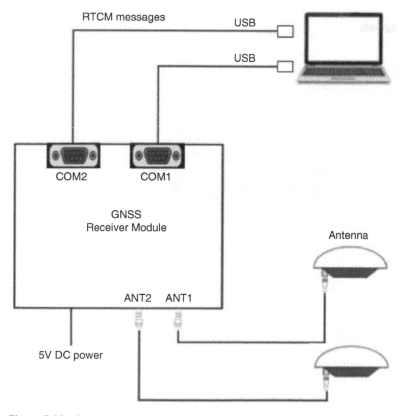

Figure 5.19   Rover hardware setup.

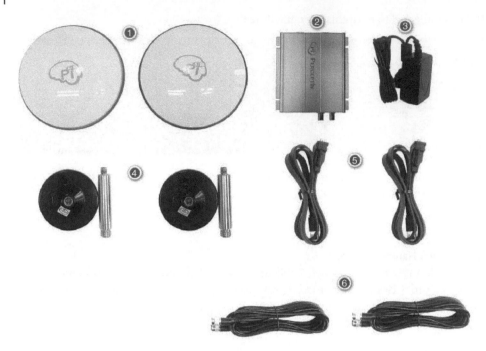

Figure 5.20 Rover hardware components: 1, GNSS antenna; 2, GNSS receiver module; 3, power supply (5 V); 4, magnetic foundation plate; 5, serial to USB connector; and 6, GNSS antenna cable (TNC male to TNC male).

Figure 5.21 Rover station antenna installation.

5.6.3.2 Rover Software Setup

Connect to GNSS module (Figure 5.23):

(5) Connect Rover station COM1 serial to PC.

(6) sudo cutecom //Open serial port tool.

(7) Check the Rover station COM1 serial device number on PC (/dev/ttyUSB0), then click "Open device".

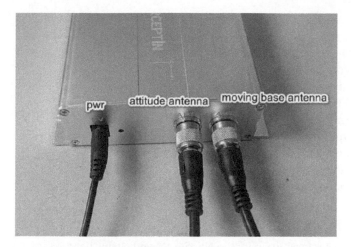

Figure 5.22 Cable connection.

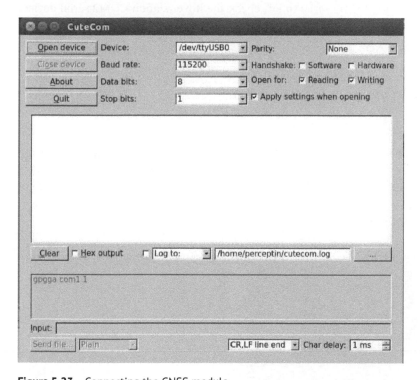

Figure 5.23 Connecting the GNSS module.

Set the com1 output frequency
(1) Enter command: gpgga com1 0.05
//set gpgga com1 output frequency to 20Hz, if command successful you will see "$command,gpgga com1 0.05, response OK * 63"

(2) Enter command: gprmc com1 0.05

//set gprmc com1 output frequency to 20Hz, if command successful you will see "$command,gprmc com1 0.05, response OK * 7E"

(3) Enter command: gphdt com1 0.05

//set gphdt com1 output frequency to 20Hz, if command successful you will see "$command,gphdt com1 0.05, response OK * 7A"

(4) Enter command: headinga com1 0.05

//set headinga com1 output frequency to 20Hz, if command successful you will see "$command,headinga com1 0.05, response OK * 1C"

(5) Enter command: saveconfig

//save config, if command successful, you will see "$command,saveconfig, response OK * 55"

Connecting to the NtripCaster in Linux:

The str2str module of RTKLIB is used to set up the NtipServer and NtripClient.

Steps to set up NtripClient in Linux:

Connect Rover station COM2 serial to PC, check the Rover station COM2 serial device number on PC (/dev/ttyUSB1).

Test Rover station COM2 receive RTCM data from NtripCaster, run the command:

```
sudo /home/perceptin/RTKLIB/RTKLIB-
master/app/str2str/gcc/str2str    -in \
ntrip://:user:password@IP:PORT/Mountpoint   -out
serial://ttyUSB1:115200:8:n:1
```

If RTCM data successfully received from NtripCaster, the data size and rate would show on the screen, and the COM1 output GPGGA message would display fix status (the value is 4).

If Rover station COM2 receives RTCM data from NtripCaster successfully, we need to plug the COM2 USB into the Rover station Raspberry Pi. Figure 5.24 illustrates the rover station output on the screen.

Figure 5.24 Rover station output on the screen.

5.7   FreeWave Radio Basic Configuration

In previous sections, we demonstrated how to set up a cloud server to stream RTK correction data from a base station. However, if we do not want to set up a cloud server, we can utilize a FreeWave radio to transmit RTCM data.

If we use FreeWave radio to transmit RTCM data, we will not need a cloud server account and Raspberry Pi, we simply need to connect the COM2 serial interface of the base station and rover station to FreeWave radio. The RTK-GNSS data transmission scheme by FreeWave radio is shown in Figure 5.25.

FreeWave 900 MHz or 2.4 GHz radios for use during evaluation of our RTK-GNSS receivers. Those radios need to be properly configured. Now we describe configuration steps for RTK base and RTK rover radios. Note that radios can be configured using a simple serial terminal program or FreeWave Tool Suite. A terminal program is used below:

(1) Install terminal program for Linux:

```
sudo apt-get install gtkterm
```

(2) Radio hardware setup

For configuration, radios should be connected to your computer via the RS-232 port using a straight RS-232 cable. If there is no RS-232 port on your computer, use a USB to RS-232 adapter. FreeWave radios require a 6–30 V DC power supply. Use the wall power adapter included with the radios, or a 12 V battery, to power the radio during configuration.

(3) Entering radio programming mode

Follow these steps to set the radio in the programming mode:
- Attach antenna to the radio board. The radio should be never powered without antenna attached.
- Connect the radio's RS-232 port to the PC, use a USB to RS-232 adapter if necessary.
- Power up the radio.
- Open terminal program and configure port parameters to 19 200 bps, 8 bits, no parity, 1 stop bit, no flow control:
  (a) In CoolTerm, click on Options button, set the parameters, then click Connect button.
  (b) In GtkTerm, click on Configuration →Port (Shift+Ctrl+s).
- Press radio Programming Button located next to the Power Input on the radio board. All three light-emitting diodes (LEDs) on the board should show solid green and you will be presented with a menu on the terminal screen as shown in Figures 5.26 and 5.27.

(4) Programming radio for RTK base station

Follow these steps to program the radio as a transmitter of RTK base station corrections. This radio will work as a Point-to-MultiPoint Master. It will be able to transmit corrections to multiple rovers simultaneously:
- Enter radio programming mode as described in point (3).

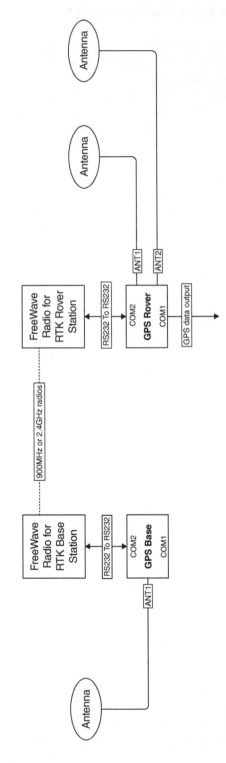

Figure 5.25 RTK-GNSS data transmission scheme by FreeWave radio.

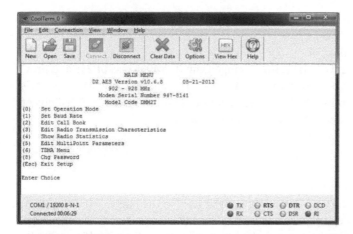

Figure 5.26   900 MHz or 2.4 GHz radio programming screen on CoolTerm.

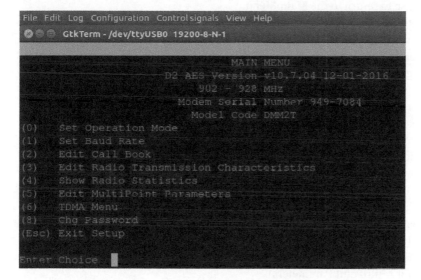

Figure 5.27   900 MHz or 2.4 GHz radio programming screen on GtkTerm.

- Press 0 (Set Operation Mode):
  (a) Press 2 (Point-to-MultiPoint Master).
  (b) Press Esc to return to the Main Menu.
- Press 1 (Set Baud Rate):
  (a) Press 1 (115200).
  (b) Press Esc to return to the Main Menu.
- Press 5 (Edit MultiPoint Parameters):
  (a) Press 0 (Number Repeaters)
    • Press 0
  (b) Press 1 (Master Packet Repeat)
    • Press 0

    (c) Press 2 (Max Slave Retry)
- Press 0

    (d) Press 6 (Network ID)
- Enter desired network ID value in range from 0 to 4095 except 255 and press Enter (value 255 will enable Call Book instead of Network ID). It is recommended to use the last three or four (when lower than 4095) digits of the base station Radio Number as the network ID.

    (e) Press Esc to return to the Main Menu.
- Optionally, to change radio power output, press 3 (Edit Radio Transmission Characteristics).

    (f) Press 5 (RF Xmit Power).
- On 900 MHz radio enter the desired power level in the range 0–10 ($0 = 5$ mW, $3 = 80$ mW, $5 = 230$ mW, $7 = 480$ mW, $10 = 1$ W).
- On 2.4 GHz radio enter the desired power level in dBm (20 dBm $= 0.1$ W, 27 dBm $= 0.5$ W).

    (g) Press Esc to return to the Main Menu.
- Press Esc to Exit Setup.
- Power off the radio. Settings are saved in the radio's non-volatile memory. The radio is ready for RTK operation.

(5) Programming radio for RTK rover

Follow these steps to program the radio as a receiver of RTK corrections. This radio will work as a Point-to-MultiPoint slave. It will not be able to transmit any data (only receive it). Use the same radio settings for all rover radios in the system with multiple rovers.

- Enter radio programming mode as described in point (3).
- Press 0 (Set Operation Mode):

    (a) Press 3 (Point-to-MultiPoint Slave).

    (b) Press Esc to return to the Main Menu.
- Press 1 (Set Baud Rate):

    (a) Press 1 (115200).

    (b) Press Esc to return to the Main Menu.
- Press 5 (Edit MultiPoint Parameters):

    (a) Press 0 (Number Repeaters)
- Press 0

    (b) Press 1 (Master Packet Repeat)
- Press 0

    (c) Press 2 (Max Slave Retry)
- Press 0 (Note: if transmission from rover to base is required, set Max Slave Retry to 1).

    (d) Press 3 (Retry Odds)
- Press 0

    (e) Press 6 (Network ID)
- Enter the same network ID value as set in RTK base station radio above and press <Enter>.

    (f) Press Esc to return to the Main Menu.

	CD	TX	CTS
Base	⬤	⬤	off
Rover	⬤	off	⬤

Figure 5.28 LED configuration.

  – Press Esc to Exit Setup.
  – Power off the radio. Settings are saved in the radio's non-volatile memory. The radio is ready for RTK operation.
(6) LED indicators
  If the radio has been configured correctly, the LEDs should illuminate as shown in Figure 5.28.
(7) Troubleshooting
  For radios to communicate with other radios in the same network, the following five settings must match on all radios: Network ID, Frequency Key, RF Data Rate, Minimum Packet Size, and Maximum Packet Size. If any of these settings do not match, the radios will not link.

References

1 Misra, P. and Enge, P. (2006). *Global Positioning System: Signals, Measurements and Performance*, 2e. Lincoln, MA: Ganga-Jamuna Press.
2 Leick, A., Rapoport, L., and Tatarnikov, D. (2015). *GPS Satellite Surveying*. Wiley.
3 Jeffrey, C. (2010). *An Introduction to GNSS*. Calgary, AB: NovAtel Inc.
4 Groves, P.D. (2013). *Principles of GNSS, Inertial, and Multisensor Integrated Navigation Systems*. Artech House.
5 Irsigler, M., Avila-Rodriguez, J.A., and Hein, G.W. (2005). Criteria for GNSS multipath performance assessment. *Proceedings of ION GNSS 2005*, Long Beach, CA (13–16 September 2005).
6 Rieder, M.J. and Kirchengast, G. (2001). Error analysis and characterization of atmospheric profiles retrieved from GNSS occultation data. *Journal of Geophysical Research: Atmospheres* 106 (D23): 31755–31770.
7 GPS Information (2017). NMEA data. https://www.gpsinformation.org/dale/nmea.htm (accessed 24 November 2019).

6

Computer Vision for Perception and Localization

6.1 Introduction

As shown in Figure 6.1, computer vision is an essential part of the modular design methodology for building autonomous vehicles and robots. Computer vision provides two essential functions: localization, which answers the question of *where I am,* and perception, which answers the question of *what is around me* [1].

In this chapter we review the details of computer vision technologies. In Section 6.2, we start with computer vision hardware design and introduce the challenges of building computer vision hardware. In Section 6.3, we introduce the concept of calibration and delve into a few calibration techniques. In Section 6.4, we explain how you can use computer vision for localization. In Section 6.5, we explain how you can use computer vision for perception. In Section 6.6, we present a case study of PerceptIn's DragonFly computer vision module.

After reading this chapter, readers should be able to understand how to use computer vision technologies in their autonomous vehicle and robot designs, as well as how to combine computer vision and other sensors to achieve better localization and perception results.

6.2 Building Computer Vision Hardware

Building computer vision hardware to perform both perception and localization tasks is extremely challenging as there are many design factors we need to consider. These include what kind of image sensors to use, what kind of lenses to use, and whether to do computing on device or off device. In this section, we review these design challenges in detail.

Engineering Autonomous Vehicles and Robots: The DragonFly Modular-based Approach,
First Edition. Shaoshan Liu.

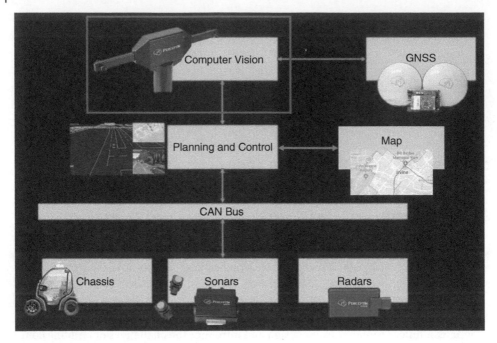

Figure 6.1 Modular design architecture.

6.2.1 Seven Layers of Technologies

As shown in Figure 6.2, to build one computer vision hardware device, you have at least seven layers of technology choices to consider:

- *Lens*: A lens decides how much light to let into to the image sensor. The simplest model of a lens is a pinhole model, which is simply a small aperture that blocks most rays of light, ideally selecting one ray to the object for each point on the image sensor. The two fundamental parameters of a lens are the focal length and the maximum aperture. The focal length determines the magnification of the image projected onto the image plane, and the

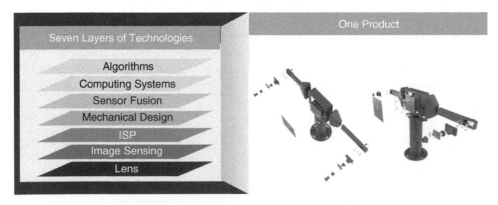

Figure 6.2 Seven layers of technologies to build computer vision hardware.

aperture the light intensity of that image. The focal length determines the field of view, short focal lengths giving a wider field of view than longer focal length lenses. On the other hand, a wider aperture allows a faster shutter speed to be used for the same exposure.

- *Image sensing*: An image sensor detects and conveys information used to make an image. It achieves this by converting the variable attenuation of light waves into digital signals. The waves can be light or other electromagnetic radiation. Cameras integrated in consumer products generally use complementary metal oxide semiconductor (CMOS) sensors, which are usually cheaper and have lower power consumption in battery-powered devices than charge-coupled devices (CCDs). CCD sensors are used for high-end cameras, such as those deployed on satellites. One example of adjusting image sensors for different usage scenarios is that you can use visible light sensors in day time, and use infrared imaging sensing to provide superior vision in the dark,

- *Image signal processor* (ISP): An ISP controls demosaicing (a digital image process used to reconstruct a full color image from the incomplete color samples output from an image sensor), autofocus, exposure, and white balance for a camera system. Especially, pixels in an image sensor are sensitive to light between some set of wavelengths, essentially they are color agnostic. The way to get a color image out is to put a filter on top, usually a Bayer pattern color filter, then interpolate the color of the adjacent pixels. Therefore, choosing the correct ISP and its parameters is extremely important for geometric feature detection under different lighting conditions.

- *Mechanical design*: When you have multiple sensors, such as a pair of cameras, mechanical design is extremely important to ensure the module's rigidity, even under a wide range of operating temperatures as well as vibrations. A great mechanical design reduces, if not completely eliminates, the need for system recalibration, which we try to minimize for commercial products.

- *Sensor fusion*: It is challenging to fuse multiple sensors together, as each new sensor would introduce more complexities on the calibration and synchronization of the system. Before we can use the fused data, we need to guarantee that data from different sensors are spatially and temporally calibrated.

- *Computing systems*: Computer vision algorithms are extremely computationally expensive, therefore it is challenging to develop a computing system that delivers high speed and good quality. Acceleration of computing workloads can be achieved through different techniques, such as parallel processing, hardware acceleration, or offloading the computing to a more powerful machine.

- *Algorithms*: Once you have your sensor system and your computing system ready, then you need to decide what algorithms to run on your computer vision system. Usually, computer vision can be used for both perception and localization. For localization, using a vision only system, you can use visual simultaneous localization and mapping (VSLAM) for localization. With a vision system and an inertial measurement unit (IMU), you can perform Visual-Inertial Odometry (VIO) for localization. With a vision system, an IMU, and a Global Navigation Satellite System (GNSS), you can perform VIO-GNSS fusion for localization, in which GNSS provides ground-truth data with good signal reception. For perception, using a stereo camera system, you can perform depth estimation by generating an accurate disparity map. In addition, with vision, you can perform image segmentation using deep learning techniques.

6.2.2 Hardware Synchronization

Next, assuming that your computer vision hardware does perform sensor fusion, then we need to consider how to synchronize different hardware sensors. For instance, if you need to perform stereo vision computation to extract object depth information, then it is essential that images from both cameras are synchronized. Otherwise, if the left image comes in 100 ms after the right image, then there is no way you can generate accurate depth information, especially when you deploy this computer vision device on a moving vehicle. The system design becomes more and more complex as you add more sensors, such as IMU and GNSS, to the system.

As shown in Figure 6.3, the latencies between CMOS image sensor and ISP, and ISP and CPU, are both roughly 10 ns through the mobile industry processor interface (MIPI). This latency number also holds for the IMU data which is triggered through the I2C interface. The image pre-processing on ISP takes ~10 ms which is still reasonable, especially the latency is consistent with little uncertainty.

The closer to sensor we perform synchronization, the less temporal variations we will observe between sensors. For instance, if we have a piece of hardware to directly synchronize the image sensors, we will get ~10 ns latency variation, which is negligible. On the other hand, if we perform synchronization at the application level, we may get up to ~100 ms latency variation, which can be catastrophic.

Therefore for stereo vision, if both image sensors are connected to the same ISP, then one efficient and simple way to synchronize the two image sensors is to use the ISP to trigger hardware synchronization between the image sensors and to trigger auto exposure and image pre-processing to improve image quality.

6.2.3 Computing

Once we are done with synchronization, we get clean sensor data, and then we have to consider computing. Computer vision based computing is extremely demanding. Eventually it becomes a tradeoff between frame rate and computing power. With commercial off-the-shelf embedded processors, it is very hard to achieve high frame rates (e.g. >15 frames per

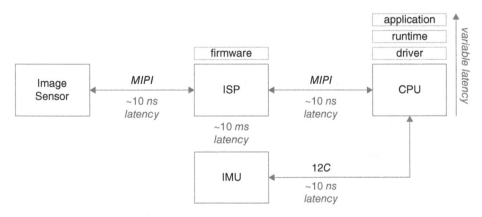

Figure 6.3 Synchronization.

second [FPS]) but low frame rates prevent the vehicle moving at a higher speed due to safety reasons.

With high-end processors, we can achieve higher frame rates but the cost and power consumption become major issues. Note that autonomous vehicles and robots are also mobile systems living on a limited onboard energy budget and thus power consumption does matter.

There are many software techniques to optimize for performance, the simplest one being reducing image resolutions but this would reduce image quality and thus negatively impact perception and localization capabilities.

Another software optimization technique is to utilize parallel computing, such as multiple processors, a graphics processing unit (GPU), or a digital signal processor (DSP) [2]. This technique involves intensive rewriting of some of the software pieces but fortunately there are many well-developed libraries, such as OpenCL [3], ARM Compute Library [4], and OpenCV on CUDA [5], etc.

If software optimization still does not satisfy your computing needs, you can try developing custom hardware, such as reported in [6, 7]. To achieve optimal hardware acceleration, you need to first identify the computing bottleneck of your computing pipeline and develop specialized hardware to accelerate the critical path of computing. However, this approach is extremely costly. A thorough review of the hardware acceleration approaches for autonomous driving workloads will be presented in Chapter 11 of this book.

6.3 Calibration

Sensor calibration is the process of determining the intrinsic (e.g. camera focal length in the pinhole model) and extrinsic (i.e. position and orientation with respect to the world, or to another sensor) parameters of a sensor. Calibration is an essential prerequisite for many applications in autonomous vehicles and robots.

For instance, in autonomous vehicles and robots, in order to fuse measurements from different sensors, such as fusing cameras and IMU for simultaneous localization and mapping (SLAM) computation, all the sensors' measurements must be expressed with respect to a common frame of reference, which requires knowing the relative pose of the sensors. In this section, we introduce the basics of sensor calibration, and present an open source calibration Kalibr [8, 9]. For those readers who want to delve into the technical details of sensor calibration, please refer to [10].

6.3.1 Intrinsic Parameters

Intrinsic parameters are those that do not depend on the outside world and how the sensor is placed in it. For instance, in the camera pinhole model, let us use u and v to represent the 2D projection of a feature point (e.g. a landmark) on the image plane, x, y, and z to represent the 3D position of the corresponding point in the world coordinate frame with origin at the focal point of the camera, and f to denote the focal length of the camera. In this simple model, the focal length f of the camera is an internal parameter which is usually unknown or only approximately known. The focal length should be estimated accurately before employing this camera model in any sensor fusion algorithm. This problem is called camera intrinsic calibration. Similar to a camera, many other sensors such as wheel encoders, IMUs, LiDARs, etc., have internal parameters that must be calibrated before you can use them.

6.3.2 Extrinsic Parameters

Extrinsic parameters are those describing the position and orientation (these two are collectively called a *pose*) of a sensor with respect to an external frame of reference. When the sensor's pose needs to be determined with respect to a global frame of reference, the problem of estimating these parameters is often called global localization, and it can be solved using efficient algorithms that exist for various sensors [10].

For instance, in 3D camera localization, the 6 degree-of-freedom camera pose can be computed from observations of at least four non-collinear landmarks whose positions are known in the global frame of reference, or at least three known lines whose directions in the 3D space are linearly independent.

Also, in many systems, multiple sensors are rigidly attached to the same device. Fusing measurements from multiple sensors may be necessary in order to ensure that the system is observable, or to increase robustness against single-sensor failure. Fusion algorithms, however, can process measurements corresponding to geometric quantities and provided from multiple sensors only if these are spatially related. Therefore, we need to perform sensor-to-sensor transformation so as to express all of the measurements with respect to a common frame of reference. The process of estimating the sensor-to-sensor transformation is called extrinsic sensor-to-sensor calibration.

Consider the case of performing IMU-to-GPS transformation. Often, the IMU is installed close to the center of rotation of the vehicle to avoid saturation, while the GPS antenna is mounted on the outer body of the vehicle, to guarantee high quality signal reception. This setup inevitably results in a large distance between the IMU and GPS. Now, consider the case where the vehicle is standing still but rotating around the IMU. In this case the GPS measurements indicate nonzero linear velocity, but the integration of the measured linear acceleration by the IMU implies zero velocity. If we do not know the transformation between the GPS and the IMU, there is no way to resolve this contradiction and any algorithm fusing measurements from these two sensors will fail.

6.3.3 Kalibr

Kalibr is an open-sourced toolbox that solves multiple commonly encountered calibration problems in robotics [8, 9]. First, Kalibr can be used for multiple camera calibration, such that intrinsic and extrinsic calibration parameters of camera systems with non-globally shared overlapping fields of view can be easily generated. Secondly, Kalibr can be used for visual-inertial calibration (camera-IMU). Visual-inertial hardware systems are commonly used for autonomous vehicle and robot localization tasks; Kalibr is a convenient tool to generate spatial and temporal calibration parameters of an IMU with respect to a camera system. Thirdly, Kalibr can be used for multiple IMU and IMU intrinsics calibration. Therefore, Kalibr is a very useful tool for calibration for visual inertial hardware systems widely used in autonomous vehicles and robots.

6.3.3.1 Calibration Target

Kalibr supports three different calibration targets. It is recommended to use the Aprilgrid (Figure 6.4) due to the following benefits: partially visible calibration boards can be used such that the pose of the target is fully resolved. The targets are configured using YAML configuration files which have to be provided to the calibration tools. Grids can be downloaded on the Downloads page or created using the following script:

```
kalibr_create_target_pdf -h
```

6.3.3.2 Multiple Camera Calibration

Step 1. Collect images: Create a Robot Operating System (ROS) bag containing the raw image data. The camera system is fixed and the calibration target is moved in front of the cameras to obtain the calibration images. It is recommended to lower the frequency of the camera streams to around 4 Hz while capturing the calibration data. This reduces redundant information in the dataset and thus lowers the runtime of the calibration.

Step 2. Run Kalibr: Run Kalibr with the following command. Note that the optimization can diverge right after processing the first few images due to a bad initial guess on the focal lengths. In this case just try to restart the calibration as the initial guesses are based on a random pick of images.

```
kalibr_calibrate_cameras --bag [filename. bag] --topics
[TOPIC_0 ... TOPIC_N] --models [MODEL_0 ... MODEL_N] --
target [target.yaml]
```

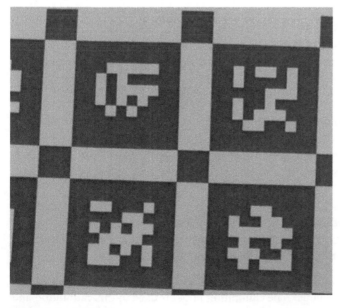

Figure 6.4 Aprilgrid.

Step 3. Understand the output: The following output is produced:

> report-cam-%BAGNAME%.pdf: report in PDF format, which contains all plots for documentation.
> results-cam-%BAGNAME%.txt: result summary as a text file.
> camchain-%BAGNAME%.yaml: results in YAML format and this file can be used as an input for the camera-IMU calibrator.

6.3.3.3 Camera IMU Calibration

Prerequisites: before we can do camera-IMU calibration, the intrinsic parameters of the IMU need to be calibrated beforehand and its corrections need to be applied to the raw measurements. Also, YAML has to be created containing the following statistical properties for the accelerometers and gyroscopes: noise density, bias random walk.

Step 1. Collect images: Create a ROS bag containing the raw image streams and a CSV file containing the IMU measurements. The calibration target is fixed in this calibration and the camera-IMU system is moved in front of the target to excite all IMU axes. It is important to ensure good illumination of the calibration target and to keep the camera shutter times low to avoid excessive motion blur. Good results have been obtained by using a camera rate of 20 Hz and an IMU rate of 200 Hz.

Step 2. Run Kalibr: Run Kalibr with the following command.

```
kalibr_calibrate_imu_camera --bag [filename. bag] --cam
[camchain.yaml] --imu [imu.yaml] --target [target.yaml]
```

Step 3. Understand the output: The following output is produced:

> report-imucam-%BAGNAME%.pdf: report in PDF format, which contains all plots for documentation.
> results-imucam-%BAGNAME%.txt: result summary as a text file.
> camchain-imucam-%BAGNAME%.yaml: results in YAML format, and this file is based on the input camchain.yaml with added transformations for all cameras with respect to the IMU.

6.3.3.4 Multi-IMU and IMU Intrinsic Calibration

Note that the extended version of Kalibr supports temporal and spatial calibration of sensor suites comprising multiple cameras and multiple IMUs. In addition, it allows for estimating IMU intrinsics as well as the displacement of the accelerometer y- and z-axis with respect to its x-axis.

Prerequisites: Before we can do camera-IMU calibration, the intrinsic parameters of the IMU need to be calibrated beforehand and its corrections need to be applied to the raw measurements. Also, YAML has to be created containing the following statistical properties for the accelerometers and gyroscopes: noise density and bias random walk.

Step 1. Collect images: Create a ROS bag containing the raw image streams and a CSV file containing the IMU measurements. The calibration target is fixed in this calibration and the camera-IMU system is moved in front of the target to excite all IMU axes. It is important to ensure good illumination of the calibration target and to keep the camera shutter times low to avoid excessive motion blur. Good results have been obtained by using a camera rate of 20 Hz and an IMU rate of 200 Hz.

Step 2. Run Kalibr: Run Kalibr with the following command.

```
kalibr_calibrate_imu_camera --bag [filename.bag] --cam
[camchain.yaml] --imu [imu.yaml] --target [target.yaml]
```

In addition, there are many additional options for the extended framework:

--IMU IMU_YAMLS [IMU_YAMLS ...]: This option now accepts a list of yaml files, one for each IMU comprised in the sensor suite. The first IMU will be the reference IMU (IMU0).
--IMU-models IMU_MODELS [IMU_MODELS ...]: This option holds a list of IMU models of the same length as the list provided to --IMU.

Currently supported models are calibrated, scale-misalignment, and scale-misalignment-size-effect. The default is calibrated, which will also be assumed when no model is provided.

Step 3. Understand the output: the following output is produced:

report-imucam-%BAGNAME%.pdf: The report pdf now contains the calibration summary in text form as well as result plots. Where residuals are plotted, three sigma bounds given the assumed noise process strengths provided in the respective yaml files or through the option --reprojection-sigma are displayed to foster an intuition about the correctness of the noise parameters and models.
results-imucam-%BAGNAME%.txt: The summary of results now also contains results specific to the chosen IMU models. The summary is identical to the one found in the pdf.
imu-%BAGNAME%.yaml: IMU calibration results in YAML format. The content of this file depends on the models chosen via the option --IMU-models.

6.4 Localization with Computer Vision

VSLAM technologies can be utilized for autonomous vehicle and robot localization tasks. VSLAM has been an active research topic for many years because it provides two fundamental components for many applications: where I am, and what I see [11]. While the theories for SLAM matured over the years, the challenge remains for VSLAM to adapt to real-world applications.

6.4.1 VSLAM Overview

VSLAM systems are highly application-specific such that each application may impose a different set of requirements. For example, a mobile robot requires mapping and localization in a large-scale environment, such as an entire building, which poses challenges for loop closing and large-scale optimization. On the other hand, augmented reality (AR) and virtual reality (VR) applications require high-precision, jitter-free position tracking with low latency to provide immersive user experiences when viewing the virtual contents. For autonomous vehicles, localization using multiple sensors to handle various environments is essential, which poses challenges for real-time sensor fusion for tracking. Thus, the challenges for SLAM to work in real-world applications become the choice of sensors, the design of the system for the targeting application, and the implementation details.

SLAM approaches evolve with the development of sensors and computation platforms. At first, SLAM was mostly applied on robots equipped with wheel encoders and range sensors. Such a SLAM system uses a Kalman filter [12] with the assumption of a linearly approximated model with Gaussian noise to jointly estimate the robot pose and a map (e.g. a set of landmarks), or a particle filter [13] to build multiple hypotheses to localize within a global map.

Passive sensors, like CCD/CMOS sensors, are becoming cost effective, better in quality, and ready for mass production, and therefore, many VSLAM approaches using sparse features (e.g. PTAM [14], ORB-SLAM [15]) have been developed. While most VSLAM approaches build a sparse point cloud with image features, some use image-to-image alignment to directly estimate pose and depth (e.g. LSD-SLAM [16]), which could produce a denser map.

VIO is a sensor-fusion method of performing localization tasks. The combination of vision sensors and IMUs is especially effective because the IMU provides high frame rate pose prediction while cameras provide accurate pose correction and map construction. There are two categories of visual-inertial systems: tightly coupled [17] and loosely coupled [18]. A tightly coupled system jointly optimizes over both inertial and visual sensor measurements, which provides higher accuracy in both mapping and tracking. A loosely coupled system provides flexibility to the combination of sensors with lower requirement of timestamp synchronization, and typically requires lower computational cost.

6.4.2 ORB-SLAM2

ORB-SLAM2 is a real-time SLAM library for monocular, stereo and RGB-D cameras that computes the camera trajectory and a sparse 3D reconstruction. It is able to detect loops and relocalize the camera in real time [19].

In [20], the authors provide examples to run the SLAM system in the KITTI dataset as stereo or monocular, in the TUM dataset as RGB-D or monocular, and in the EuRoC dataset as stereo or monocular. The authors also provide a ROS node to process live monocular, stereo or RGB-D streams. The library can be compiled without ROS. In addition, ORB-SLAM2 provides a graphical user interface to change between a SLAM mode and Localization mode.

6.4.2.1 Prerequisites

There are a few prerequisites before you can install ORB-SLAM2 on your own system. First, ORB-SLAM2 has been successfully run on a system with Ubuntu 14.04 or 16.04. Secondly, a C++11 or C++0x compiler is required as ORB-SLAM2 uses the new thread and chrono functionalities of C++11. Thirdly, ORB-SLAM2 uses Pangolin for visualization and user interface. Fourthly, ORB-SLAM2 uses OpenCV for image and feature processing. Fifthly, ORB-SLAM2 uses Eigen3 for matrix computation, which is required by g2o for nonlinear optimization. Sixthly, ORB-SLAM2 uses DBoW2 and g2o, which are already included in ORB-SLAM2's third party folder. Note that the DBoW2 library is for performing place recognition and the g2o library is for performing nonlinear optimizations.

6.4.2.2 Building the ORB-SLAM2 Library

Next, you can start building the ORB-SLAM2 library locally. First, you can clone the repository by using the following command:

```
git clone https://github.com/raulmur/ORB_SLAM2.git ORB_SLAM2
```

ORB-SLAM2 provides a very-easy-to-use script build.sh to build the third party libraries as well as ORB-SLAM2. Before you build, please make sure you have installed all the required dependencies listed in Section 6.4.2.1. Then you can execute:

```
cd ORB_SLAM2
chmod +x build.sh
./build.sh
```

These steps will create libORB_SLAM2.so in the lib folder and the executables mono_tum, mono_kitti, rgbd_tum, stereo_kitti, mono_euroc, and stereo_euroc in the Examples folder.

6.4.2.3 Running Stereo Datasets

KITTI is a dataset for algorithm developments in autonomous driving [21]. KITTI contains six hours of traffic scenarios at 10–100 Hz using a variety of sensor modalities such as high-resolution color and grayscale stereo cameras, a Velodyne 3D laser scanner and a high-precision GPS/IMU inertial navigation system. The scenarios presented in KITTI are diverse, capturing real-world traffic situations, and range from freeways over rural areas to inner-city scenes with many static and dynamic objects. In addition, sensor data in KITTI is calibrated, synchronized, and timestamped, and both rectified and raw image sequences are provided.

In this subsection we show how to run ORB-SLAM2 on KITTI's stereo image dataset. The dataset can be downloaded from the following link:

http://www.cvlibs.net/datasets/kitti/eval_odometry.php

Then you can execute the following command, note that you can change KITTIX.yaml to KITTI00-02.yaml, KITTI03.yaml, or KITTI04-12.yaml for sequence 0–2, 3, and 4–12, respectively. Then you can change PATH_TO_DATASET_FOLDER to the uncompressed dataset folder, and change SEQUENCE_NUMBER to 00, 01, 02, ..., 11.

./Examples/Stereo/stereo_kitti Vocabulary/ORBvoc.txt Examples/Stereo/KITTIX.yaml PATH_TO_DATASET_FOLDER/dataset/sequence

6.5 Perception with Computer Vision

In this section, we introduce two techniques for perception using computer vision: estimating depth from binocular imagery and object instance segmentation. Using object instance segmentation, you can extract semantic information of a detected object, such as a vehicle or a pedestrian. On top of that, with depth estimation, you can extract the depth information of the detected objects. Combining these two techniques, you can correctly identify spatial and semantic information of all interested objects in your environment, which is crucial for the planning and control module to make intelligent decisions in real time.

In order to be of practical use for applications such as autonomous driving, binocular depth estimation methods should run at a fast speed, e.g. >30 FPS. On the other hand, since depth errors increase quadratically with the distance, high-resolution images are often needed to obtain accurate 3D representations [22] but high resolution also imposes high computation burden. Therefore, the key challenge is to achieve high speed without sacrificing depth quality.

Stereo algorithms based on local correspondences are typically fast but require an adequate choice of window size [23]. Hence this leads to a trade-off between low matching ratios for small window sizes and border bleeding artifacts for larger ones. As a consequence, poorly textured and ambiguous surfaces cannot be matched consistently. On the other hand, dense and accurate matching can be obtained by global methods, which enforce smoothness explicitly by minimizing an MRF-based energy function [24]. However, global methods are often computationally expensive. Later in this section, we introduce ELAS (Efficient LArge-scale Stereo), a binocular depth estimation approach for fast matching of high-resolution images [25].

On object detection, R-CNN is a bounding-box object detection approach to attend to a manageable number of candidate object regions and evaluate convolutional networks independently on each region of interest (ROI) [26]. Faster R-CNN advanced R-CNN by learning the attention mechanism with a Region Proposal Network [27]. In these methods, segmentation precedes recognition, which is slow and less accurate. In Section 6.5.2 we introduce Mask R-CNN, which is based on parallel prediction of masks and class labels, which is simpler and more flexible [28].

6.5.1 ELAS for Stereo Depth Perception

As introduced in [25], ELAS is a generative probabilistic model for stereo matching, which allows for dense matching with small aggregation windows by reducing ambiguities on the correspondences. ELAS builds a prior over the disparity space by forming a triangulation on a set of robustly matched correspondences, named "support points." Since the prior is piecewise linear, ELAS does not suffer in the presence of poorly textured and slanted surfaces. Hence, ELAS is an efficient algorithm that reduces the search space and can be easily parallelized. The authors of ELAS demonstrated that ELAS is able to achieve state-of-the-art performance with significant speedups of up to three orders of magnitude when compared with prevalent approaches.

LIBELAS (LIBrary for Efficient LArge-scale Stereo matching) is a cross-platform C++ library for computing disparity maps of large images [29]. You can input to a pair of rectified grayscale stereo images of the same size to LIBELAS for it to generate the corresponding disparity map.

Before you can compile LIBELAS, make sure you have installed CMake (available at: http://www.cmake.org), which is required to compile LIBELAS using C++. Assuming that you are using a Linux system, you can perform the following steps to compile LIBELAS:

```
Move to LIBELAS root directory

Type 'cmake .'

Type 'make'

Run './elas demo'
```

The above steps will compute disparity maps for images from the "img" directory.

6.5.2 Mask R-CNN for Object Instance Segmentation

In essence, Mask R-CNN extends Faster R-CNN by adding a branch for predicting segmentation masks on each ROI, in parallel with the existing branch for classification and bounding box regression [28]. Mask R-CNN is simple to implement and train given the Faster R-CNN framework, which facilitates a wide range of flexible architecture designs. Additionally, the mask branch only adds a small computational overhead, enabling a fast system and rapid experimentation.

In principle Mask R-CNN is an intuitive extension of Faster R-CNN, yet constructing the mask branch properly is critical for good results. Most importantly, Faster RCNN was not designed for pixel-to-pixel alignment between network inputs and outputs. Specifically, Mask R-CNN proposes a simple, quantization-free layer, called ROIAlign, which faithfully preserves exact spatial locations and improves mask accuracy by 10–50%. In addition, Mask R-CNN decouples mask and class prediction, such that it predicts a binary mask for each class independently, without competition among classes, and relies on the network's ROI classification branch to predict the category.

An open-sourced version of Mask R-CNN can be found in [30], which contains an implementation of Mask R-CNN on Python 3, Keras, and TensorFlow. The model generates bounding boxes and segmentation masks for each instance of an object in the image. It is based on a Feature Pyramid Network (FPN) and a ResNet101 backbone. The code repository includes source code of Mask R-CNN built on FPN and ResNet101, training code for MS COCO, pre-trained weights for MS COCO, parallel model class for multi-GPU training, and evaluation on MS COCO metrics (application processor).

Installation of this code repository can be done with the following steps:

git clone https://github.com/matterport/Mask_RCNN
pip3 install -r requirements.txt
python3 setup.py install
Download pre-trained COCO weights (mask_rcnn_coco.h5) from https://github.com/matterport/Mask_RCNN/releases

To train or test on MS COCO install pycocotools from https://github.com/waleedka/coco.

6.6 The DragonFly Computer Vision Module

As shown in Figure 6.5, the PerceptIn DragonFly system utilizes computer-vision-based sensor fusion to achieve reliable localization and perception results to enable outdoor low-speed autonomous vehicles and robots [31, 32]. Specifically, DragonFly integrates four hardware-synchronized high-definition global-shutter cameras (a stereo pair in the front, and a stereo pair in the back), an IMU device, and a Jetson TX1 computing module, as well as an interface to connect to the GNSS receiver module.

Different from other off-the-shelf computer vision modules, the DragonFly module not only provides hardware synchronization for the camera data but for the IMU data as well. Thus, it is SLAM ready such that developers can easily perform visual SLAM computations with this device. Also, the stereo pairs of the DragonFly module have a baseline of 50 cm, which is significantly longer than other off-the-shelf computer vision modules. This allows the DragonFly module to perform long-range perception to detect objects as far as 300 m away [33]. The multiple sensor and long baseline design makes calibration of the DragonFly module difficult. A detailed instruction video on the calibration of the DragonFly modules can be found in [34].

6.6.1 DragonFly Localization Interface

Internally, the DragonFly sensor module runs PerceptIn's proprietary VIO algorithm to provide accurate vehicle position and heading in real time. However, VIO suffers from cumulative errors, such that the longer the distance the vehicle travels, the more inaccurate the position. Hence, VIO alone is not sufficient to provide reliable and accurate position updates.

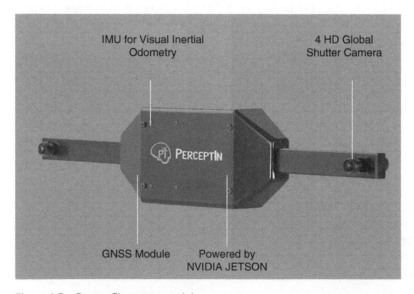

Figure 6.5 DragonFly sensor module.

To solve this problem, we can perform sensor fusion on real-time kinematic (RTK) GNSS and VIO results. When the GNSS signal is good, RTK GNSS provides very accurate position updates, and these updates can correct and alleviate the VIO cumulative errors. On the other hand, when the GNSS signal is bad and when multipath problems occur, VIO can still provide accurate position updates. In the past few years, we have verified the effectiveness of this system design.

The following data structure shows how we fuse VIO and GNSS results. VIO continuously provides position (*tx, ty, tz*) and quaternion updates (*qx, qy, qz, qw*) relative to the starting location. Each time these results are updated, we transform them into Universal Transverse Mercator (UTM) format (*utm_x, utm_y, heading*), which is an absolute coordinate commonly used by GNSS devices.

When we get a good GNSS signal, the GNSS updates are directly fed to the planning and control module, and also fed to the extended Kalman filter in the localization module to reduce VIO errors. When the GNSS signal is suboptimal, the VIO updates are transformed to UTM format and then fed to the planning and control module.

```
typedef struct PILocalizationVioMsg_
{
  // Sensor module's timestamp, in the unit of second
  double stamp;
  double gstamp; // gps global timestamp

  // position of DragonFly under the world coordinate
  double tx;
  double ty;
  double tz;

  // orientation (quaternion) of DragonFly under the world coordinate
  double qx;
  double qy;
  double qz;
  double qw;

  // UTM coordinates, valid when gnss_fusion is enabled
  double utm_x;
  double utm_y;
  int utm_zone;
  double gheading;      // heading from GPS

  // gnss fusion pos_status
  int fusion_mode;      // 0: gps bypass; 1: vio fusion
  int pos_status;       // position status under gps bypass mode
  int heading_status;   // heading status under gps bypass mode
  double accuracy;      // 0.0 under gps bypass mode; represents
the accuracy
                        // under vio fusion mode.
} PILocalizationVioMsg;
```

6.6.2 DragonFly Perception Interface

Internally, the DragonFly sensor module runs PerceptIn's proprietary perception algorithm to provide accurate obstacle spatial and semantic information. By spatial information, we mean that we use stereo vision to detect the distance of an object relative to the center of the front of the vehicle. By semantic information, we mean that we use deep learning models to extract the types of obstacles (e.g. pedestrians, bikes, vehicles, etc.). By combining this information, the perception system can understand the distances of different types of obstacles relative to the current vehicle. Then the planning and control system can combine this information, along with the current vehicle status (e.g. speed) to make intelligent decisions to guarantee the safety of the vehicle.

In addition, the perception system combines active perception results from the DragonFly sensor module, along with passive perception results from radars and sonars to provide a comprehensive understanding of the vehicle's current surroundings.

The Perception application program interface (API) along with the associated data structures are:

```
Perception API:

unsigned int GetObstacles(Perception_Obstacles *perceptionObs);

Return value:
The return value is a 32bit unsigned int. The meaning of each type
in the return data is defined as follows,

reserved    |  sonar      |  radar      |  vision
bit[31-24]  |  bit[23-16] |  bit[15-8]  |  bit[7-0]

Data structure:
typedef struct _PerceptionObstacle {
  SensorType sensor_type;          // SensorType: Enum Type to represent
                     // Radar, Sonar, Vision
  int sensor_id;                   // There are multiple Radars/Sonars
  int obj_id;                      // Obstacle id
  double timestamp;
  Pose3D pose;                     // Obstacle position in vehicle
                     // coordinate
  Arc2D arc;                       // Sonar output arc
  Velocity3D velocity;             // Obstacle velocity
  float power;                     // Reflection power of Radar
  ObstacleType obs_type;           // ObstacleType: Enum type to represent
                     // the class of an obstacle
  double confidence;               // Confidence level of the detection type
                     // and result in terms of percentage
  std::vector<Point2D> obs_hull;   // 2D Vision detected obstacle

  // ostream operator overload enable std::cout
  friend std::ostream &operator<<(std::ostream &os,
                           const _Perception_Obstacle &pObs);
} Perception_Obstacle, *PPerception_Obstacle;
```

Details of the definitions inside struct Perception_Obstacle:

```
typedef struct _Pose3D {
  double x;           // unit: meter
  double y;           // unit: meter
  double z;           // unit: meter
  double heading;     // in vehicle coordinate, unit: radian
} Pose3D, *PPose3D;


typedef struct _Arc2D {
  // (x, y) is center of the arc.
  double x;                // unit: meter
  double y;                // unit: meter
  double start_angle;   // unit: radian
  double end_angle;     // unit: radian
  double radius;           // unit: meter
} Arc2D, *PArc2D;


typedef struct _Velocity3D {
  double vel_x;  // unit: meter/s
  double vel_y;  // unit: meter/s
  double vel_z;  // unit: meter/s
} Velocity3D, *PVelocity3D;


enum ObstacleType : char {
  UNKNOWN = 0,
  UNKNOWN_MOVABLE = 1,
  UNKNOWN_UNMOVABLE = 2,
  PEDESTRIAN = 3,   // Pedestrian
  BICYCLE = 4,      // bike, motor bike.
  VEHICLE = 5,      // Passenger car, bus or truck.
};
```

6.6.3 DragonFly+

To achieve affordability and reliability, we have four basic requirements for the next generation of DragonFly:

- *Modular*: Independent hardware module for computer-vision-based localization and map generation.
- *SLAM ready*: Hardware synchronization of four cameras and IMU.
- *Low power*: The total power budget for this system is less than 10 W.
- *High performance*: DragonFly needs to process four-way 720P YUV images with >30 FPS.

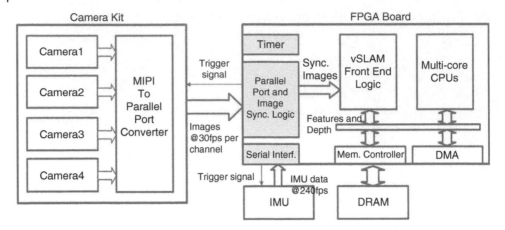

Figure 6.6 DragonFly+ hardware architecture.

Note that, with this design, at 30 FPS, it generates more than 100 MB of raw image data per second and thus imposes tremendous stress on the computing system. After initial profiling, we found out that the image processing frontend (e.g. image feature extraction) accounts for >80% of the processing time.

To achieve the aforementioned design goals, we designed and implemented DragonFly+, a field-programmable gate array (FPGA)-based real-time localization module [35]. As shown in Figure 6.6, the DragonFly+ system features: (i) hardware synchronizations among the four image channels as well as the IMU; (ii) a direct IO architecture to reduce off-chip memory communication; and (iii) a fully pipelined architecture to accelerate the image processing frontend of our localization system. In addition, parallel and multiplexing processing techniques are employed to achieve a good balance between bandwidth and hardware resource consumption.

We have thoroughly evaluated the performance and power consumption of our proposed hardware, and compared it against a Nvidia TX1 GPU system on chip (SoC), as well as an Intel core i7 processor. The results demonstrate that, for processing four-way 720p images, DragonFly+ achieves 42 FPS performance while consuming only 2.3 W of power, thus exceeding our design goals. In comparison, Nvidia Jetson TX1 GPU SoC achieves 9 FPS at 7 W and Intel Core i7 achieves 15 FPS at 80 W. Therefore, DragonFly+ is 3× more power efficient and delivers 5× the computing power compared with Nvidia TX1 and is 34× more power efficient and delivers 3× the computing power compared with Intel Core i7.

References

1 YouTube (2017). Enabling Computer-Vision-Based Autonomous Vehicles. https://www.youtube.com/watch?v=89giovpaTUE&t=62s (accessed 1 October 2019).

2 Tang, J., Sun, D., Liu, S., and Gaudiot, J.L. (2017). Enabling deep learning on IoT devices. *Computer* 50 (10): 92–96.

3 Khronos (2019). OpenCL Overview. https://www.khronos.org/opencl (accessed 1 October 2019).

4 Arm (2017). ARM Compute Library. https://www.arm.com/why-arm/technologies/compute-library (accessed 1 October 2019).

5 OpenCV (2019). CUDA. https://opencv.org/cuda (accessed 1 October 2019).

6 Fang, W., Zhang, Y., Yu, B., and Liu, S. (2017). FPGA-based ORB feature extraction for real-time visual SLAM. In: *2017 International Conference on Field Programmable Technology (ICFPT)*, 275–278. IEEE.

7 Tang, J., Yu, B., Liu, S. et al. (2018). π-SoC: heterogeneous SoC architecture for visual inertial SLAM applications. In: *2018 IEEE/RSJ International Conference on Intelligent Robots and Systems (IROS)*, 8302–8307. IEEE.

8 Rehder, J., Nikolic, J., Schneider, T. et al. (2016). Extending kalibr: calibrating the extrinsics of multiple IMUs and of individual axes. In: *2016 IEEE International Conference on Robotics and Automation (ICRA)*, 4304–4311. IEEE.

9 GitHub (2017). Kalibr. https://github.com/ethz-asl/kalibr (accessed 1 May 2019).

10 Mirzaei, F.M. (2013). Extrinsic and intrinsic sensor calibration. PhD thesis. University of Minnesota.

11 Cadena, C., Carlone, L., Carrillo, H. et al. (2016). Past, present, and future of simultaneous localization and mapping: toward the robust-perception age. *IEEE Transactions on Robotics* 32 (6): 1309–1332.

12 Kalman, R.E. (1960). A new approach to linear filtering and prediction problems. *Journal of Basic Engineering* 82 (1): 35–45.

13 Thrun, S. (2002). Particle filters in robotics. In: *Proceedings of the Eighteenth Conference on Uncertainty in Artificial Intelligence*, 511–518. Morgan Kaufmann Publishers Inc.

14 Klein, G. and Murray, D. (2007). Parallel tracking and mapping for small AR workspaces. In: *Proceedings of the 2007 6th IEEE and ACM International Symposium on Mixed and Augmented Reality*, 1–10. IEEE Computer Society.

15 Mur-Artal, R., Montiel, J.M.M., and Tardos, J.D. (2015). ORB-SLAM: a versatile and accurate monocular SLAM system. *IEEE Transactions on Robotics* 31 (5): 1147–1163.

16 Engel, J., Schöps, T., and Cremers, D. (2014). LSD-SLAM: large-scale direct monocular SLAM. In: *European Conference on Computer Vision*, 834–849. Cham: Springer.

17 Qin, T., Li, P., and Shen, S. (2018). Vins-mono: a robust and versatile monocular visual-inertial state estimator. *IEEE Transactions on Robotics* 34 (4): 1004–1020.

18 Lynen, S., Achtelik, M.W., Weiss, S. et al. (2013). A robust and modular multi-sensor fusion approach applied to MAV navigation. In: *2013 IEEE/RSJ International Conference on Intelligent Robots and Systems*, 3923–3929. IEEE.

19 Mur-Artal, R. and Tardós, J.D. (2017). ORB-SLAM2: an open-source SLAM system for monocular, stereo, and RGB-D cameras. *IEEE Transactions on Robotics* 33 (5): 1255–1262.

20 GitHub (2017). ORB-SLAM2. https://github.com/raulmur/ORB_SLAM2 (accessed 1 May 2019).

21 Geiger, A., Lenz, P., Stiller, C., and Urtasun, R. (2013). Vision meets robotics: the KITTI dataset. *The International Journal of Robotics Research* 32 (11): 1231–1237.

22 Gallup, D., Frahm, J.M., Mordohai, P., and Pollefeys, M. (2008). Variable baseline/resolution stereo. In: *2008 IEEE Conference on Computer Vision and Pattern Recognition*, 1–8. IEEE.

23 Scharstein, D. and Szeliski, R. (2002). A taxonomy and evaluation of dense two-frame stereo correspondence algorithms. *International Journal of Computer Vision* 47 (1–3): 7–42.

24 Felzenszwalb, P.F. and Huttenlocher, D.P. (2006). Efficient belief propagation for early vision. *International Journal of Computer Vision* 70 (1): 41–54.

25 Geiger, A., Roser, M., and Urtasun, R. (2010). Efficient large-scale stereo matching. In: *Asian Conference on Computer Vision*, 25–38. Berlin: Springer.

26 Girshick, R., Donahue, J., Darrell, T., and Malik, J. (2014). Rich feature hierarchies for accurate object detection and semantic segmentation. In: *Proceedings of the IEEE Conference on Computer Vision and Pattern Recognition*, 580–587. IEEE.

27 Ren, S., He, K., Girshick, R., and Sun, J. (2015). Faster R-CNN: towards real-time object detection with region proposal networks. In: *Advances in Neural Information Processing Systems*, 91–99. Neural Information Processing Systems Foundation, Inc.

28 He, K., Gkioxari, G., Dollár, P., and Girshick, R. (2017). Mask R-CNN. In: *Proceedings of the IEEE International Conference on Computer Vision*, 2961–2969. IEEE.

29 Geiger, A. (2019). LibELAS. http://www.cvlibs.net/software/libelas (accessed 1 May 2019).

30 GitHub (2017). Mask R-CNN. https://github.com/matterport/Mask_RCNN (accessed 1 May 2019).

31 YouTube (2018). DragonFly Sensor Module. https://www.youtube.com/watch?v=WQUGB-IqbgQ (accessed 1 October 2019).

32 PerceptIn (2018). PerceptIn's DragonFly Sensor Module. https://www.perceptin.io/products (accessed 1 May 2019).

33 YouTube (2019). 300-meter Visual Perception Systems for Autonomous Driving. https://www.youtube.com/watch?v=2_VfLZLy7Eo&t=21s (accessed 1 October 2019).

34 YouTube (2018). (DragonFly Calibration. https://www.youtube.com/watch?v=tRhGStjnS6M&feature=youtu.be (accessed 1 October 2019).

35 Fang, W., Zhang, Y., Yu, B., and Liu, S. (2018). DragonFly+: FPGA-based quad-camera visual SLAM system for autonomous vehicles. *HotChips 2018*, Cupertino, CA (19–21 August 2018). IEEE.

7

Planning and Control

7.1 Introduction

As shown in Figure 7.1, in order to generate real-time vehicle motions, the planning and control module combines perception inputs, which detect dynamic obstacles in real time, localization inputs, which generate real-time vehicle poses, and mapping inputs, which capture road geometry and static obstacles, and then based on these inputs, generates action plans for the vehicle.

As detailed in [1, 2], a typical planning and control system has the following architecture (Figure 7.2). First, as the user enters the destination, the routing module checks the map for road network information and generates a route. Then the route is fed to the behavioral planning module, which checks the traffic rules to generate motion specifications. Next, the generated route along with motion specifications are passed down to the motion planner, which combines real-time perception and localization information to generate trajectories. Finally, the generated trajectories are passed down to the control system, which reactively corrects errors in the execution of the planned motions.

In this chapter, we delve into the planning and control module, and introduce routing planning algorithms, behavioral planning algorithms, motion planning algorithms, and feedback control algorithms. Also, we present a real-world case study of Apollo's Iterative Expectation–Maximization (EM) Planner, which was designed for L4 autonomous driving passenger vehicles. In addition, we introduce PerceptIn's planning and control framework, which was developed to enable low-speed autonomous driving in controlled environments, such as university campuses, entertainment parks, industrial parks, etc.

7.2 Route Planning

The first submodule is the route planner, which selects an optimal route by checking the road network information from the map. Note that representing the road network as a directed graph with edge weights corresponding to the cost of traversing a road segment, such a route can be formulated as the problem of finding a minimum-cost path on a road network graph.

Engineering Autonomous Vehicles and Robots: The DragonFly Modular-based Approach,
First Edition. Shaoshan Liu.
© 2020 John Wiley & Sons Ltd. Published 2020 by John Wiley & Sons Ltd.

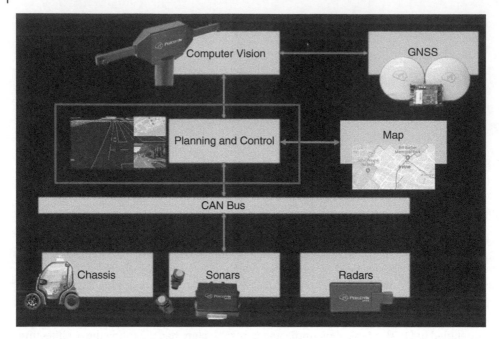

Figure 7.1   Modular design architecture.

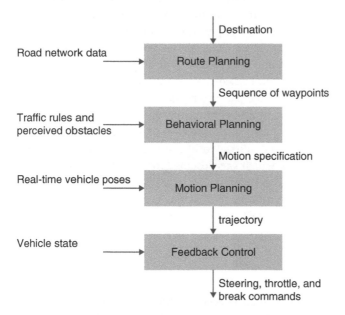

Figure 7.2   Planning and control module architecture.

7.2.1   Weighted Directed Graph

In formal terms, a directed graph is an ordered pair $G = (V, E)$, where V is a set whose elements are called vertices; and E is a set of ordered pairs of vertices, called directed edges. It differs from an undirected graph, in that the latter is defined in terms of unordered pairs of vertices, which are usually called edges. An example of a weighted directed graph is shown in Figure 7.3.

Weighted directed graphs can be used to represent road networks, for instance, a vertex can represent San Francisco, another vertex can represent New York, and an edge connecting these two vertices records the distance between these two cities. A routing algorithm can then be applied to this road network graph to search for the shortest route between the two cities.

7.2.2 Dijkstra's Algorithm

The first shortest-path routing algorithm we introduce here is Dijkstra's algorithm [3], which works by visiting vertices in the graph starting with the object's starting point. It then repeatedly examines the closest not-yet-examined vertex, adding its vertices to the set of vertices to be examined. It expands outwards from the starting point until it reaches the goal.

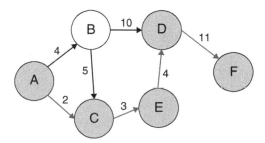

Figure 7.3 Weighted graph data structure.

```
1:    function Dijkstra(Graph, source):
2:        for each vertex v in Graph:               // Initialization
3:            dist[v] := infinity                    // initial distance from source to vertex v is set to infinite
4:            previous[v] := undefined               // Previous node in optimal path from source
5:        dist[source] := 0                          // Distance from source to source
6:        Q := the set of all nodes in Graph         // all nodes in the graph are unoptimized - thus are in Q
7:        while Q is not empty:                      // main loop
8:            u := node in Q with smallest dist[ ]
9:            remove u from Q
10:           for each neighbor v of u:              // where v has not yet been removed from Q.
11:               alt := dist[u] + dist_between(u, v)
12:               if alt < dist[v]                   // Relax (u,v)
13:                   dist[v] := alt
14:                   previous[v] := u
15:       return previous[ ]
```

Figure 7.4 Dijkstra's algorithm pseudocode.

In detail, as shown in Figure 7.4, Dijkstra's algorithm continuously calculates the shortest distance beginning from a starting point, and excludes longer distances when making an update. Dijkstra's algorithm consists of the following steps:

1. Initialization of all nodes with distance "infinite"; initialization of the starting node with 0.
2. Marking the distance of the starting node as permanent, all other distances as temporary.
3. Setting of the starting node as active.
4. Calculation of the temporary distances of all neighbor nodes of the active node by summing up its distance with the weights of the edges.
5. If such a calculated distance of a node is smaller than the current one, update the distance and set the current node as antecessor. This step is also called "update" and is Dijkstra's central idea.
6. Setting of the node with the minimal temporary distance as active. Mark its distance as permanent.
7. Repeating steps 4–7 until there are no nodes left with a permanent distance, whose neighbors still have temporary distances.

7.2.3 A* Algorithm

Although Dijkstra's algorithm guarantees to find a shortest path, when there is a large graph, Dijkstra's algorithm can be extremely computationally expensive. A much faster algorithm, called the Greedy Best-First-Search algorithm works in a similar way: instead of selecting the vertex closest to the starting point, it selects the vertex closest to the goal. However, Greedy Best-First-Search relies on a heuristic function and is not guaranteed to find the shortest path.

In this subsection, we introduce the A* algorithm, which combines the benefits of Dijkstra's algorithm and the Greedy Best-First-Search algorithm [4]. A* is like Dijkstra's algorithm in that it can be used to find a shortest path. A* is also like Greedy Best-First-Search in that it can use a heuristic function to guide itself.

Dijkstra's algorithm wastes time exploring in directions that are not promising. Greedy Best-First-Search explores in promising directions but it may not find the shortest path. As shown in Figure 7.5, the A* algorithm uses both the actual distance from the start and the estimated distance to the goal. A great introduction to the A* algorithm can be found in [5].

7.3 Behavioral Planning

After a route plan has been found, the autonomous vehicle must be able to navigate the selected route and interact with other traffic participants according to driving conventions and rules of the road. Given a sequence of road segments specifying the selected route, the behavioral planner is responsible for selecting an appropriate driving behavior at any point in time based on the perceived behavior of other traffic participants, road conditions, and signals from infrastructure.

For instance, when an autonomous vehicle is reaching the stop line before an intersection, the behavioral planner will command the vehicle to stop, observe the behavior of

```
frontier = PriorityQueue()
frontier.put(start, 0)
came_from = {}
cost_so_far = {}
came_from[start] = None
cost_so_far[start] = 0

while not frontier.empty():
    current = frontier.get()

    if current == goal:
        break

    for next in graph.neighbors(current):
        new_cost = cost_so_far[current] + graph.cost(current, next)
        if next not in cost_so_far or new_cost < cost_so_far[next]:
            cost_so_far[next] = new_cost
            priority = new_cost + heuristic(goal, next)
            frontier.put(next, priority)
            came_from[next] = current
```

Figure 7.5 A* algorithm pseudocode.

other vehicles, bikes, and pedestrians at the intersection, and let the vehicle proceed once it is its turn to go.

Real-world driving, especially in an urban setting, is however characterized by uncertainty over the intentions of other traffic participants. The problem of intention prediction and estimation of future trajectories of other vehicles, bikes, and pedestrians has also been studied. Among the proposed solution techniques are machine learning based techniques, e.g. Gaussian mixture models (GMMs) [6].

The uncertainties in the behaviors of other traffic participants (e.g. generated by GMMs), is then commonly considered in the behavioral layer for decision making using probabilistic planning formalisms, such as Markov decision processes (MDPs). For instance, the partially observable Markov decision process (POMDP) framework can be applied to model unobserved driving scenarios and pedestrian intentions explicitly, and generates specific approximate solution strategies [7].

Specifically, a POMDP is a generalization of a MDP. A POMDP models an agent decision process in which it is assumed that the system dynamics are determined by an MDP but the agent cannot directly observe the underlying state. Instead, it must maintain a probability distribution over the set of possible states, based on a set of observations and observation probabilities, and the underlying MDP.

7.3.1 Markov Decision Process

When we are confronted with a decision, there can be a number of different actions that we can choose from, and each leads to a different outcome. Choosing the best action requires thinking about more than just the immediate effects of an action. The immediate effects are often easy to see; however the long-term effects are not always as clear. Thus actions with poor immediate effects may have better long-term ramifications.

MDP can be used to model the decision process so that we can automate this process. By using MDP to formalize the decision-making process, a number of algorithms can be used to automatically solve the decision problem. The four components of an MDP model are: a set of states, a set of actions, the effects of the actions, and the immediate value of the actions.

- *S*: a set of states. The state is the way the world currently exists, and an action will have the effect of changing the state of the world. If we think about the set of every possible way the world could be, then this is the set of state of the world. Each of these states would be a state in the MDP.
- *A*: a set of actions. The problem is to know which of the available actions to take in for a particular state of the world.
- *T*: transitions. The transitions specify how each of the actions change the state. Since an action could have different effects, depending upon the state, we need to specify the action's effect for each state in the MDP. Note that in MDP the effects of an action can be probabilistic.
- *R*: immediate rewards. If we want to automate the decision-making process, then we must be able to have some measure of an action's value so that we can compare different actions. We specify the immediate value for performing each action in each state.

The solution to an MDP is called a policy and it simply specifies the best action to take for each of the states. To derive a policy, we need a value function to optimize for. A value function specifies a numerical value for each state. Therefore, with MDPs we have a set of states, a set of actions to choose from, an immediate reward function, and a probabilistic transition matrix. Our goal is to derive a mapping from states to actions, which represents the best actions to take for each state.

7.3.2 Value Iteration Algorithm

As shown in Figure 7.6, value iteration is a method of computing an optimal MDP policy and its value [8]. The value iteration algorithm computes this value function by finding a sequence of value functions, each one derived from the previous one.

The value iteration algorithm starts by trying to find the value function for a horizon length of 1. This will be the value of each state given that we only need to make a single decision. There is not much to do to find this in an MDP. Recall that we have the immediate rewards, which specify how good each action is in each state. Since our horizon length is 1, we can simply look at the immediate rewards and choose the action with the highest immediate value for each state.

The next step, which is the second iteration of the algorithm, is to determine the value function for a horizon length of 2. The value of acting when there are two steps to go, is the immediate reward for the immediate action you will take, plus the value of the next action you choose. Conveniently, we have already computed the values of each state for a horizon length of 1. So, to find the value for horizon 2, we can just add the immediate effects of each of the possible actions to the already computed value function to find the action with the best value given that there will be two decisions to be made.

```
1: Procedure Value_Iteration(S,A,P,R,θ)
2:        Inputs
3:              S is the set of all states
4:              A is the set of all actions
5:              P is state transition function specifying P(s'|s,a)
6:              R is a reward function R(s,a,s')
7:              θ a threshold, θ>0
8:        Output
9:              π[S] approximately optimal policy
10:             V[S] value function
11:       Local
12:             real array Vₖ[S] is a sequence of value functions
13:             action array π[S]
14:       assign V₀[S] arbitrarily
15:       k ←0
16:       repeat
17:             k ←k+1
18:             for each state s do
19:                   Vₖ[s] = maxₐ Σₛ' P(s'|s,a) (R(s,a,s')+ γVₖ₋₁[s'])
20:       until vs |Vₖ[s]−Vₖ₋₁[s]| < θ
21:       for each state s do
22:             π[s] = argmaxₐ Σₛ' P(s'|s,a) (R(s,a,s')+ γVₖ[s'])
23:       return π,Vₖ
```

Figure 7.6 Value iteration algorithm pseudocode.

Now the algorithm iterates again; it finds the horizon 3 value function using the horizon 2 value function. This iterates until we have found the value function for the desired horizon.

7.3.3 Partially Observable Markov Decision Process (POMDP)

The main difference between a MDP and a POMDP is in whether or not we can observe the current state of the process. In a POMDP we add a set of observations to the model. So instead of directly observing the current state, the state gives us an observation which provides a hint about what state it is in.

Note that the observations can be probabilistic such that we need to specify an observation model. This observation model simply tells us the probability of each observation for each state in the model. Since we have no direct access to the current state, our decisions require keeping track of the entire history of the process. Specifically, the history at a given point in time is composed of our knowledge about our starting situation, all actions performed, and all observations seen.

Maintaining a probability distribution over all of the states provides us with the same information as if we maintained the complete history. In a POMDP we have to maintain this probability distribution over states. When we perform an action and make an observation, we have to update the distribution. Updating the distribution involves using the transition and observation probabilities.

As illustrated in Figure 7.7, a POMDP can be formalized as follows:

- S, a set of states of the world.
- A, a set of actions.
- O, a set of possible observations.
- $P(S_0)$, which gives the probability distribution of the starting state.

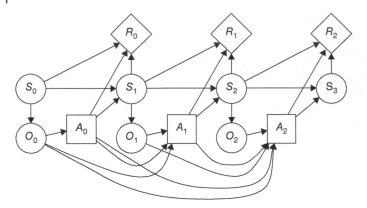

Figure 7.7 Example of a POMDP.

- $P(S'|S, A)$, which specifies the dynamics – the probability of getting to state S' by doing action A from state S.
- $R(S, A, S')$, which gives the expected reward of starting in state S, doing action A, and transitioning to state S'.
- $P(O|S)$, which gives the probability of observing O given the state is S.

7.3.4 Solving POMDP

Before solving a POMDP, let us first understand the concept of a "belief state," which is a probability distribution over all possible model states. Assume that there are only two possible states, 0 and 1, and the belief state at time t is $\Pr(s=0) = 0.75$ and $\Pr(s=1) = 0.25$.

If we are given a belief state, b, for time "t," and we perform an action "a" and get observation "z" we can compute a new belief state for time "$t+1$" by simply applying Bayes' rule and using the following equation, where S = set of states, A = set of actions, Z = set of observations, $T(s, a, s')$: $S \times A \times S \rightarrow \Pr(s'|s, a)$, $O(s, a, z)$: $S \times A \times Z \rightarrow \Pr(z|s, a)$, $R(a, s)$: $S \times A$.

$$
\begin{aligned}
b_z^a(s') &= \Pr(s' \mid b, a, z) \\[6pt]
&= \frac{\Pr(s', b, a, z)}{\Pr(b, a, z)} \\[6pt]
&= \frac{\Pr(z \mid s', b, a)\Pr(s' \mid b, a)\Pr(b, a)}{\Pr(z \mid b, a)\Pr(b, a)} \\[6pt]
&= \frac{\Pr(z \mid s', a)\Pr(s' \mid b, a)}{\sum_{s,s''}\Pr(z \mid b, a, s, s'')\Pr(s, s'' \mid b, a)} \\[6pt]
&= \frac{\Pr(z \mid s', a)\sum_{s}\Pr(s' \mid b, a, s)\Pr(s \mid b, a)}{\sum_{s,s''}\Pr(z \mid a, s'')\Pr(s'' \mid b, a, s)\Pr(s \mid b, a)} \\[6pt]
&= \frac{\Pr(z \mid s', a)\sum_{s}\Pr(s' \mid a, s)\Pr(s \mid b)}{\sum_{s,s''}\Pr(z \mid a, s'')\Pr(s'' \mid a, s)\Pr(s \mid b)},
\end{aligned}
$$

Then we could compute exactly how much expected reward we could achieve from any given belief state, and for each belief state you get a single expected value, which if done for all belief states, would yield a value function defined over the belief space. Then using the value iteration algorithm presented in Figure 7.6, we could solve a POMDP. Interested readers who want to explore advanced POMDP algorithms, papers, examples, and source codes can find more information at www.pomdp.org.

7.4 Motion Planning

When the behavioral layer decides on the driving behavior to be performed in the current context, which could be, e.g. cruise-in-lane, change lane, or turn right, the selected behavior has to be translated into a path or trajectory that can be tracked by the low-level feedback controller.

The resulting path or trajectory must be dynamically feasible for the vehicle, comfortable for the passenger, and avoid collisions with obstacles detected by the onboard sensors. The task of finding such a path or trajectory is the responsibility of the motion planning system.

Exact solutions to the motion planning problem are in most cases computationally intractable. Thus, numerical approximation methods are typically used in practice [1]. Among the most popular numerical approaches are variational methods that pose the problem as nonlinear optimization in a function space (www.pomdp.org), graph-search approaches that construct graphical discretization of the vehicle's state space and search for a shortest path using graph search methods [9], and incremental tree-based approaches that incrementally construct a tree of reachable states from the initial state of the vehicle and then select the best branch of such a tree [10].

In this section, we present rapidly exploring random tree (RRT) and RRT* algorithms, both are incremental tree-based approaches widely used in motion planning.

7.4.1 Rapidly Exploring Random Tree

As shown in Figure 7.8, a RRT is an algorithm designed to efficiently search nonconvex, high-dimensional spaces by randomly building a space-filling tree. The tree is constructed incrementally from samples drawn randomly from the search space and is inherently biased to grow towards large unsearched areas of the problem. RRTs can be viewed as a technique to generate open-loop trajectories for nonlinear systems with state constraints. A detailed discussion of RRT algorithms can be found in [11].

As shown in Figure 7.9, RRT grows a tree rooted at the starting configuration by using random samples from the search space. As each sample is drawn, a connection is attempted between it and the nearest state in the tree. If the connection is feasible, this results in the addition of the new state to the tree.

With uniform sampling of the search space, the RRT tree preferentially expands towards large unsearched areas. The length of the connection between the tree and a new state is frequently limited by a growth factor. If the random sample is further from its nearest state in the tree than this limit allows, a new state at the maximum distance from the tree along the line to the random sample is used instead of the random sample itself.

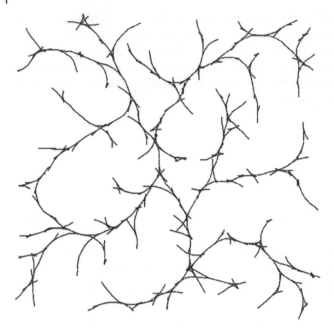

Figure 7.8 RRT algorithm illustration.

```
Algorithm BuildRRT
    Input: Initial configuration q_init, number of vertices in RRT K, incremental distance Δq)
    Output: RRT graph G

    G.init(q_init)
    for k = 1 to K
        q_rand ← RAND_CONF()
        q_near ← NEAREST_VERTEX(q_rand, G)
        q_new ← NEW_CONF(q_near, q_rand, Δq)
        G.add_vertex(q_new)
        G.add_edge(q_near, q_new)
    return G
```

Figure 7.9 RRT algorithm pseudocode.

The random samples can then be viewed as controlling the direction of the tree growth while the growth factor determines its rate. This maintains the space-filling bias of the RRT while limiting the size of the incremental growth.

Note that RRT growth can be biased by increasing the probability of sampling states from a specific area. Most practical implementations of RRTs make use of this to guide the search towards the planning problem goals. This is accomplished by introducing a small probability of sampling the goal to the state sampling procedure. The higher this probability, the more greedily the tree grows towards the goal.

7.4.2   RRT*

Although RRT has been shown to work well in practice and possesses theoretical guarantees such as probabilistic completeness, it has been proved that RRT may not converge to optimal values. RRT* is an improved version of RRT, which is provably asymptotically optimal such that the cost of the returned solution converges almost surely to the optimum [9].

As shown in Figure 7.10, the basic principle of RRT* is the same as RRT, but two key additions to the algorithm result in significantly different results [12]. First, RRT* records the distance each vertex has traveled relative to its parent vertex. This is referred to as the cost of the vertex. After the closest node is found in the graph, a neighborhood of vertices in a fixed radius from the new node are examined. If a node with a lower cost than the proximal node is found, the lower-cost node replaces the proximal node. The effect of this feature can be seen with the addition of fan-shaped twigs in the tree structure. The cubic structure of RRT is eliminated.

The second difference RRT* adds is the rewiring of the tree. After a vertex has been connected to the lowest-cost neighbor, the neighbors are again examined. Neighbors are checked if being rewired to the newly added vertex will make their cost decrease. If the cost does indeed decrease, the neighbor is rewired to the newly added vertex. This feature makes the path smoother.

7.5 Feedback Control

In order to execute the reference path or trajectory from the motion planning system a feedback controller is used to select appropriate actuator inputs to carry out the planned motion and correct tracking errors. The tracking errors generated during the execution of a planned motion are due in part to the inaccuracies of the vehicle model.

As shown in Figure 7.11, the role of a feedback controller is to stabilize the reference path or trajectory in the presence of modeling error and other forms of uncertainty. Specifically, the controller compares measured system output against reference to generate measured errors. Based on measured errors, the controller then generates a new system input.

```
Rad = r
G(V,E) //Graph containing edges and vertices
For itr in range(0…n)
    Xnew = RandomPosition()
    If Obstacle(Xnew) == True, try again
    Xnearest = Nearest(G(V,E),Xnew)
    Cost(Xnew) = Distance(Xnew,Xnearest)
    Xbest,Xneighbors = findNeighbors(G(V,E),Xnew,Rad)
    Link = Chain(Xnew,Xbest)
    For x' in Xneighbors
        If Cost(Xnew) + Distance(Xnew,x') < Cost(x')
            Cost(x') = Cost(Xnew)+Distance(Xnew,x')
            Parent(x') = Xnew
            G += {Xnew,x'}
    G += Link
Return G
```

Figure 7.10 RRT* algorithm pseudocode.

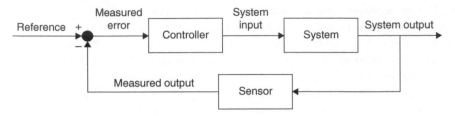

Figure 7.11 Feedback control.

7.5.1 Proportional–Integral–Derivative Controller

A proportional–integral–derivative (PID) controller is a control loop feedback mechanism widely used in autonomous driving [13]. As shown in Figure 7.12, a PID controller continuously calculates an error value as the difference between a desired setpoint and a measured process variable and applies a correction based on proportional, integral, and derivative terms (denoted P, I, and D, respectively).

A common example of a PID controller is the cruise control on a car, where ascending a hill would lower speed if only constant engine power is applied. The controller's PID algorithm restores the measured speed to the desired speed with minimal delay and overshoot, by increasing the power output of the engine.

The distinguishing feature of the PID controller is the ability to use the three control terms of proportional, integral, and derivative influence on the controller output to apply accurate and optimal control. The controller attempts to minimize the error over time by adjustment of a control variable such as the opening of a control valve, to a new value determined by a weighted sum of the control terms. The pseudocode of PID is shown in Figure 7.13 and is self-explanatory.

7.5.2 Model Predictive Control

Model predictive control (MPC) is an advanced method of control that is used to control a process while satisfying a set of constraints [14,15]. As shown in Figure 7.14, MPC relies on

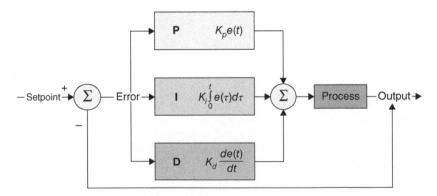

Figure 7.12 A PID controller.

```
previous_error = 0
integral = 0
Start:
        error = setpoint – input
        integral = integral + error*dt
        derivative = (error – previous error)/dt
        output = Kp*error + Ki*integral + Kd*derivative
        previous_error = error
        wait (dt)
Goto Start
```

Figure 7.13 PID pseudocode.

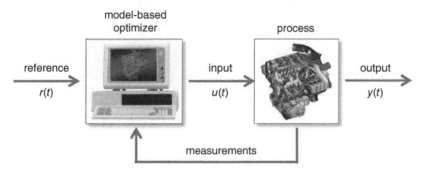

Figure 7.14 Model predictive control.

dynamic models of the process, most often linear empirical models obtained by system identification. The main advantage of MPC is that it allows the current timeslot to be optimized, while keeping future timeslots in account. Specifically, MPC has the ability to anticipate future events and can take control actions accordingly, whereas PID controllers do not have this predictive ability.

A detailed example of utilizing MPC for an autonomous vehicle can be found in [16], and the example contains the following components.

- *Vehicle control interface*: The vehicle adjusts the steering and throttle every 100 ms.
- *Cost function*: On a high level, the cost function represents the difference between the target trajectory point and the actual vehicle trajectory. In detail, the cost function is a weighted sum of cross-track error, heading error, speed cost, steering cost, acceleration cost, steering rate change, and acceleration rate change.
- *Constraint*: The vehicle wheel cannot be steered more than 25°.

In this example, MPC can be utilized to minimize the cost function while satisfying the constraints. At each period (100 ms), MPC reads from the sensors to determine the current state of the vehicle including: position of the vehicle (x, y), speed v, heading ψ, the steering angle δ, and the acceleration a.

MPC reads sensor inputs to determine the current vehicle state, including position, heading, speed, etc. Then MPC generates possible actions within a short period of time, such as one second, based on sensor readings.

For example, assume that the optimal plan generated by MPC is to steer the wheel by 20° clockwise and then reduces steering by 1° every 100 ms, and these actions are expected to minimize the cost function at the end of the one second period.

MPC then applies the first action of stirring the wheel 20°. In the next cycle (100 ms later), MPC reads the sensor inputs again. With the new readings, instead of performing the remaining actions, MPC recomputes the next optimal actions and repeats this process.

The beauty of MPC is that, instead of simply generating a one-step action, it repeatedly generates the next actions by considering a longer future plan, in this case one second, or 10 steps ahead. As a result, unlike PID, MPC is less vulnerable to short-sighted gain in a greedy method and therefore leads to a smoother trajectory.

The following steps provide the details of solving this MPC problem:

1. Read the current vehicle state, including position (x, y), speed v, heading ψ, the steering angle δ, and the acceleration a.
2. Use the optimizer to generate throttle and steering actions for the next 10 steps (100 ms per step) by minimizing the cost function under defined constraints.
3. Execute only the first throttle and steering action.
4. Go back to step 1.

7.6 Iterative EM Plannning System in Apollo

In previous sections, we have introduced the basics of path, behavioral, and motion planning; in this section we present a case study of an open source planning and control system, the Apollo Iterative EM Planning System [17]. The planned trajectory is usually specified and represented as a sequence of planned "trajectory points." Each of these points contains attributes such as location, time, speed, and curvature. Before we dive into the details of our Apollo autonomous driving system, it is important to illustrate some important terminologies in Apollo's planning system

7.6.1 Terminologies

7.6.1.1 Path and Trajectory
A path indicates the route which is usually represented by a series of "waypoints." Such waypoints depict the shape of a path. The attributes of a path include position, curvature, and curvature derivative with respect to the arc. However, a path only describes the shape and contains no information regarding vehicle velocity and time.

On the other hand, a trajectory consists of a path, as well as the speed profile along the path. Detailed information regarding the data definition of path and trajectory is illustrated in Figure 7.15.

7.6.1.2 *SL* Coordinate System and Reference Line
One of the most significant characteristic of planning is that motion planning for autonomous vehicles has to comply with the "road structure." Since autonomous vehicles are running on structured roads rather than on free spaces, the planning module in Apollo takes place in the road coordinate system as specified by the high-definition map.

```
 1  message PathPoint {
 2        // coordinates
 3        optional double x = 1;
 4        optional double y = 2;
 5        optional double z = 3;
 6
 7        // direction on the x-y plane
 8        optional double theta = 4;
 9        // curvature on the x-y plane
10        optional double kappa = 5;
11        // accumulated distance
12        optional double s = 6;
13
14        // derivative of kappa w.r.t s
15        optional double dkappa = 7;
16        // derivative of derivative of kappa w.r.t s
17        optional double ddkappa = 8;
18        // the lane ID where the path point is on
19        optional string lane_id = 9;
20  }
21
22  message TrajectoryPoint {
23        // path point
24        optional PathPoint path_point = 1;
25        // linear velocity
26        optional double v = 2;   // in [m/s]
27        // linear acceleration
28        optional double a = 3; // in [m/s^2]
29        // relative time from the beginning of the trajectory
30        optional double relative_time = 4;
31  }
```

Figure 7.15 Path and trajectory definition.

Specifically, the road coordinate system is represented by a reference line. Along the direction of the reference line is referred to as the "s" direction, while perpendicular to the reference line is the "l" direction. While the common-sense space coordinate system is referred to as the "cartesian" space, the sl space coordinate system given a reference line is referred to as the "Frenet" frame space [18].

Given a predefined reference line, there exists a bidirectional mapping for any point between its Cartesian space representation (x, y) and its Frenet space representation (s, l). The most important merit for planning on the Frenet space instead of cartesian space is that the sl coordinate system contains semantics. For example, it is very easy to refer to a leading vehicle in front, or a vehicle by the left side, in the sl coordinate system, while it is very difficult to clearly depict such semantic objects in the xy system.

7.6.1.3 ST Graph
Given the sl coordinate system, the movement along a certain reference path with respect to time can be illustrated by a graph called an ST graph, where the x-axis is the time and the y-axis is the s direction. To understand the use of an ST graph, we can refer to Figure 7.16, where our autonomous vehicle is going to make a right turn through a junction. Note, there are other vehicles: one already entering the lane that our vehicle wants to enter (vehicle 2),

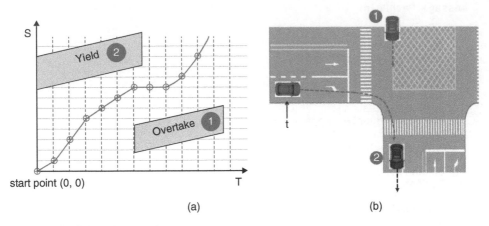

Figure 7.16 ST-graph example.

and the other moving from the lane across the junction (vehicle 1). An example of an ST graph is shown in Figure 7.16.

If the autonomous vehicle's motion is to yield to vehicle 2 and to overtake vehicle 1, the speed profile of our vehicle, as shown in the ST graph, will be the dotted trajectory in the graph which stays above 1 and below 2. The ST graph is a very useful but simple tool to facilitate the computations of speed profile along a given path.

7.6.2 Iterative EM Planning Algorithm

With the concept of the *sl* coordinate system and the reference line, the planning algorithm in Apollo takes place in an iterative fashion in the (s, l, t) space, as shown in Figure 7.17.

The first round of optimization is a Dynamic Programming (DP)-based approach (DP Path and DP Speed), which first generates and optimizes the path (s, l) and then generates and optimizes the speed profile (s, t).

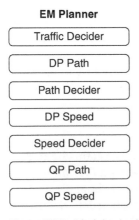

Figure 7.17 Modules in the Iterative EM planning.

The characteristics of the DP-based approach are interpreted and memorized by the path and speed deciders. Then the second round of optimization formulates the problem as a Quadratic Programming (QP) problem, where the optimization also happens in first (s, l) space for shape and then (s, t) space for speed.

The linear constrains of these QP optimizers are interpreted constraint results from the DP speed and path deciders. After these two rounds of iterative speed and path planning, the final trajectory is output and published to the downstream control module. We now describe these iterative optimizers in more details.

7.6.2.1 Traffic Decider

The traffic decider is responsible for the "traffic rules." Such traffic rules are usually hard-coded rules specified in the traffic laws; for example, if there is a stop sign or pedestrian crosswalk. The traffic rule decider will retrieve a stop line from the high-definition map and passes the stop position to the downstream layers.

One way to implement such a hard-coded stop rule is to create "virtual" objects to the path and speed deciders such that the planned trajectory will always stay behind such "virtual walls." The output of a traffic decider are constraints which have to be obeyed while performing the downstream path and speed planning.

Following the traffic decider is the first round of optimization which uses DP. As the first step, the DP model samples points along the (s, l) coordinate system. For each two points $(s_1, s_1' = 0, s_1'' = 0)$ and $(s_2, s_2' = 0, s_2'' = 0)$ at adjacent layers, we can fit a unique quantic polynomial $S(l)$ to connect them. Then we use smooth polynomial spirals to connect these sampling points in a layer-by-layer fashion. For each spiral connecting the sampled points in two layers, costs are incurred not only due to the spiral itself but also the points it is connecting. Figure 7.18 shows an example of DP-based path planning in the Iterative EM planning algorithm.

To formulate this, let $A_{(i,j)}$ denote the ith point at level j. The function $\text{Cost}(A_{(i,j)})$ represents the minimum cumulative cost of all the path connecting to the ith point at level j. Then $\text{Cost}(A_{(i,j)})$ could be written as:

$$\text{Cost}(A_{(i,j)}) = \min_{i' \text{ from level } j-1} \left(\text{Cost}(A_{(i',j-1)}) + \text{Spiral}_{\text{Cost}(A_{(i',j-1)}, A_{(i,j)})} \right)$$

The cost structure of the optimal path connecting to a specific point naturally forms a recursive structure which could be solved by the classical DP approach. The cost of each

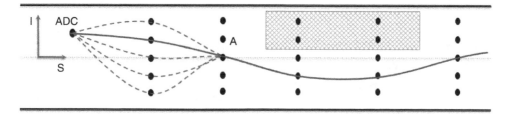

Figure 7.18 DP-based path planning in the Iterative EM planning algorithm.

spiral is designed to consider two aspects: (i) cumulative lateral distance to the central reference line; and (ii) static obstacle avoidance. Assuming there are n sampling points per layer, and we sample m points at the lateral directions, the DP program could find the optimal solution in $O(nm^2)$ time.

The DP path algorithm is mainly to compute a rough path for the autonomous vehicle to follow. Only static obstacles are considered in the DP path stage since there is no speed information being computed.

The DP speed solves a similar problem, and the only difference is that the problem space becomes the (s, t) space since the (s, l) space solution has already been found. The algorithm in DP speed takes place in a (s, t)-based grid, where some grids are occupied by the projections of dynamic obstacles. The goal of the algorithm is also to find a series of spirals connecting layer-by-layer sampled (s, t) points reaching to a certain desired position.

As shown in Figure 7.19, the results of both DP path and DP speed are interpreted by the path and speed deciders. As shown in the figure, the potential actions to avoid a static obstacle include "left nudge" or "right nudge" or "stop," while potential actions for avoiding dynamic obstacles are "yield" or "overtake."

7.6.2.2 QP Path and QP Speed
Even though the DP-based path and speed approaches are able to find a safe and collision-free path, the smoothness requirements are not specifically addressed and guaranteed.

The QP part mainly addresses the smoothness requirement by formulating the costs into a quadratic function and utilizes QP methods to find an optimal and smooth enough trajectory. We will use QP path problem formulization as a detailed example. The QP speed problem is similar and interested readers can refer to Apollo 2.0's detailed QP programming documentation [17].

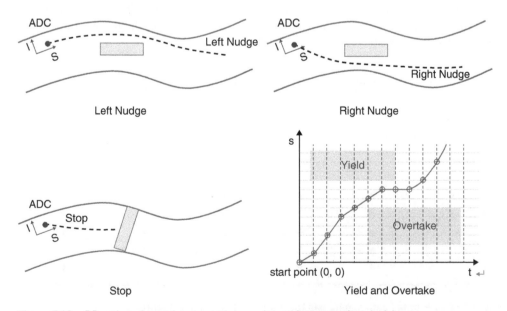

Figure 7.19 DP path and speed computation results are interpreted as decisions.

The QP path problem is formulated as l being a function of s:

$$l = f_i(s) = a_{i0} + a_{i1}s + a_{i1}s^2 + a_{i2}s^2 + a_{i3}s^3 + a_{i4}s^4 + a_{i5}s^5$$

And the cost to optimize is the cumulative lateral speed along with its higher order derivatives:

$$\text{Cost} = \sum_{i=1}^{n} \left(w_0 \int_0^{d_i} f(s)ds + w_1 \int_0^{d_i} (f_i')^2(s)ds + w_2 \int_0^{d_i} (f_i'')^2(s)ds + w_3 \int_0^{d_i} (f_i''')^2(s)ds \right)$$

The equality constraints in the QP problem consists of two aspects. First, the starting point has to be fixed:

$$f_i(s_0) = l_0, \ f_i'(s_0) = l_0', \ f_i''(s_0) = l_0'' .$$

Secondly, strict enforcement of smoothness requires that the poses at the connecting knots or joints have to be continuous up to certain degree level, usually:

$$f_k(s_k) = f_{k+1}(s_0), \ f_k'(s_k) = f_{k+1}'(s_0), \ f_k''(s_k) = f_{k+1}''(s_0), \ f_k'''(s_k) = f_{k+1}'''(s_0)$$

Now remember that we have already been informed by the DP optimizers how to avoid the static obstacles with ether "left nudge," "right nudge," or "stop." And these previous path computation results per object can be written as inequality constraints for the QP problem.

More specifically, the evaluated l value at specific s values where the obstacle spans has to be "constrained" between the lane boundary and the obstacle boundary, thus forming an inequality constraint for the QP problem. Given these equality constraints and inequality constraints, the whole QP path optimization problem is similar to the classical QP problem of the following form:

Minimize $\dfrac{1}{2} \cdot x^2 \cdot H \cdot x + f^T \cdot x$

s.t. $\quad LB \leq x \leq UB$

$A_{eq}x = b_{eq}$

$Ax \geq b$

Taking the $\int_0^{d_i} (f_i')^2(s)ds$ part for example to expand, the QP optimization cost for the second-order derivative is written as:

$$f_i'(s)^2 = \begin{vmatrix} a_{i0} & a_{i1} & a_{i2} & a_{i3} & a_{i4} & a_{i5} \end{vmatrix} \cdot \begin{vmatrix} 0 \\ 1 \\ 2s \\ 3s^2 \\ 4s^3 \\ 5s^4 \end{vmatrix} \cdot \begin{vmatrix} 0 & 1 & 2s & 3s^2 & 4s^3 & 5s^4 \end{vmatrix} \cdot \begin{vmatrix} a_{i0} \\ a_{i1} \\ a_{i2} \\ a_{i3} \\ a_{i4} \\ a_{i5} \end{vmatrix}$$

$$\int_0^{d_i} f_i'(s)^2 ds = \begin{vmatrix} a_{i0} & a_{i1} & a_{i2} & a_{i3} & a_{i4} & a_{i5} \end{vmatrix} \cdot \begin{vmatrix} 0 & 0 & 0 & 0 & 0 & 0 \\ 0 & d_i & d_i^2 & d_i^3 & d_i^4 & d_i^5 \\ 0 & d_i^2 & \frac{4}{3}d_i^3 & \frac{6}{4}d_i^4 & \frac{8}{5}d_i^5 & \frac{10}{6}d_i^6 \\ 0 & d_i^3 & \frac{6}{4}d_i^4 & \frac{9}{5}d_i^5 & \frac{12}{6}d_i^6 & \frac{15}{7}d_i^7 \\ 0 & d_i^4 & \frac{8}{5}d_i^5 & \frac{12}{6}d_i^6 & \frac{16}{7}d_i^7 & \frac{20}{8}d_i^8 \\ 0 & d_i^5 & \frac{10}{6}d_i^6 & \frac{15}{7}d_i^7 & \frac{20}{8}d_i^8 & \frac{25}{9}d_i^9 \end{vmatrix} \cdot \begin{vmatrix} a_{i0} \\ a_{i1} \\ a_{i2} \\ a_{i3} \\ a_{i4} \\ a_{i5} \end{vmatrix}$$

With the QP path algorithm, the planned trajectory will be smooth enough in terms of shape. The QP speed is very similar to the QP path, and the whole process takes place in the (s, t) space given the previous obtained QP path result. Within both DP and QP optimizations, we first optimize the path and then optimize the speed given the shape. The process is similar to the EM approach to find the posterior maximum, and that is why we name our planner an "EM" planner.

7.7 PerceptIn's Planning and Control Framework

In this section, we introduce PerceptIn's planning and control framework, which was developed to enable low-speed autonomous driving in controlled environments, such as university campuses, entertainment parks, and industrial parks.

Figure 7.20 shows the architecture diagram of PerceptIn's planning and control framework. It consists of a mission planner, a behavior planner, a motion planner, and a vehicle controller:

- *Mission planner*: The mission planner defines two basic missions. "A→B" defines the mission of traveling from an arbitrary point A to an arbitrary point B, and "parking" defines the mission of the vehicle parking itself at a designated parking spot. These two simple missions are enough for controlled environments, as in most usage cases, people want to use autonomous vehicles to travel from point A to point B, and also expect the vehicles to park themselves when needed.
- *Behavior planner*: The behavior planner defines all possible behaviors needed to complete a mission. Once a mission is defined, a lane is also generated for the vehicle to travel on. The most popular behavior is "lane keeping," or having the vehicle stay in the designated lane. If there is a vehicle traveling in front of the current vehicle on the same lane, then we can enter the "car follow" behavior to follow the car in front. On the other hand, if an obstacle is detected blocking the lane, we can enter the "avoidance" behavior to slow down the current vehicle and to go around the obstacle. Once our target destination is reached, we transition from "lane keeping behavior" to "mission_complete" behavior, which stops the current vehicle.
- *Motion planner*: To implement the aforementioned behaviors, we have defined multiple motions. First is "attach lane," which maintains the vehicle on the designated lane. If we

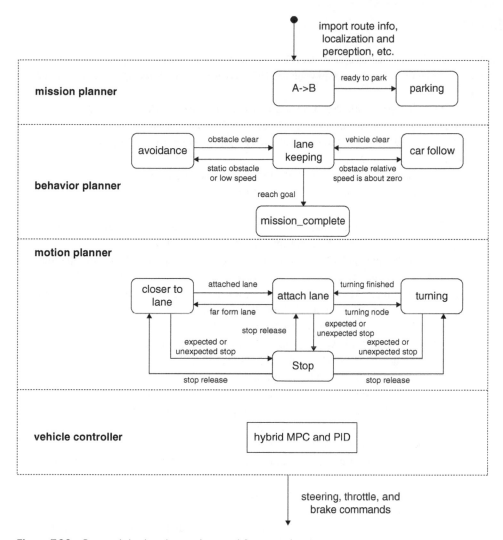

Figure 7.20 PerceptIn's planning and control framework.

detect that the vehicle is out of lane, we apply the motion "closer to lane" to bring the vehicle back on the designated lane. If the current vehicle is about to make a turn, either left or right, we apply the motion "turning." If the target is reached, or if we have to stop the current vehicle for any reason, we apply the motion "stop" to pause the current vehicle.

- *Vehicle controller*: At the lowest level, to translate the aforementioned motions into control actions, such as steering, throttle, and brake, we define a vehicle controller, which applies MPC and PID algorithms (please refer to previous sections) for vehicle control.

The PerceptIn planning and control framework generates control commands at 10 Hz, or each 100 ms, and we keep the end-to-end (from perception and localization inputs to control outputs) computing latency below 50 ms to ensure safe and reliable real-time planning.

References

1 Paden, B., Čáp, M., Yong, S.Z. et al. (2016). A survey of motion planning and control techniques for self-driving urban vehicles. *IEEE Transactions on Intelligent Vehicles* 1 (1): 33–55.

2 Liu, S., Li, L., Tang, J. et al. (2017). *Creating Autonomous Vehicle Systems*, Synthesis Lectures on Computer Science, 1–186. Morgan & Claypool Publishers.

3 Dijkstra, E.W. (1959). A note on two problems in connexion with graphs. *Numerische Mathematik* 1 (1): 269–271.

4 Hart, P.E., Nilsson, N.J., and Raphael, B. (1968). A formal basis for the heuristic determination of minimum cost paths. *IEEE Transactions on Systems Science and Cybernetics* 4 (2): 100–107.

5 Red Blob Games (2014). Introduction to the A* Algorithm. https://www.redblobgames.com/pathfinding/a-star/introduction.html (accessed 1 June 2019).

6 Havlak, F. and Campbell, M. (2013). Discrete and continuous, probabilistic anticipation for autonomous robots in urban environments. *IEEE Transactions on Robotics* 30 (2): 461–474.

7 Ulbrich, S. and Maurer, M. (2013). Probabilistic online POMDP decision making for lane changes in fully automated driving. In: *16th International IEEE Conference on Intelligent Transportation Systems (ITSC 2013)*, 2063–2067. IEEE.

8 Poole, D.L. and Mackworth, A.K. (2010). *Artificial Intelligence: Foundations of Computational Agents*. Cambridge University Press.

9 Karaman, S. and Frazzoli, E. (2011). Sampling-based algorithms for optimal motion planning. *The International Journal of Robotics Research* 30 (7): 846–894.

10 LaValle, S.M. and Kuffner, J.J. Jr. (2001). Randomized kinodynamic planning. *The International Journal of Robotics Research* 20 (5): 378–400.

11 LaValle, S. (n.d.). The RRT Page. http://msl.cs.uiuc.edu/rrt/ (accessed 1 June 2019).

12 Medium. Robotic Path Planning: RRT and RRT*. https://medium.com/@theclassytim/robotic-path-planning-rrt-and-rrt-212319121378 (accessed 1 June 2019).

13 Marino, R., Scalzi, S., and Netto, M. (2011). Nested PID steering control for lane keeping in autonomous vehicles. *Control Engineering Practice* 19 (12): 1459–1467.

14 Garcia, C.E., Prett, D.M., and Morari, M. (1989). Model predictive control: theory and practice—a survey. *Automatica* 25 (3): 335–348.

15 Bemporad, A. Model Predictive Control. http://cse.lab.imtlucca.it/~bemporad/teaching/ac/pdf/AC2-10-MPC.pdf (accessed 1 June 2019).

16 Hui, J. (2018). Lane keeping in autonomous driving with Model Predictive Control & PID. https://medium.com/@jonathan_hui/lane-keeping-in-autonomous-driving-with-model-predictive-control-50f06e989bc9 (accessed 1 June 2019).

17 GitHub. Apollo Auto. https://github.com/ApolloAuto (accessed 1 June 2019).

18 Werling, M., Ziegler, J., Kammel, S., and Thrun, S. (2010). Optimal trajectory generation for dynamic street scenarios in a Frenet frame. In: *2010 IEEE International Conference on Robotics and Automation*, 987–993. IEEE.

8

Mapping

8.1   Introduction

As shown in Figure 8.1, a mapping module provides essential geographical information, such as lane configurations and static obstacle information, to the planning and control module. In order to generate real-time motion plans, the planning and control module can combine perception inputs, which detect dynamic obstacles in real time, localization inputs, which generate real-time vehicle poses, and mapping inputs, which capture road geometry and static obstacles.

Hence it is essential to have highly accurate maps to aid autonomous navigation. Specifically, the planning and control module projects the real-time vehicle pose (from the localization module) onto the map to derive which lane the vehicle is currently on. Also, the planning and control module projects detected dynamic obstacles (from the perception module) onto the map, and decides whether the vehicle shall keep going, stop, or change lane. If the map is not accurate enough, accidents can easily happen.

Currently, fully autonomous cars (such as Waymo's and Uber's autonomous cars) use high definition (HD) 3D maps. Such high precision maps are extremely complex and contain trillion bytes of data to represent not only lanes and roads but also semantic information and locations of 3D landmarks in the real world [1]. With HD maps, autonomous vehicles are able to localize themselves and navigate in the mapped area.

In this chapter, we delve into mapping technologies, and we introduce traditional digital maps, HD maps, and a case study of enhancing existing digital maps for autonomous driving applications.

8.2   Digital Maps

Digital maps, such as Google map, Bing map, and Open Street Map (OSM), were developed for humans instead of for machines, as these digital maps rely heavily on human knowledge and observations. For instance, Google map tells you in real time which street/road you are on but not which lane you are on, and thus you have to make intelligent decisions based on what you know (e.g. traffic rules) and what you observe

Engineering Autonomous Vehicles and Robots: The DragonFly Modular-based Approach,
First Edition. Shaoshan Liu.
© 2020 John Wiley & Sons Ltd. Published 2020 by John Wiley & Sons Ltd.

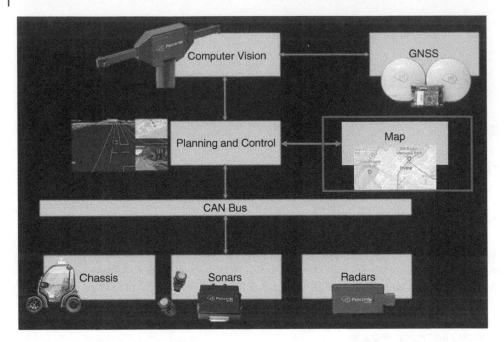

Figure 8.1 Modular design architecture.

(e.g. current traffic situation). In this section, using OSM as an example, we introduce the details of digital mapping. In Section 8.3, we will discuss details of building HD maps.

8.2.1 Open Street Map

OSM is a free, editable map of the whole world that is being built by volunteers largely from scratch and released with an open-content license (www.openstreetmap.org). OSM consists of raw geographical data from third-party suppliers, and a suite of software tools for creating and sharing map information.

8.2.1.1 OSM Data Structures

First, let us examine the data structures of the OSM data. OSM data are made of the following basic elements:

- *Node*: Nodes are dots used to mark locations. Nodes can be separate or can be connected.
- *Way*: Ways are a connected line of nodes used to create roads, paths, rivers, and so on.
- *Closed way*: Closed ways are ways that form a closed loop. They usually form areas.
- *Area*: Areas are closed ways which are also filled. An area is usually implied when making a closed way.
- *Relation*: Relation can be used to create more complex shapes, or to represent elements that are related but not physically connected. We will not go into this now.

All these basic elements can be annotated with tags to give element semantic informa-tion. A tag is a <key, value> pair describing the element. For instance, mapping a restau-rant can be done by creating a node, and adding the following tags: *shop = restaurant. name = John's Mexican Food*.

Note that many keys, like *Key:building* or *Key:amenity* will make OSM automatically assume a closed way when it should be an area. It is relatively uncommon to create an area explicitly (using an area = yes tag on a closed way).

There are several important tag keys as follows:

- *Key:highway* – For tagging highways, roads, paths, footways, cycleways, bus stops, etc.
- *Key:place* – Used for tagging countries, cities, towns, villages, etc.
- *Key:amenity* – Used for tagging useful amenities such as restaurants, drinking water spots, parking lots, etc.
- *Key:shop* – Used for tagging shops that you buy products from.
- *Key:building* – Used for tagging buildings.
- *Key:landuse* – Used for tagging land being used by humans.
- *Key:natural* – Used for tagging natural land such as a forest.

8.2.1.2   OSM Software Stack

OSM provides a suite of software tools to import, export, store, modify, render, and visualize map data. The architecture of OSM is shown in Figure 8.2, which is divided into five groups:

- *Geodata*. This is information about geographic locations that is stored in a format that can be used with a geographic information system (GIS). Geodata can be stored in a database, geodatabase, shapefile, coverage, raster image, or even a dbf table. For instance, a Web Map Service (WMS) is a standard protocol developed by the Open Geospatial Consortium in 1999 for serving georeferenced map images over the Internet.
- *Editing*. There is a lot of editing software, such as ID, Java OpenStreetMap Editor (JOSM), and Vespucci, that can be used to edit OSM. We will introduce JOSM in Section 8.2.2.
- *Backend*. The OSM backend consists of a set of tools to store and retrieve geodata. For instance, you can store geodata in PostgreSQL, and then use Nominatim to search the database. We will introduce Nominatim in Section 8.2.3.
- *Rendering*. This is the process involved in the generation of a 2D or 3D image from raw geographical data. A suite of rendering tools is provided by OSM.
- *Visualization*. The suite of tools to display OSM graphics, the most popular one being the OSM website, in which you can navigate through the maps.

8.2.2   Java OpenStreetMap Editor

As shown in Figure 8.3, JOSM is an interactive open source OSM editor that you can use to modify and update OSM data (josm.openstreetmap.de). Note that JOSM is an offline editor which means everything you do will not be visible for anyone else until you upload it to the server. This makes it possible to experiment and repeatedly move, tag, add and delete elements without breaking anything. Subsequent actions on a single element will go into the database as a single modification when uploaded. You can also find the source code of JOSM in [2] in case you want to modify JOSM functionalities.

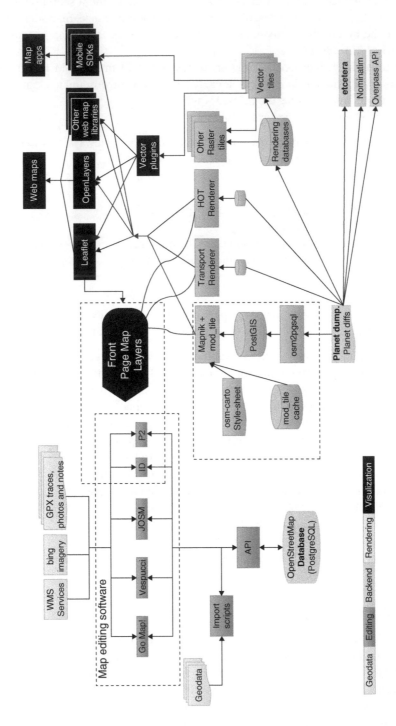

Figure 8.2 OSM architecture.

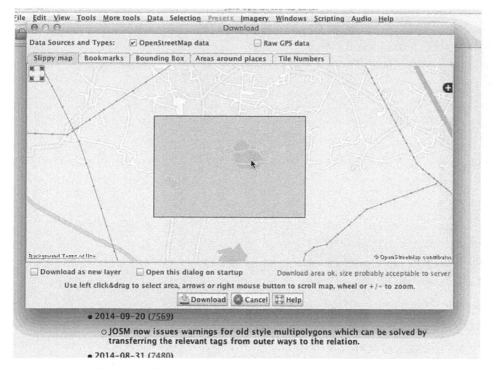

Figure 8.3 JOSM user interface.

8.2.2.1 Adding a Node or a Way

The first step is to add a node or way to the OSM data. You can add standalone nodes or you can add nodes to ways, especially where there is a junction between two ways. To add a node, activate "Draw Nodes" mode by hitting the "A" key on the keyboard. Then move the mouse cursor over where you want the node, over a way or over your GPS track (if you uploaded one) and left click wherever you want to place the node. A red dot (a selected node) should appear and a rubber-line spans from that node to the mouse cursor. If you create subsequent nodes, the earlier nodes will be shown as yellow nodes. A series of joined nodes forms a way.

8.2.2.2 Adding Tags

Figure 8.4 shows the JOSM user interface of adding tags. Ways or nodes on their own are not much use unless they are tagged to provide semantic information (the Map Features page shows some popular tags you can refer to).

The first step in adding tags is to be sure the Tags/Membership window is open on the right-hand side of JOSM. To edit the properties of a node or way (such as adding a tag) in the Tags/Membership window, the way or node must be selected. Enter Select mode by hitting the S key. Highlight the way or point you wish to select. A dialog box will appear, and you will be asked to select a key and a value for each tag. Type in the key/value pair that represents the tag you are creating. For example, for the key you might type "amenity" and for the value "fountain" (without quotes). Click OK. You have now tagged your way. You can also add several tags to one object.

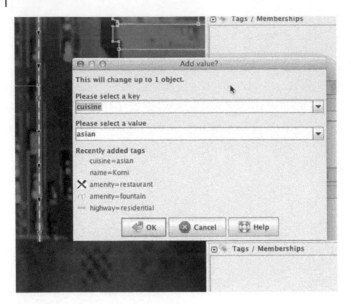

Figure 8.4 Adding a tag in JOSM.

8.2.2.3 Uploading to OSM

Once you are done with the edits, you can contribute them back to the OSM community. If you are happy with all that you have done then you can upload your work to the OSM server. Click on the upload button. This will automatically trigger a validation of your changes. Review all validation warnings and try to resolve them before you upload. This will prevent unfortunate mistakes such as untagged objects or unconnected roads. Note that validator warnings can also be wrong in special cases. Before you upload, add a proper changeset comment and specify which source you used. This is important as it will show other users who see your changesets what this changeset was intended to modify and from where you took the information. Note that in Section 8.4 we will show how we use JOSM to construct a map for autonomous vehicles.

8.2.3 Nominatim

Nominatim is an OSM tool to search OSM data by name and address (geocoding) and to generate synthetic addresses of OSM points (reverse geocoding). An instance with up-to-date data can be found at nominatim.openstreetmap.org. Nominatim is also used as one of the sources for the Search box on the OSM home page. You can find the source code of Nominatim in [3] in case you want to modify JOSM functionalities.

8.2.3.1 Nominatim Architecture

Nominatim provides geocoding based on OSM data. It uses a PostgreSQL database as a backend for storing the data. There are three basic parts to Nominatim's architecture: the data import, the address computation, and the search frontend.

The data import stage reads the raw OSM data and extracts all information that is useful for geocoding. This part is done by osm2pgsql, the same tool that can also be used to import a rendering database.

The address computation or indexing stage takes the data from a place and adds additional information needed for geocoding. It ranks the places by importance, links objects that belong together and computes addresses and the search index. Most of this work is done in PostgreSQL via database triggers and can be found in the file sql/functions.sql.

The search frontend implements the actual application program interface. It takes queries for search and reverse geocoding queries from the user, looks up the data and returns the results in the requested format. This part is written in PHP and can be found in the lib/ and website/ directories.

8.2.3.2 Place Ranking in Nominatim

Nominatim uses two metrics to rank a place: search rank and address rank. Both can be assigned a value between 0 and 30. They serve slightly different purposes.

The search rank describes the extent and importance of a place. It is used when ranking the search result. Simply put, if there are two results for a search query which are otherwise equal, then the result with the lower search rank will be appear higher in the result list. Search ranks are not so important these days because many well-known places use the Wikipedia importance ranking instead.

The address rank describes where a place shows up in an address hierarchy. Usually only administrative boundaries and place nodes and areas are eligible to be part of an address. All other objects have an address rank of 0. Note that the search rank of a place plays a role in the address computation as well. When collecting the places that should make up the address parts then only places that have a lower address rank than the search rank of the base object are taken into account.

Search and address ranks are assigned to a place when it is first imported into the database. There are a few hard-coded rules for the assignment:

- Postcodes follow special rules according to their length.
- Boundaries that are not areas and railway = rail are dropped completely.
- The following are always search rank 30 and address rank 0:

    - highway nodes
    - land use that is not an area.

Other than that, the ranks can be freely assigned via the json file defined with CONST_ Address_Level_Config according to their type and the country they are in.

8.3 High-Definition Maps

HD maps provide highly accurate, fresh, and comprehensive geometric information and semantics of the driving environment. Since the inception of the Defense Advanced Research Projects Agency challenges in the 2000s, HD maps have already been widely used for precise localization of autonomous vehicles [4, 5].

In addition to localization, HD maps contain precomputed data for perception, prediction, motion planning, vehicle control, etc. One example of the precomputed data is the 3D locations of traffic lights, thus allowing autonomous vehicles running on the road to only examine a small region instead of the whole field of view to efficiently detect traffic lights. While there are still debates about the possibility of building a fully autonomous vehicle system without using pre-built HD maps, no existing highly automated driving (HAD) systems we know of are running in urban environments without using some kind of HD map.

8.3.1 Characteristics of HD Maps

8.3.1.1 High Precision
As the name suggests, HD maps for autonomous driving systems need to have high precision, usually at centimeter level. While there is no standard about what exactly the precision should be, it is common to assume HD maps have precisions between 5 cm and 20 cm.

8.3.1.2 Rich Geometric Information and Semantics
HD maps also contain rich geometric and semantic information of the road network and surrounding environment for use by localization, perception, prediction, motion planning and vehicle control, etc. The most common content includes lane/road model, 3D locations of traffic control devices (mainly traffic lights and traffic signs), and geometry and semantics of other static road elements such as curbs, crosswalk, railway tracks, guardrails, poles, bus stops, speed bumps, potholes, and overpass.

8.3.1.3 Fresh Data
HD maps need to be updated with changes in a timely fashion. TomTom estimates about 15% of US roads change every year in some way. Although not all of those changes are of concern for autonomous vehicles, we could infer the order of magnitude of relevant changes that need to be updated to ensure the safety of all parties on the roads where autonomous vehicles are operating. The industry standard is that HD maps be updated weekly. In comparison, traditional digital maps, such as Google map, have an update cycle of 6–12 months. Therefore, it is extremely costly to maintain HD maps, as we have to deploy a large fleet of data collection vehicles as well as a significant cloud computing infrastructure to maintain the weekly refresh rate.

8.3.2 Layers of HD Maps

HD maps usually have multiple layers and together they provide a full stack of information for autonomous vehicles. On account of the size of all the layers, they are usually being served to autonomous vehicles from the cloud [6, 7], and only a few nearby small areas of the HD map (called submaps) are downloaded to the vehicle when needed.

Layers of HD maps are quite different from each other and have different representations, data structures, and purposes. Although HD map builders do not necessarily follow the same practice, HD maps usually contain the following four layers.

8.3.2.1   2D Orthographic Reflectivity Map

The orthographic reflectivity map leverages the fact that different materials (e.g. different types of road pavement, road marking paints, etc.) on the road surface have different infrared reflective intensities from laser. This layer is a 2D planar view of the road surface extracted from Light Detection and Ranging (LiDAR) point clouds. The reflectivity map actually may look photorealistic after combining multiple scans of the same area and texturing the intensity values onto the points. Visualizations of reflectivity maps can be found in [8, 9].

8.3.2.2   Digital Elevation Model

A digital elevation model (DEM) is a 3D model and contains the height information of the surface of the driving environment, such as the height of the road curbs, and the grade/steepness of a ramp or hilly road. It is useful for localization (in situations where the road surface is lacking features), motion planning, and vehicle control. An example DEM visualization could be found in [10].

8.3.2.3   Lane/Road Model

The lane/road model is a very important vectorized layer that contains the semantics of lane segments and road segments. The road model includes parts of the road that are not part of the lanes, such as edges of the road. However, since autonomous vehicle builders always try to center the autonomous vehicles in the lane, in reality autonomous vehicles only need to deal with the lane model except on rare occasions when they need to travel outside the lane boundaries. The lane model contains information on lane geometrics (boundaries, width, curvature, etc.), lane type (car lane, bike lane, bus-only lane, etc.), lane directionalities, lane marking/divider types (solid vs. dashed, single vs. double, etc.), restrictions (e.g. left/right turn only), speed limits, connectivity between lanes, etc. The lane/road model is critical for motion planning, vehicle control, etc.

8.3.2.4   Stationary Map

This is a layer that is not well-defined. It is usually a versatile layer that stores the semantics of static elements in the driving environment that are not captured in other layers (e.g. traffic lights and their association with lanes, road obstacles, etc.).

8.3.3   HD Map Creation

As shown in Figure 8.5, the HD map creation process can be broken down into four stages: data collection, HD map generation, quality control and validation, and update and maintenance.

8.3.3.1   Data Collection

Mobile Mapping Systems (MMSs) are usually equipped with multiple sensors including LiDARs, cameras, GPS, IMU (inertial measurement unit), and wheel odometer. MMSs then go on field trips to collect data and log them into solid-state storage device hard drives (or send the data to servers or cloud storage via a cellar network after some kind of processing, filtering, and compression). The data collection process is usually carried out by zones

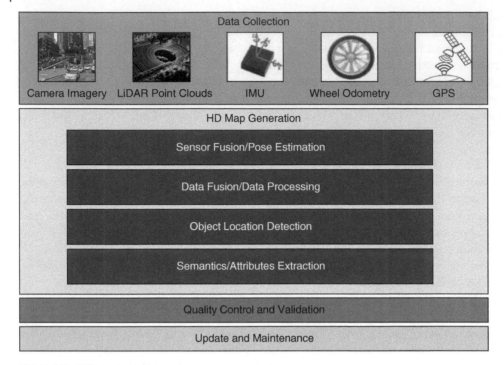

Figure 8.5 HD map creation.

of a city and involves careful route planning as well as optimized data storage and transmission. Cost of equipment, human labor, data storage and transmission are the major concerns in the data collection process; and overdrive (i.e. re-collection for the same road segment) reduction is of great interest to practitioners.

The data collected for HD map creation belong to two categories: (i) HD map data: LiDAR point clouds and camera images containing geometries and semantic information that will become content of the HD maps; and (ii) auxiliary data: logs of GPS/IMU/wheel odometer that are useful for creating the HD maps but not containing the geometric and semantic information for the HD maps. The use of the auxiliary data is mainly for pose optimizations for the data-collecting vehicles.

8.3.3.2 Offline Generation of HD Maps
This is the back-office work that processes the collected data and generates the HD maps. Roughly it can be further broken down into four steps (Figure 8.5).

8.3.3.2.1 Sensor Fusion and Pose Estimation Knowing the accurate poses (location and orientation) of the MMS vehicles is key to generating HD maps. If the poses of the vehicles are inaccurate, it is impossible to produce precise maps. Once we have the accurate poses of the data-collecting vehicles, and given we know where the sensors are mounted and their relative angles to the vehicle frame, we could infer the accurate poses of the collected point cloud and image frames.

Although accurate poses could not be acquired directly at runtime due to the limitation of GPS, IMU, and wheel odometry, etc., accurate poses can be estimated by utilizing offline optimizations such as fusing logs of different sensors with graph-based SLAM (simultaneous localization and mapping) [8, 11].

8.3.3.2.2 *Map Data Fusion and Data Processing* Once we have accurate poses, we then could perform map data fusion. Map data here mean LiDAR 3D point clouds and camera images; note that for HD mapping, the resolutions and qualities of videos are usually not satisfactory, and we do not need such a high frame rate from videos, so higher resolution images taken in <10 FPS are commonly used. During the data fusion process, multiple scans of point clouds are aligned and calibrated to get denser point clouds. Also, point clouds and camera images are registered to each other so that we could use the point clouds to get the 3D locations of objects and use the registered images to extract semantic information. This is because although point clouds provide accurate 3D positions, they do not provide semantic information, whereas images do provide accurate semantic information.

In addition, other data processing steps are also carried out, including road plane generation, removal of irrelevant objects (e.g. dynamic objects and objects too far away from the road), and texturing to generate photorealistic orthographic images.

8.3.3.2.3 *3D Object Location Detection* For road elements whose geometrics and precision locations are important (e.g. lane boundaries, curbs, traffic lights, overpasses, railway tracks, guardrails, light poles, speed bumps, and potholes), we need to map their precise 3D locations. LiDAR point clouds provide 3D location information directly and 3D object detection on point clouds is performed either using a geometry-based method [12–15] or deep learning on 3D point clouds [16–18]. We could also detect 3D object locations without using point clouds through triangulation with multiple images of the same objects. One such example can be found in [19].

8.3.3.2.4 *Semantics/Attributes Extraction* The last and also the most laborious step is to extract semantics and attributes from data for the HD maps. The process includes lane/ road model construction, traffic sign recognitions, associations of traffic lights with lanes, road marking semantics extraction, and road element (e.g. light poles) detections. There is actually other work that needs to be done before a large-scale HD map could be generated but the aforementioned steps are the major steps involved.

8.3.3.3 Quality Control and Validation

Once the HD maps are generated, predefined quality metrics must be met, and HD maps must be validated by different means including testing on road and verified by using more traditional survey methods.

8.3.3.4 Update and Maintenance

This stage is the ongoing work to keep the HD maps updated timely with changes and also fixing issues discovered during the use of them.

8.3.3.5 Problems of HD Maps

Although HD maps bring many benefits, the complexities of building HD maps also present several problems. First, to collect raw data, a large number of MMS vehicles need to be deployed. These MMS vehicles are equipped with very expensive sensors, such as LiDAR, highly accurate Global Navigation Satellite System (GNSS), HD cameras, etc. Each MMS vehicle could cost over 0.5 million USD. Secondly, a very powerful cloud computing infrastructure needs to be deployed to consume the raw data and generate updated HD maps [7]. Thirdly, since HD maps need to be updated weekly, HD map providers need to maintain an operation team to constantly rescan areas that have already been captured. Note that the refresh rate of digital maps, such as Google map, is 6–12 months, whereas the refresh rate of HD maps is a week. This adds additional operation costs to the already extremely expensive HD map production costs.

8.4 PerceptIn's π-Map

As shown in the previous section, HD maps are extremely expensive to construct and to maintain, making it extremely hard for ubiquitous deployment. For certain scenarios, such as low-speed (e.g. <20 MPH) autonomous driving in highly structured environments (e.g. university campuses, industrial parks), we may not need full-fledged HD maps, we can simply extend existing digital maps to provide accurate lane information to enable autonomous driving. In this section, we present a case study on PerceptIn's mapping technology, in which existing OSM is extended for autonomous robot and vehicle navigation.

To achieve this, PerceptIn have developed a graph-based data structure to represent lanes' topology, and a methodology to construct a map by only using a real-time kinematic (RTK) GNSS receiver [20] and the JOSM toolchain (https://josm.openstreetmap.de). PerceptIn's map, or π-map, can be easily integrated into the off-the-shell digital map, such as OSM, to form a two-layered map. With lanes' physical information provided by the layered map, the planning and control module is able to plan a global route for navigation, and to generate a local trajectory and a series of control commands to maneuver the vehicle.

8.4.1 Topological Map

π-Map uses a set of nodes and edges to represent lanes' structure. Without loss of generality, we use a simplified road model here only for illustrative purposes. A road contains one or multiple directional lanes, such that a vehicle can travel on one direction on the lane. Figure 8.6 shows a simple map that consists of four nodes and four edges. In practice, nodes are physical points centered in a lane, whereas edges between nodes represent the connectivity between nodes. For example, the edge between node 0 and node 1 represents that node 1 is reachable from node 0.

π-Map uses the following data structure to describe the topology of the above map. Each row represents a node. The first row contains information on node 0, the second row contains information on node 1, and so on. In a particular row, the first and second columns

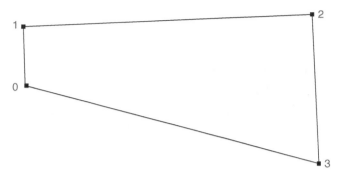

Figure 8.6 Example of our map's topology.

arc the x and y coordinates (under Universal Transverse Mercator coordinates) of the node, respectively, the third column is the number of nodes connected to this node (i.e. adjacent nodes of this node), and the rest of the columns list the ID of adjacent nodes.

	Column 1	Column 2	Column 3	Column 4	Column 5
Row 1	X1	Y1	2	1	3
Row 2	X2	Y2	2	0	2
Row 3	X3	Y3	2	1	3
Row 4	X4	Y4	2	2	0

Take the first row as an example to explain the data structure:

- This row contains information on node 0.
- X1 and Y1 are the x and y coordinates of node 0.
- 2 represents the number of adjacent nodes,
- 1 and 3 are IDs of the adjacent nodes to node 0.

8.4.2 π-Map Creation

This subsection illustrates our method of creating a map. As shown in Figure 8.7, we use a subarea of the University of California, Irvine campus as an example and create a map of roads around the Anteater Recreation Center.

According to maps' data structures discussed in the previous subsection, to compose a map, coordinates of nodes and connectivity among nodes need to be determined. In practice, we can use a RTK GNSS receiver and JOSM to obtain the coordinates of nodes, and use JOSM to draw nodes and edges between nodes.

Figure 8.8 shows the map of lanes around the Anteater Recreation Center as an example. To create the map, first, we mount the RTK GNSS module on the PerceptIn DragonFly Pod [21]. Then, we drive the DragonFly Pod along the center of the lanes that we want to map, and use the RTK GNSS device to obtain the trajectory of the car. Secondly, we load the trajectory into JOSM and draw nodes along the trajectory. Finally, we use JOSM to draw the edges between nodes.

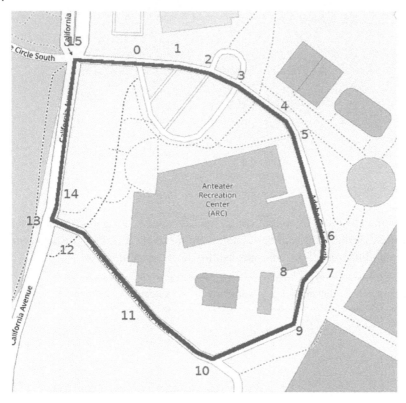

Figure 8.7 The Anteater Recreation Center. The solid line is the lane map that we want to make.

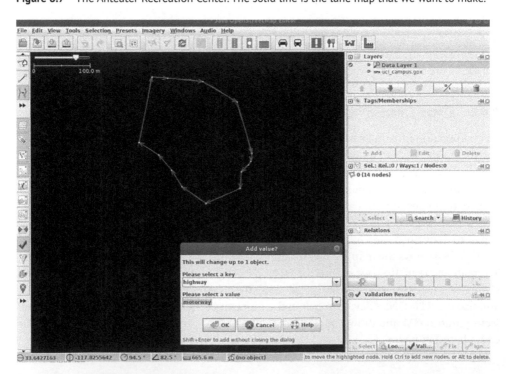

Figure 8.8 The resulting map in the JOSM.

This generated map, which consists of nodes to represent the topology of the target location, is then fed to the planning and control module for operation. For instance, a user can click anywhere on the map to call the autonomous vehicle for pick up, and then click a new location on the map for drop off.

References

1 Jiao, J. (2018). Machine Learning assisted High-Definition Map creation. *2018 IEEE 42nd Annual Computer Software and Applications Conference (COMPSAC)*, Tokyo, Japan (23–27 July 2018). IEEE.

2 GitHub (2017). JOSM source code. https://github.com/openstreetmap/josm (accessed 1 December 2018).

3 GitHub (2017). Nominatim source code. https://github.com/openstreetmap/Nominatim (accessed 1 December 2018).

4 Buehler, M., Iagnemma, K., and Singh, S. (eds.) (2007). *The 2005 DARPA Grand Challenge: The Great Robot Race*, vol. 36. Springer Science & Business Media.

5 Buehler, M., Iagnemma, K., and Singh, S. (eds.) (2009). *The DARPA Urban Challenge: Autonomous Vehicles in City Traffic*, vol. 56. Springer.

6 Liu, S., Li, L., Tang, J. et al. (2017). Creating autonomous vehicle systems. *Synthesis Lectures on Computer Science* 6 (1): 1–186.

7 Liu, S., Tang, J., Wang, C. et al. (2017). A unified cloud platform for autonomous driving. *Computer* 50 (12): 42–49.

8 Levinson, J., Montemerlo, M., and Thrun, S. (2007). Map-based precision vehicle localization in urban environments. In: *Robotics: Science and Systems*, vol. 4, 1. MIT Press.

9 Levinson, J. (2011). Automatic laser calibration, mapping, and localization for autonomous vehicles. PhD thesis. Stanford University.

10 Waymo Team (2016). Building maps for a self-driving car. https://medium.com/waymo/building-maps-for-a-self-driving-car-723b4d9cd3f4 (accessed 1 June 2019).

11 Thrun, S. and Montemerlo, M. (2006). The graph SLAM algorithm with applications to large-scale mapping of urban structures. *The International Journal of Robotics Research* 25 (5–6): 403–429.

12 Yu, Y., Li, J., Guan, H. et al. (2015). Semiautomated extraction of street light poles from mobile LiDAR point-clouds. *IEEE Transactions on Geoscience and Remote Sensing* 53 (3): 1374–1386.

13 Zheng, H., Wang, R., and Xu, S. (2017). Recognizing street lighting poles from mobile LiDAR data. *IEEE Transactions on Geoscience and Remote Sensing* 55 (1): 407–420.

14 Ordóñez, C., Cabo, C., and Sanz-Ablanedo, E. (2017). Automatic detection and classification of pole-like objects for urban cartography using mobile laser scanning data. *Sensors* 17 (7): 1465.

15 Fukano, K. and Masuda, H. (2015). Detection and classification of pole-like objects from mobile mapping data. *ISPRS Annals of Photogrammetry, Remote Sensing & Spatial Information Sciences*, La Grande Motte, France (28 September–3 October 2015). ISPRS.

16 Qi, C.R., Su, H., Mo, K., and Guibas, L.J. (2017). PointNet: deep learning on point sets for 3D classification and segmentation. In: *Proceedings of Computer Vision and Pattern Recognition (CVPR)*, vol. 1, 4. IEEE.

17 Qi, C.R., Yi, L., Su, H., and Guibas, L.J. (2017). PointNet++: deep hierarchical feature learning on point sets in a metric space. In: *Advances in Neural Information Processing Systems*, 5105–5114. NeurIPS.

18 Zhou, Y. and Tuzel, O. (2017). VoxelNet: End-to-End Learning for Point Cloud Based 3D Object Detection. arXiv preprint arXiv:1711.06396.

19 Fairfield, N. and Urmson, C. (2011). Traffic light mapping and detection. In: *2011 IEEE International Conference on Robotics and Automation (ICRA)*, 5421–5426. IEEE.

20 PerceptIn (2018). PerceptIn DragonFly RTK GNSS Module. https://www.perceptin.io/products (accessed 1 December 2018).

21 Perceptin (2018). PerceptIn DragonFly Pod. https://www.perceptin.io/products (accessed 1 December 2018).

9

Building the DragonFly Pod and Bus

9.1 Introduction

In this chapter, we provide a thorough case study of PerceptIn's DragonFly Pod and DragonFly bus, which were developed using the modular design approach introduced in this book [1, 2]. A few video demos of the autonomous vehicles can be found in [3, 4].

The two-seater DragonFly Pod was developed for private autonomous driving transportation services such that passengers can enjoy privacy during their trip. Typical usages of DragonFly Pods include entertainment parks, industrial parks, tourist attractions, and senior living societies. The eight-seater DragonFly bus was designed for public autonomous driving transportation solutions, usually with a distance less than 5 mi. Typical usages of DragonFly buses include university campuses, city bus routes, and transportation within airports and train stations.

First, we introduce the chassis specifications of these two vehicles, so that readers can understand the physical differences of these vehicles. Secondly, we reveal the sensor configurations on these two chassis, so that readers can understand how perception and localization modules are deployed. Thirdly, we introduce the "anatomy" of the DragonFly system, or the software architecture enabling autonomous driving on these vehicles, so that readers can understand how different modules work together to form a system. Fourthly, we introduce the "physiology" of the DragonFly system, or the mechanism of the autonomous vehicles, so that readers understand the life cycle of the autonomous driving software. Fifthly, we go through the data structures used for communications between different modules, so that readers understand how different modules interact with each other. Finally, we show how users can interact with the autonomous vehicles through a simple user interface (UI).

After reading this chapter, readers should have a basic understanding of how to build their own autonomous vehicles or robots from scratch.

9.2 Chassis Hardware Specifications

Figure 9.1 shows a DragonFly Pod and Table 9.1 lists the details of the chassis specifications. A DragonFly Pod is 2.18 m long, 1.38 m wide, and 1.675 m high, weighs 580 kg, and has a

Engineering Autonomous Vehicles and Robots: The DragonFly Modular-based Approach,
First Edition. Shaoshan Liu.

Figure 9.1 DragonFly two-seater pod.

maximum speed of 25 kilometers per hour. While in autonomous driving mode, we typically keep the speed around 10 kilometers per hour for safety reasons. Its battery allows the vehicle to function continuously for 10 hours at normal speed (10 kilometers per hour). A DragonFly Pod chassis is drive-by-wire-enabled, such that the planning and control module can maneuver the vehicle by sending control commands. Also, the chassis is able to provide real-time vehicle status information such as angular speed, linear speed, brake pressure, etc.

Figure 9.2 shows a DragonFly bus and Table 9.2 lists the details of the chassis specifications. A DragonFly bus is 3.93 m long, 1.51 m wide, and 2.04 m high, weighs 910 kg, and has a maximum speed of 30 kilometers per hour. While in autonomous driving mode, we typically keep the speed around 10 kilometers per hour for safety reasons. Its battery allows the vehicle to function continuously for eight hours at normal speed (10 kilometers per hour). A DragonFly bus chassis is drive-by-wire-enabled, such that the planning and control module can maneuver the vehicle by sending control commands. Also, the chassis is able to provide real-time vehicle status information such as angular speed, linear speed, brake pressure etc.

9.3 Sensor Configurations

Once we understand the chassis capability, we need to figure out how to deploy sensors on the autonomous vehicles for perception and localization. Figure 9.3 shows how sensors are deployed on a DragonFly Pod. The four major types of sensors we use include the DragonFly vision module, GPS receivers, radars, and sonars.

The DragonFly vision module is used for both localization and active perception. It is mounted on top of the vehicle, at the center location, in order to get an open field of view

Table 9.1 DragonFly Pod chassis specification.

	DragonFly Pod
Suspension (F/R)	McPherson independent front suspension: spiral spring + cylinder hydraulic shock absorption Integral rear axle, speed ratio 12.49:1 helical spring damping + cylinder hydraulic shock absorption
Frame material	Carrier frame structure
Driving method	Front wheel steering
Brake (F/R)	Front disc rear hub, double tube double circuit hydraulic brake
Parking system	Electric park brakes electronic parking and hand brake parking
Control method	CAN bus
Length/width/height	2180/1380/1675 mm
Wheelbase	Back 1190 mm, front 1170 mm
Ground clearance	145 mm
Minimum turning radius	≤4.4 m
Gradeability	15% (≥8.5°)
Tire	155 65/R13 13
Total weight	580 kg
Maximum speed	25 kilometers per hour
Battery pack type	Lead-acid
Battery capacity	120 Ah
Battery specification	12 V/120 Ah
Number of batteries	4
Charger type	External charger
Charging voltage	220 V
Vehicle power output	12 V, 700 W
Urban range	100 km
Recharge time	10 h, 80%
Communication method	CAN protocol
Chassis information	Angular speed, linear speed, brake pressure, voltage, electric current, power
Number of seats	2
Drive type	Center motor

to allow it to capture surrounding spatial features. Also, by placing the DragonFly vision module at the center of the vehicle, we can easily align different sensors' coordinates with the DragonFly vision module when doing spatial sensor calibrations.

We also deploy two GPS receivers along the horizontal axis. The two GPS receivers form a differential pair to provide not only accurate real-time positions of the vehicle but accurate

Figure 9.2 DragonFly eight-seater bus.

real-time headings as well. The center of the differential GPS receivers is exactly the center of the DragonFly vision module, thus simplifying the spatial calibration process.

Around the vehicle, we deploy six radars and eight sonars to maximize perception detection coverage. This way, we can use radars and sonars for passive perception with two layers of protection: radar at the mid-range, and sonar at the close-range. In addition, radars can provide object distance, object speed information, as well as object tracking capability, which can be fused with visual perception for more accurate active perception.

Figure 9.4 shows how sensors are deployed on a DragonFly bus, which is very similar to the DragonFly Pod deployment except:

- Due to the length of the vehicle, instead of using six radars and eight sonars, we need to deploy eight radars and eight sonars.
- Due to the length of the vehicle, the DragonFly vision module is placed at the front part of the vehicle instead of at the center of the vehicle in order to get an unobstructed field of view.
- Due to the length of the vehicle, the differential GPS receivers are deployed in the vertical dimension to fully utilize the length of the vehicle in order to get more accurate real-time headings.

9.4 Software Architecture

Once we understand the sensor deployment scheme, we can delve into the software stack to introduce the "anatomy," or the software architecture, of the DragonFly system.

Table 9.2 DragonFly bus chassis specification.

	DragonFly bus
Controller	InBol electronic control/AC MC3336
Battery	Lvtong maintenance-free battery 6 V/170 Ah * 8 only (3 h rate)
Electric motor	Lvtong special AC asynchronous motor 33 V/5 kW
Charger	Computer intelligent charger 48 V/25 A, charging time <10 h (discharge rate 80%)
DC converter	High Power Isolated DC Converter 48 V/12 V, 400 W
Lighting and warning system	Front light, turn signal, fog light, reverse light, rear tail light, snail horn, reverse voice horn
Steering system	Bidirectional rack and pinion steering system, automatic gap compensation function: optional electric power
Braking system	Front disc and rear hub four-wheel hydraulic brake + handbrake parking: electric vacuum assisted brake system is optional
Front suspension system	McPherson independent front suspension: helical spring + cylinder hydraulic damping
Rear suspension system	Integral rear axle, speed ratio 16:1, steel leaf spring + cylinder hydraulic shock absorption
Tire diameter	165/70r13c vacuum tire (diameter 560 mm): 13 steel ring
Length/width/height	3930/510/2040 mm
Number of seats	8
Maximum speed	30 kilometers per hour
Driving mileage km	75–95 km (flat road)
Energy consumption per hundred kilometers	9 kWh
Maximum gradation	0.15
In the slope performance	0.2
Minimum turning radius	5.6 m
Vehicle weight	910 kg
Brake stability	1900 mm
Minimum ground clearance	155 mm
Wheelbase	Back 1330 mm, front 1300 mm
Communication method	CAN protocol

Figure 9.5 shows the details of the DragonFly system software architecture. Note that each dotted box represents an independent process.

First, let us review the data collection processes. The first process is the GPS Daemon process which continuously acquires the latest Global Navigation Satellite System (GNSS) data and sends the data to the localization process. Similarly, the image and inertial measurement unit (IMU) dispatcher process continuously acquires the latest image and IMU data and sends the data to the localization process and the perception process.

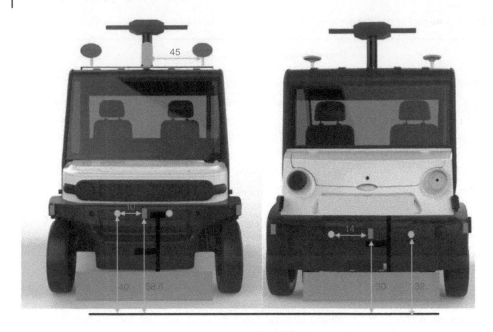

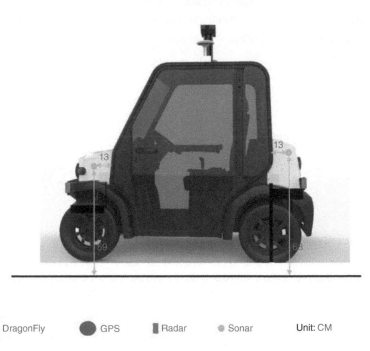

DragonFly   GPS   Radar   Sonar   Unit: CM

Figure 9.3 DragonFly two-seater pod sensor configuration.

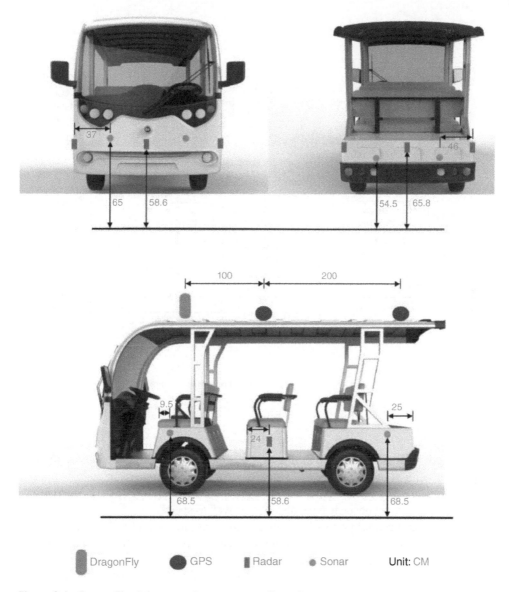

DragonFly   GPS   Radar   Sonar   Unit: CM

Figure 9.4   DragonFly eight-seater bus sensor configuration.

The localization process receives image, IMU, and GNSS data and generates real-time localization results. Note that in our design, we use GNSS data as the ground truth, and when the GNSS data are not available or not accurate due to multipath problems or other problems, then Visual-Inertial Odometry (VIO) will take over to generate accurate localization results.

The perception process receives image data, as well as radar and sonar data from the chassis, and combines these pieces of information to generate real-time perception results. When stereo vision data comes in, the perception process applies a deep learning model to extract obstacle semantic information, and applies stereo matching techniques to generate

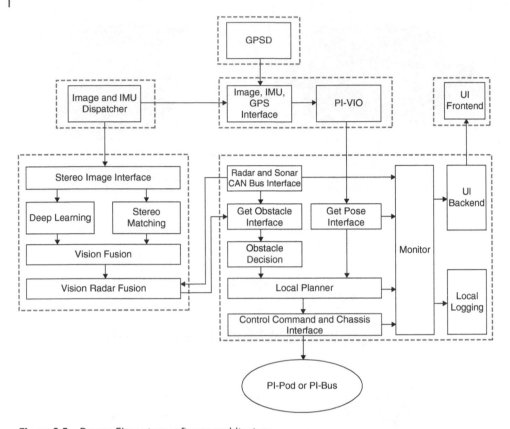

Figure 9.5 DragonFly system software architecture.

obstacle depth information. By combining the obstacle semantics and depths, the perception process can identify exact obstacle type and distance information. In addition, radar provides obstacle speed information, and by fusing radar and vision results, the perception process is able to extract obstacle type, distance, as well as speed.

The planning and control process is the most important process and is the "brain" of the DragonFly system. It consumes outputs from the perception process and the localization process, and generates real-time control commands through the local planner module, and sends these commands to the chassis for execution. Also, a monitor module continuously checks the health status of the whole system and stops the vehicle if any module malfunctions. In addition, a UI backend continuously sends status data to the UI frontend process to keep riders/operators informed of the real-time status of the system. Similarly, a local logging module also continuously logs system information to a local disk or a remote cloud for debugging purposes.

9.5 Mechanism

After understanding the "anatomy" of the DragonFly system, we delve into the "physiology" or the system mechanism. Figure 9.6 illustrates the detailed steps of the DragonFly system initialization process.

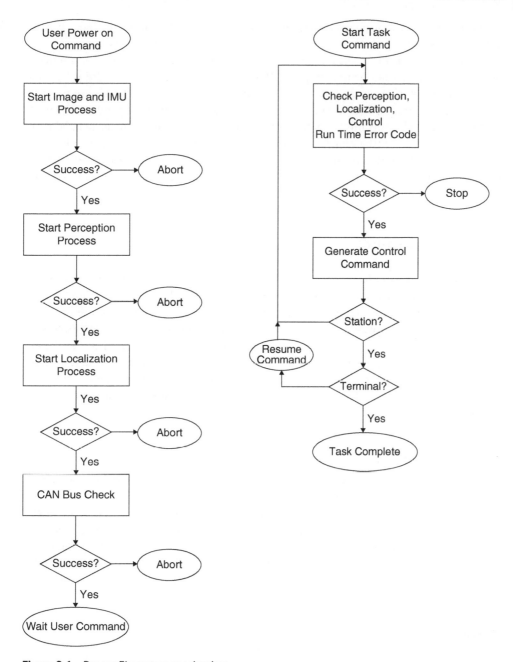

Figure 9.6 DragonFly system mechanism.

One the left-hand side of Figure 9.6, once a user powers on the system, the system first launches the image and IMU collection stream on the DragonFly vision module. If this is unsuccessful, then the system aborts and stops execution. Otherwise, the system starts the perception process. Next, the system starts the localization process. Once these are successful, the system checks the Controller Area Network (CAN) bus to make sure communication with the chassis is acceptable and the chassis' status is satisfactory. After all checks have been passed, the system spins to wait for user commands.

On the right-hand side of Figure 9.6, once a user task has been initiated (e.g. command the vehicle to move from point A to point B), the planning and control module checks to ensure that the perception module, the localization module, and the chassis are properly functioning and no error code has been raised. If successful, the planning and control module continuously issues control commands to drive the vehicle along the designated path. If a station is reached, the planning and control module then checks the health of the system again and continuously commands the vehicle along the designated path. If the destination is reached, the planning and control process terminates and waits for the next task command.

9.6 Data Structures

After understanding the "anatomy" and "physiology" of the DragonFly system, in this section, we introduce the data structures used in the system so that readers can understand what information is provided by each module, as well as how different modules interact with each other. Note that all data structures are encoded using Protocol Buffers (Protobuf), which is a method of serializing structured data. Protobuf is widely used in developing programs to communicate with each other and this method involves an interface description language that describes the structure of some data and a program that generates source code from that description for generating or parsing a stream of bytes that represents the structured data.

9.6.1 Common Data Structures

First, we introduce the common data structures that are shared between all modules. Common.proto defines the common header used in all modules, which includes timestamp, a system timestamp used to synchronize all data; module name, the name of the current module; sequence number, a counter to keep track of the number of data sent since boot time; and a hardware timestamp, which is the timestamp from the sensor that is different from the system timestamp. By keeping track of both the sensor timestamp and the system timestamp, we also keep track of the time difference between the system and the sensor.

Common.proto

```
syntax = "proto3";

package piauto.common;

message Header {
  // message publishing time in milliseconds since 1970.
  uint64 timestamp = 1;
```

```
  // module name
  string module_name = 2;

  // sequence number for each message: each module maintains its
own counter for
  // sequence_num, always starting from 1 on boot.
  uint32 sequence_num = 3;

  // hardware sensor timestamp in milliseconds since 1970
  uint64 hardware_timestamp = 4;
}
```

Geometry.proto stores commonly used geometries for the perception and the planning and control modules. These geometries include 2D points, 3D points, velocity, and polygons (collection of 3D points).

Geometry.proto

```
syntax = "proto3";

package piauto.common;

// A general 3D point, in meter
message Point3D {
  double x = 1;
  double y = 2;
  double z = 3;
}

// A general 2D point, in meter
message Point2D {
  double x = 1;
  double y = 2;
}

// General speed, in m/s
message Velocity3D {
  double vel_x = 1;
  double vel_y = 2;
  double vel_z = 3;
}

// A general polygon, points are counter clockwise
message Polygon {
  repeated Point3D point = 1;
}
```

9.6.2 Chassis Data

Chassis.proto stores the enormous amount of data generated by the chassis. These pieces of data are continuously sent to the planning and control module, so that the planning and control module can combine these pieces of data, along with the pieces of data from the perception and localization modules, and generate real-time control commands. The chassis data are also sent to the UI module to inform riders/operators about the current status of the vehicle. The more commonly used pieces of chassis data include error code, vehicle speed, vehicle odometer, fuel range, steering angle, and steering velocity.

Chassis.proto

```
syntax = "proto3";

package piauto.chassis;

import "header.proto";

// next id :31
message Chassis {
    enum DrivingMode {
        COMPLETE_MANUAL = 0;             // manual mode
        COMPLETE_AUTO_DRIVE = 1;         // auto mode
        AUTO_STEER_ONLY = 2;             // only steer
        AUTO_SPEED_ONLY = 3;             // include throttle and brake

        // security mode when manual intervention happens, only
response status
        EMERGENCY_MODE = 4;
        MANUAL_INTERVENTION = 5;         // human manual intervention
    }

    enum ErrorCode {
        NO_ERROR = 0;

        CMD_NOT_IN_PERIOD = 1;           // control cmd not in period

        // receive car chassis can frame not in period
        CHASSIS_CAN_NOT_IN_PERIOD = 2;

        // car chassis report error, like steer, brake, throttle,
gear fault
        CHASSIS_ERROR = 3;

        // classify the types of the car chassis errors
```

```
        CHASSIS_ERROR_ON_PARK = 4;
        CHASSIS_ERROR_ON_LIGHT = 5;
        CHASSIS_ERROR_ON_STEER = 6;
        CHASSIS_ERROR_ON_BRAKE = 7;
        CHASSIS_ERROR_ON_THROTTLE = 8;
        CHASSIS_ERROR_ON_GEAR = 9;

        UNKNOWN_ERROR = 10;
}

enum GearPosition {
        GEAR_NEUTRAL = 0;
        GEAR_DRIVE = 1;
        GEAR_REVERSE = 2;
        GEAR_PARKING = 3;
        GEAR_LOW = 4;
        GEAR_INVALID = 5;
        GEAR_NONE = 6;
}

common.Header header = 1;

bool engine_started = 3;

// engine speed in RPM.
float engine_rpm = 4;

// vehicle speed in meters per second.
float speed_mps = 5;

// vehicle odometer in meters.
float odometer_m = 6;

// fuel range in meters.
int32 fuel_range_m = 7;

// real throttle location in [%], ranging from 0 to 100.
float throttle_percentage = 8;

// real brake location in [%], ranging from 0 to 100.
float brake_percentage = 9;

// real steering location in degree, ranging from about -30 to 30.
// clockwise: negative
// counter clockwise: positive
float steering_angle = 11;
```

```
    // applied steering velocity in [degree/second].
    float steering_velocity = 12;

    // parking brake status.
    bool parking_state = 13;

    // battery voltage
    float battery_voltage = 14;

    //battery power in [%], ranging from 0 to 100.
    float battery_power = 15;

    // signals.
    bool high_beam_signal = 16;
    bool low_beam_signal = 17;
    bool left_turn_signal = 18;
    bool right_turn_signal = 19;
    bool flash_signal = 20;
    bool horn = 21;

    bool wiper = 22;
    bool disengage_status = 23;
    DrivingMode driving_mode = 24;
    ErrorCode error_code = 25;
    GearPosition gear_location = 26;

    // timestamp for steering module
    double steering_timestamp = 27; // In seconds, with 1e-6 accuracy

    WheelSpeed wheel_speed = 30;
}

message WheelSpeed {
    enum WheelSpeedType {
        FORWARD = 0;
        BACKWARD = 1;
        STANDSTILL = 2;
        INVALID = 3;
    }

    bool is_wheel_spd_rr_valid = 1;
    WheelSpeedType wheel_direction_rr = 2;
    double wheel_spd_rr = 3;
    bool is_wheel_spd_rl_valid = 4;
    WheelSpeedType wheel_direction_rl = 5;
    double wheel_spd_rl = 6;
    bool is_wheel_spd_fr_valid = 7;
    WheelSpeedType wheel_direction_fr = 8;
```

```
    double wheel_spd_fr = 9;
    bool is_wheel_spd_fl_valid = 10;
    WheelSpeedType wheel_direction_fl = 11;
    double wheel_spd_fl = 12;
}

message License {
    string vin = 1;
}
```

9.6.3   Localization Data

Localization.proto stores the localization data, which are continuously sent to the planning and control module for processing. The key pieces of data include the vehicle position in Universal Transverse Mercator format (utm_x, utm_y), as well as the vehicle heading. Each piece of localization data includes details regarding whether the current localization data are generated solely by the GPS or by the fusion of GPS and other techniques, e.g. VIO.

Localization.proto

```
syntax="proto3";

package piauto.localization;

import "header.proto";

enum LocalizationStatus{
    GPS = 0;                    // postion:GPS heading:GPS
    BOTH_FUSION = 1;            // postion:FUSION heading:FUSION
    GPS_FUSION = 2;             // postion:GPS heading:FUSION
    FUSION_GPS = 3;             // postion:FUSION heading:GPS
    INIT=4;
    ERROR=5;
}

enum FusionType{
    ORIGIN_GPS = 0;
    FUSION = 1;
}

enum GPSStatus{
    FLOAT = 0;
    FIXED = 1;
}
```

```
enum ErrorType{
    // sensor failed
    IMAGE_OPEN_FAILED=0;
    IMU_OPEN_FAILED=1;
    GPS_OPEN_FAILED=2;

    // init failed
    GRAVITY_INIT_FAILED=11;
    GPS_INIT_FAILED=12;
    GPS_INVALID_DATA=13;

    // run error
    CONNECT_FAILED=20;
}

message LocalizationData{
    // header
    common.Header header = 1;

    // position
    double utm_x = 2;
    double utm_y = 3;
    double utm_x_variance = 4;
    double utm_y_variance = 5;
    sint32 utm_zone = 6;
    FusionType position_type = 7;
    GPSStatus gps_position_status = 8;

    // heading
    double heading = 9;
    double heading_variance = 10;
    FusionType heading_mode = 11;
    GPSStatus gps_heading_status = 12;

    // system status
    LocalizationStatus localization_status = 13;
    ErrorType error_code = 14;
}
```

9.6.4 Perception Data

Perception.proto stores the perception data, which are continuously sent to the planning and control module for processing. The key pieces of data include object position, object velocity, and object type. Each piece of perception data includes details regarding whether the current perception data are generated by vision, sonar, radar, or the fusion of them.

Perception.proto

```
syntax = "proto3";

package piauto.perception;

import "geometry.proto";
import "header.proto";


message PerceptionObstacle {
  // timestamp
  common.Header header = 1;

  // we assume the basic sensors include radar, sonar, and
stereo_camera
  enum SensorType {
    UNKNOWN_SENSOR = 0;
    RADAR = 1;
    VISION = 2;
    ULTRASONIC = 3;
    FUSION = 4;
  };

  SensorType sensor_type = 2;

  // identify different sonar and radar
  int32 sensor_id = 3;

  // each obstacle has an unique id
  int32 obstacle_id = 4;

  common.Point3D position = 5;

  common.Velocity3D velocity= 6;

  // obstacle semantic type
  enum ObstacleType {
    UNKNOWN_OBSTACLE = 0;
    UNKNOWN_MOVABLE = 1;
    UNKNOWN_UNMOVABLE = 2;
    CAR = 3;
    VAN = 4;
    TRUCK = 5;
```

```
   BUS = 6;
   CYCLIST = 7;
   MOTORCYCLIST = 8;
   TRICYCLIST = 9;
   PEDESTRIAN = 10;
   TRAFFIC_CONE = 11;
   TRAFFIC_LIGHT = 12;
};

ObstacleType obstacle_type = 7;

// confidence level regarding the detection result
double confidence = 8;

enum ConfidenceType {
  CONFIDENCE_UNKNOWN = 0;
  CONFIDENCE_CNN = 1;
  CONFIDENCE_STEREO = 2;
  CONFIDENCE_RADAR = 3;
};

ConfidenceType confidence_type = 9;

repeated common.Polygon polygons = 10;

// traffic light detection result
enum TrafficLightColor {
  UNKNOWN = 0;
  RED = 1;
  YELLOW = 2;
  GREEN = 3;
  BLACK = 4;
};

TrafficLightColor traffic_light_color = 11;

// historical points on the trajectory path
message TrajectoryPathPoint {
  common.Point3D path_point = 1;

  // in milliseconds since 1970
  uint64 timestamp = 2;
```

```
    // in millisecond by hardware sensor
    uint64 hardware_timestamp = 3;
  }

  repeated TrajectoryPathPoint trajectory_points = 12;

  // confidence level of the trajectory prediction
  double trajectory_probability = 13;

  enum IntentType {
    UNKNOWN_INTENT = 0;
    STOP = 1;
    STATIONARY = 2;
    MOVING = 3;
    CHANGE_LANE = 4;
    LOW_ACCELERATION = 5;
    HIGH_ACCELERATION = 6;
    LOW_DECELERATION = 7;
    HIGH_DECELERATION = 8;
  }

  // estimated obstacle intent
  IntentType intent_type = 14;

  enum ErrorCode {
    OK = 0;
    IMAGE_TIMEOUT_ERROR = -1;
  }

  ErrorCode error_code = 15;
}

message PerceptionObstacles {
  repeated PerceptionObstacle perception_obstacle = 1;
}
```

9.6.5 Planning Data

The planning and control module consumes data from the perception module, the localization module, and the chassis module, and generates real-time control commands. Decision. proto defines the vehicle behaviors, including to follow a front vehicle, to yield to another vehicle, to stop the current vehicle, and to avoid an obstacle. The reasons for stopping the current vehicle are defined in Decision.proto as well.

Decision.proto

```
syntax = "proto3";

package piauto.plannning;

import "geometry.proto";

message EStop {
  // is_estop is true when emergency stop is required
  bool is_estop = 1;
  string reason = 2;
}

message MainEmergencyStop {
  // unexpected event happened, human driver is required to take over
  enum ReasonCode {
    ESTOP_REASON_INTERNAL_ERR = 0;
    ESTOP_REASON_COLLISION = 1;
    ESTOP_REASON_SENSOR_ERROR = 2;
  }
  ReasonCode reason_code = 1;
}

enum StopReasonCode {
  STOP_REASON_HEAD_VEHICLE = 0;
  STOP_REASON_DESTINATION = 1;
  STOP_REASON_PEDESTRIAN = 2;
  STOP_REASON_OBSTACLE = 3;
  STOP_REASON_PREPARKING = 4;
  STOP_REASON_SIGNAL = 5;                    // only for red light
  STOP_REASON_STOP_SIGN = 6;
  STOP_REASON_YIELD_SIGN = 7;
  STOP_REASON_CLEAR_ZONE = 8;
  STOP_REASON_CROSSWALK = 9;
  STOP_REASON_CREEPER = 10;
  STOP_REASON_REFERENCE_END = 11;            // end of the reference line
  STOP_REASON_YELLOW_SIGNAL = 12;       // yellow light
  STOP_REASON_LANE_CHANGE_URGENCY = 13;
}

message MainStop {
  StopReasonCode reason_code = 1;

  string reason = 2;

  // when stopped, the front center of vehicle should be at this point.
  common.Point3D stop_point = 3;
```

```
  // when stopped, the heading of the vehicle should be stop_heading.
  double stop_heading = 4;
}


// strategy to ignore objects
message ObjectIgnore {
  string ignore_strategy = 1;
  double distance_s = 2;        // in meters
}


message ObjectStop {
  StopReasonCode reason_code = 1;

  double distance_s = 2;        // in meters

  // when stopped, the front center of vehicle should be at this point.
  common.Point3D stop_point = 3;

  // when stopped, the heading of the vehicle should be stop_heading.
  double stop_heading = 4;

  repeated string wait_for_obstacle = 5;
}

// strategy to follow objects
message ObjectFollow {
  string follow_strategy = 1;
  double distance_s = 2;        // in meters
}

// strategy to yield objects
message ObjectYield {
  string yield_strategy = 1;
  double distance_s = 2;        // in meters
}

// strategy to avoidance objects, such as double-lane changing or
floating-lane
// avoidance
message ObjectAvoid {
  string avoid_strategy = 1;
  double distance_s = 2;        // in meters
}

message ObjectDecisionType {
  oneof object_tag {
    ObjectIgnore ignore = 1;
    ObjectStop stop = 2;
```

```
      ObjectFollow follow = 3;
      ObjectYield yield = 4;
      ObjectAvoid avoid = 5;
   }
}

message ObjectDecision {
   string id = 1;
   int32 perception_id = 2;
   repeated ObjectDecisionType object_decision = 3;
}

// decisions based on each object
message ObjectDecisions {
   repeated ObjectDecision decision = 1;
}

message MainLaneKeeping {
   string lane_id = 1;
   string sec_id = 2;
}

message MainNotReady {
   // decision system is not ready. e.g. wait for routing data.
   string reason = 1;
}

message MainParking {
   // parking_lot
   string parking_lot = 1;
}

message MainMissionComplete {
   // arrived at routing destination
   // when stopped, the front center of vehicle should be at this point.
   common.Point3D stop_point = 1;

   // when stopped, the heading of the vehicle should be stop_heading.
   double stop_heading = 2;
}

message MainDecision {
   oneof task {
      MainLaneKeeping lane_keeping = 1;
      MainStop stop = 2;
      MainEmergencyStop estop = 3;
      MainMissionComplete mission_complete = 4;
```

```
      MainNotReady not_ready = 5;
      MainParking parking = 6;
   }
}

message DecisionResult {
   // decisions based on task and motion planning
   MainDecision main_decision = 1;

   // decisions based on each object
   ObjectDecisions object_decision = 2;
}
```

Planning.proto encapsulates decision.proto, and also contains the current vehicle's control state as well as vehicle state. These pieces of information can be sent to the UI module for display, and also recorded in the log for future debugging needs.

Planning.proto

```
syntax = "proto3";

package piauto.plannning;

import "decision.proto";
import "header.proto";
import "geometry.proto";

message Planning {
   common.Header header = 1;
   ControlState control_state = 2;        // control state
   VehicleState state = 3;                // vehicle state

   // decision of the vehicle, lane follow, stop by obstacle and
etc..
   DecisionResult decision = 4;

   repeated common.Point3D trajectory_point = 5; // predict
trajectory

   // signal status of the current vehicle
   ADCSignals adc_signals = 6;

   bool autonomous_mode = 7;
}
```

```
enum ControlState {
  // attach to current lane
  AttachLane = 0;

  // turning left and right state
  Turnning = 1;

  // no attach lane, need slow down and try to attach lane
  CloserToLane = 2;

  // Stop
  Stop = 3;
}

message VehicleState {
  // Current pose of the vehicle
  common.Point3D pose = 1;
  double body_angle = 2;
  double front_wheel_angle = 3;
  double rear_wheel_speed = 4;
}

message ADCSignals {
  enum SignalType {
    LEFT_TURN = 0;
    RIGHT_TURN = 1;
    LOW_BEAM_LIGHT = 2;
    HIGH_BEAM_LIGHT = 3;
    FOG_LIGHT = 4;
    EMERGENCY_LIGHT = 5;
    HORN = 6;
  }
  repeated SignalType signal = 1;
}
```

9.7 User Interface

At last, we come to the UI to show how easy it is for users to interact with the autonomous vehicles. Figure 9.7 shows the UI when the vehicle is static. On the left-hand side of the UI, users can see the current time, the current speed of the vehicle, the next station, as well as the estimated time to the destination. On the right-hand side of the UI, the map of the deployment environment is displayed, as well as the fixed route along with the stations in between. Users can interact with the map by choose their destination and then click "Start" on the left-hand side to trigger the vehicle to move.

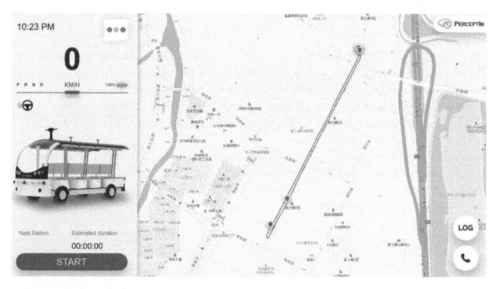

Figure 9.7 DragonFly UI when the vehicle is static.

Figure 9.8 shows the UI when the vehicle is moving. On the left-hand side of the UI, users can see the current speed of the vehicle and detected obstacles will also be projected onto the UI. Users can also click the "Stop" button on the UI to stop the vehicle at any time.

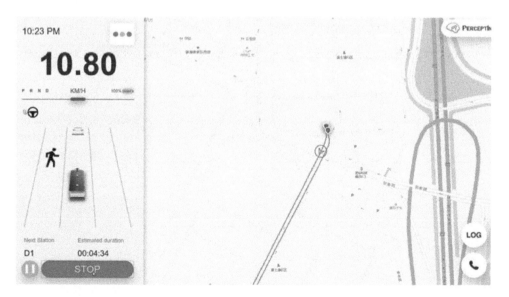

Figure 9.8 DragonFly UI when the vehicle is moving.

References

1 Kite-Powell, J. (2018). This company says you can design your own autonomous vehicle. https://www.forbes.com/sites/jenniferhicks/2018/09/24/this-company-says-you-can-design-your-own-autonomous-vehicle/#33733dab2009 (accessed 1 October 2019).

2 PerceptIn (2018). Build your own autonomous vehicles with DragonFly technologies. https://www.perceptin.io/post/build-your-own-autonomous-vehicle-with-dragonfly-technologies (accessed 1 October 2019).

3 YouTube (2019). PerceptIn DragonFly Autonomous Pod in Extreme Traffic Environments. https://www.youtube.com/watch?v=KhzwnJ8ayYg&t=42s (accessed 1 October 2019).

4 YouTube (2019). Autonomous Shuttle Service Provided by PerceptIn. https://www.youtube.com/watch?v=6twW4EoiThk (accessed 1 October 2019).

10

Enabling Commercial Autonomous Space Robotic Explorers

10.1 Introduction

In Chapter 9, we presented a case study on building autonomous low-speed electric vehicles (LSEVs). In this chapter, we will explore a very interesting topic, building commercial autonomous space robotic explorers. With the recent emergence of commercial space exploration companies such as SpaceX and Blue Origin, we envision commercial space robotic explorers will become a reality in the near future.

In the past, robots have been sent into space for varied purposes, e.g. taking photographs and performing mineral composition analysis. In contrast to manned missions, the application of autonomous robots for space exploration missions decreases the safety concerns of the exploration missions while extending the exploration distance since returning transportation is not necessary for robotics missions. In addition, the employment of robots in these missions also decreases mission complexities and costs because there is no need for onboard life support systems: robots can withstand and operate in harsh conditions, for instance, extreme temperature, pressure, and radiation, where humans cannot survive.

Most of the space robotic exploration missions today rely on remote control from Earth. This method suffers from extremely long communication latencies, leading to lack of efficiency for an operator to receive information, make a decision on how to respond, and issue commands to the spacecraft. To improve the efficiency of robotic exploration missions, there have been several attempts by NASA to enable autonomous robotic navigation on Mars [1].

As shown in Figure 10.1, we envision a future where commercial autonomous robotic explorers will explore and construct basic infrastructure on Mars, making it habitable for mankind. While there have been a few successful attempts to deliver exploration robots to planets such as Mars, how to develop autonomous robots suitable for commercial space exploration missions still requires a lot more research.

In this chapter, we explore the autonomous driving technologies, including localization, perception, planning, and control, required to enable a commercial space exploration robot, as well as how to integrate these technologies into a working system.

This chapter is organized as follows: in Section 10.2 we introduce the environments of Mars, and explore the challenges of enabling autonomous robotic explorers on Mars. In

Engineering Autonomous Vehicles and Robots: The DragonFly Modular-based Approach,
First Edition. Shaoshan Liu.
© 2020 John Wiley & Sons Ltd. Published 2020 by John Wiley & Sons Ltd.

Figure 10.1 The future of commercial space exploration.

Section 10.3, we explore technologies required to enable future commercial autonomous space robotic explorers. In Section 10.4, we present one urgent challenge for space exploration mission, namely, computing power. We conclude in Section 10.5.

10.2 Destination Mars

Mars is a potential destination for autonomous space robotic explorers. Currently, the main focus of space exploration is Mars, for it is relatively close to the Earth and shares many macro level similarities to Earth, such as the existence of atmosphere and the evidence of past flowing water.

The purpose of Mars exploration can be categorized into understanding the evolution of the Martian environment, examining the current conditions of Mars, and searching for past, present, and future potential for life. Mars exploration also lays the foundation for potential exploitation of Martian resources and, ultimately, mankind expansion.

Up until now, uncertainties about the Martian environment and the associated high cost has prevented human exploration of Mars. Therefore, Mars surface exploration is currently accomplished with robot explorers. Explorers collect and send back scientific data on the Martian surface and thus pave the way for future human exploration.

The Martian environment is drastically different from that of Earth, especially in terms of atmospheric composition, temperature, and geologic features. These differences pose potential challenges for robot design.

The Martian atmosphere is 96% carbon dioxide compared with less than 1% on Earth. The temperature on Mars can be as high as 70 °F or as low as about −225 °F. Because the atmosphere is so thin, heat from the Sun easily escapes this planet, and thus temperatures at different altitudes have tremendous variations. In addition, occasionally, winds on Mars are strong enough to create dust storms that cover much of the planet. After such storms, it can be months before all of the dust settles [2].

The geological features on Mars are generally more extreme than those on Earth. For instance, the deepest canyon on Mars is around 7 km in depth whereas on Earth, it is 1.8 km [3]. Martian soil is also different from soil on Earth; it is composed of fine regolith, or unconsolidated rock powder, which lacks traction and also affects visibility during Martian storms and that has huge implications for sensors used in autonomous movement.

The extreme geological features combined with low traction soil and low gravity pose challenging design questions for autonomous explorers, in terms of both hardware and software.

10.3 Mars Explorer Autonomy

The above introduced technologies and methods work well on Earth. However, when it comes to space explorers, the environment in which the vehicle operates in is vastly different from the environment on Earth. As a result, autonomous driving and navigation methods also have to be modified.

On planets other than Earth, there is no set traffic system nor other maneuverable objects. This simplifies the autonomous driving system in the sense that explorers do not have to localize at a centimeter level precision and can maneuver without any restriction and plan paths without concerns of crashing into another vehicle. However, the underdeveloped infrastructure in space also poses challenges on the design of autonomous driving systems.

In space, there is no available GPS or detailed surface map. The condition of the terrain is also much more complex and requires greater consideration compared with driving on Earth, for there is no road infrastructure in space.

We shall now examine the autonomous driving technologies and challenges for Mars explorers with a focus on perception and decision. This environment is particularly challenging for localization and path planning of the robot explorers.

10.3.1 Localization

Without the availability of GPS and known maps, localization for a Mars explorer robot is keeping track of its motion trajectory while observing the surrounding environment and estimating its position in the environment. Mars explorer localization relies on the camera and inertial measurement unit (IMU) for localization. One additional sensor that has been applied to Mars explorers is a star tracker, an optical device that measures the position of stars. There are mainly three methods for localization: vision-based simultaneous localization and mapping (SLAM), dead reckoning based on IMU, and star tracking.

The lack of detailed maps of Mars leaves the robot explorer having to navigate in an unknown environment while keeping track of its path. SLAM is a method for the robot to construct a map of its environment and localizing with regard to its surroundings simultaneously. While driving, an explorer can estimate its trajectory with a structure-from-motion algorithm. This trajectory is then used to create a layout of the environment by incorporating matching and triangulation. This constructed environment layout can then in turn be used for further localization with regard to the environment [1].

Specifically, visual odometry is a popular SLAM technique. Visual odometry is the estimation of the motion of the explorer using camera vision. It first detects the salient features on the image and then estimates the 3D positions of selected features by stereo matching. It tracks the salient features through a sequence of optical images and thus determines the change of positions of the explorer. Note that visual odometry has already been applied on the NASA Mars Exploration Mission in 2003 with promising results.

The second method to achieve localization on Mars is dead reckoning, the process of estimating the explorer's current position using its previous position and updating based on estimated information such as the velocity. IMU and wheel encoder are commonly used in dead reckoning [4]. By incorporating a gyroscope and accelerometer, IMU estimates the linear acceleration and rotation rate of the explorer. Then through integration over time, these measurements are used for dead reckoning and pose estimation. However, since dead reckoning relies on integration over time, the accuracy of such a method also decreases over time and thus cannot be used for effective localization in long-distance operations. Likewise, another dead-reckoning technique, wheel odometry, also has drawbacks when operating on Mars. Since the surface of Mars is covered with fine regolith, and since the explorer often has to pass through rugged terrain, wheel slip is common, which makes wheel odometry inaccurate.

Star tracking is another localization method available for use during planetary exploration [5]. On Mars, the lack of GPS and global magnetic field add to the challenge for determining the orientation of the explorer. Using the star tracking method, a camera-based star tracker identifies the position of a known set of stars and then compares them with the absolute known position of stars stored in memory. As many star positions have been measured to high accuracy, star tracking allows the explorer to determine its orientation. However, star trackers would only work at night and may fail when used in bright environments, and thus this method fails to enable accurate localization at all times.

10.3.2 Perception

The complex terrain on Mars makes terrain assessment a crucial component of autonomous navigation. Similar to the methods applied in autonomous driving on Earth, Mars explorers use an obstacle avoidance system that is divided into two layers: proactive and reactive.

In the proactive layer, the 3D point cloud generated by stereo vision and triangulation constructs the shape of the environment and thus detects obstacles and hazards. With robust and efficient onboard processors and the reliable algorithm for perception of hazards of current processors, it is fair to say that the challenge for terrain assessment does not lie in the geometry of the terrain, e.g. rocks, but rather in non-geometric aspects where hazards are not obvious for detection, such as the load-bearing properties of the terrain.

In the reactive layer, basic level information such as current vehicle tilt and the feedback from wheels and suspension are taken into consideration. As the last line of defense, if any feedback from sensors is abnormal, the explorer's emergency response will be immediately triggered. For instance, if the discrepancy between wheel odometry and visual odometry exceeds a set limit, the vehicle can conclude that it is experiencing severe wheel slippage and thus generate an alternative path.

10.3.3 Path Planning

In order to navigate from one point to another, the explorer generates a series of direction-oriented waypoints, leading up to the goal destination. Each waypoint is reached by repeating the process of terrain assessment and path selection.

The basic hazard avoidance capabilities discussed above are sufficient to stop a vehicle once it is in a risky situation. However, in order to achieve efficiency and to increase safety, terrain assessment is also incorporated into the path planning process.

Various methods have been applied for explorer path planning. One such method transforms the environment information gained from analyzing stereo images into grid cells, which cover the area surrounding the explorer and thus building a local traversability map stored in the explorer's memory system.

This map is centered around the explorer and is updated constantly as the explorer moves and gains new terrain assessment information. Then, plane fitting is applied to the traversability map to assess how safe the explorer will be at each point in the map. The plane models the explorer body, and it is roughly the size of the explorer plus an additional margin for safety.

Centered in every grid cell, a set of 3D points representing the explorer plane are sampled from the point cloud generated by the stereo image. The 3D data are analyzed for information regarding the traversability of the explorer, such as tilt and roughness of the terrain. If at a grid cell the explorer plane has excessive tilt, too much residual (indicating that the underlying terrain is too rough), or deviations from the best fit (greater than explorer clearance), the grid cell is then marked as impassable.

In ideal conditions, the explorer plane lays flat on the surface. Based on the above-discussed assessment process, each grid cell is assigned a value that serves as a safety index, reflecting the terrain safety there. This method can be visualized as the difference in colors of grid cells reflecting a safety index of the environment which is used in path selection (Figure 10.2).

Path selection for explorers follows two principles: safety and efficiency. When candidate motion paths are generated, they are projected onto the traversability map. Each path is assigned an overall safety or traversability evaluation based on the safety index given to the individual grid cells in the path. Paths are also evaluated for efficiency. The one directly leading to the waypoint is preferred. The efficiency is reduced as the candidate paths deviate from the direct path. By combining safety and efficiency evaluation, the explorer can ultimately select the optimal path to reach the goal destination.

10.3.4 The Curiosity Rover and Mars 2020 Explorer

As detailed in [6], Mars robotic explorers were also built using the modular design methodology, for instance the Curiosity rover consists of the following basic modules:

Chassis. The rover chassis is a strong, outer layer that protects the rover's computer and electronics (which are basically the equivalent of the rover's brains and heart). The rover

Figure 10.2 Grid-based traversability map.

chassis thus keeps the rover's "vital organs" protected and temperature controlled. The warm electronics box is closed on the top by a piece called the Rover Equipment Deck. The Rover Equipment Deck makes the rover like a convertible car, allowing a place for the rover mast and cameras to sit out in the Martian air, taking pictures and clearly observing the Martian terrain as it travels.

Power system. The Curiosity rover requires power to operate. The Curiosity rover carries a radioisotope power system that generates electricity from the heat of plutonium's radioactive decay. This power source gives the mission an operating lifespan on Mars' surface of at least a full Martian year (687 Earth days) or more while also providing significantly greater mobility and operational flexibility, enhanced science payload capability, and exploration of a much larger range of latitudes and altitudes than was possible on previous missions to Mars.

Communication system. The Curiosity rover has multiple antennas that serve as both its "voice" and its "ears." They are located on the Rover Equipment Deck. Having multiple antennas provides back-up options just in case they are needed.

Most often, Curiosity sends radio waves through its ultra-high frequency antenna (about 400 MHz) to communicate with Earth through NASA's Mars Odyssey and Mars Reconnaissance Orbiters. Using orbiters to relay messages is beneficial because they are closer to the rover than the Deep Space Network (DSN) antennas on Earth and they have Earth in their field of view for much longer time periods than the rover does on the ground.

Curiosity also uses its high-gain antenna to receive commands for the mission team back on Earth. The high-gain antenna can send a "beam" of information in a specific direction, and it is steerable, so the antenna can move to point itself directly to any antenna on Earth.

In addition, Curiosity uses its low-gain antenna primarily for receiving signals. This antenna can send and receive information in every direction; that is, it is "omni-directional." The antenna transmits radio waves at a low rate to the DSN antennas on Earth.

Perception system. The Curiosity rover relies on four pairs of engineering hazard avoidance cameras (Hazcams) for perception. These black-and-white cameras use visible light to capture 3D imagery. The rover uses pairs of Hazcam images to map out the shape of the terrain as far as 3 m in front of it, in a "wedge" shape that is over 4 m wide at the farthest distance. The cameras need to see far either side because unlike human eyes, the Hazcam cameras cannot move independently; they are mounted directly to the rover body.

Localization system. The rover also relies on two pairs of engineering navigation cameras (Navcams) for localization. Mounted on the mast (the rover "neck and head"), these black-and-white cameras use visible light to gather panoramic, 3D imagery. The navigation camera unit is a stereo pair of cameras that capture images to support visual SLAM algorithms to enable ground navigation planning by scientists and engineers.

The latest Mars explorer project is Mars 2020 by NASA, which is set to launch in July 2020. The new explorer relies solely on camera-based systems for navigation. As shown in Figure 10.3, it is equipped with 23 different cameras responsible for autonomous driving, including six Hazcams, mainly for perception purposes, and one pair of Navcams, mainly for localization purposes.

With one pair mounted in the back and two pairs mounted in the front, the Hazcams monitor the surrounding environment of the explorer. They take stereo images and assess the terrain traversability. Hazcams have a broad field of view of 120°. The Navcams have a field of view of 45° and are mounted on top of the mast. They also take stereo images but are responsible for macro-level observation.

Compared with the previously sent explorer, Curiosity, the Mars 2020 explorer has a major upgrade in image processing power, increasing the speed for stereo image and visual

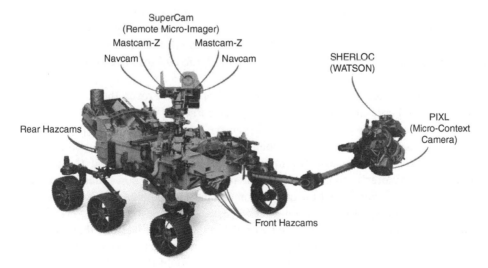

Figure 10.3　Mars 2020 explorer.

odometry calculations. As a result, the explorer will be able to operate at a higher speed, around 152 miles per hour, outperforming its predecessors.

10.4   Challenge: Onboard Computing Capability

In multiple space exploration missions, NASA has demonstrated autonomous rover capabilities. As detailed in [7], autonomous navigation not only improved target approach efficiency, it also proved crucial to maintaining vehicle safety. However, onboard autonomy is often constrained by processor computing power because of the number of sensor inputs that have to be evaluated in real time.

For instance, the Opportunity rover is equipped with an IBM RAD6000, a radiation-hardened single board computer, based on the IBM RISC Single Chip CPU [7]. For reliability reasons, the RAD6000 on the Opportunity rover was implemented on a radiation-hardened field programmable gate array (FPGA) and runs only at 20 MHz, delivering over 22 MIPS (million instructions per second). In comparison, a commercial Intel Core i7 can easily deliver 50 000 MIPS running at 2.7 GHz.

Unfortunately, we cannot use these powerful commercial central processing units or graphics processing units for space exploration missions since these fabrics are not radiation hardened and thus cannot operate in the harsh environments in space or on other planets. Nonetheless, a few FPGA manufacturers provide radiation-hardened and space-ready FPGA substrates and we can optimize autonomous navigation workloads on these substrates to enable future commercial space exploration missions.

Due to the computing power constraints, only limited autonomous navigation capabilities were turned on in the Opportunity rover. For instance, only low-resolution low-throughput cameras were used for localization, and each update of rover location would take a nontrivial amount of time, up to three minutes for a single location update, as opposed to 30 updates per second for autonomous vehicles on Earth, thus leading to the average speed of rover autonomous navigation under 0.1 miles per hour.

To make matters worse, in order for the Opportunity rover to make long-distance autonomous navigation, ground truth data (e.g. 3D reconstruction of the Mars surface for rover localization) on Mars was needed but missing, and this limited the distance the Opportunity rover could travel.

To generate the needed ground-truth data for the Opportunity rover, the rover needs to collect a large number of images on Mars and then perform surface reconstruction or map optimization, an extremely computationally expensive step. As discussed in [8], ground-truth data reconstruction is achieved through employing structure-from-motion algorithms. However, processing structure-from-motion algorithms is beyond the current capabilities of an explorer's onboard computer. To provide an idea of how much computing power it consumes: to reconstruct the city of Rome using 150 000 images would require a 500-node cluster running fully for 24 hours [9].

As shown in Figure 10.4, what happened with the Opportunity rover was that the rover would run for a very short distance (e.g. a few meters) and collect images, then send the images back to Earth for further processing. The rover would then wait for the reconstructed surface map to be transmitted back before it could take the next action.

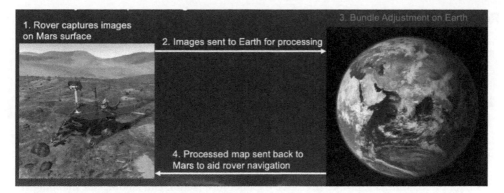

Figure 10.4 Mars navigation map generation.

This is extremely inefficient, as a one-way communication to Mars has a delay of up to 20 minutes, depending on the orbital alignment of the planets. In addition, communication is available only twice per sol (Martian day) due to the limited spacecraft around Mars.

We believe the solution lies in developing better computing systems for space explorers. It is thus imperative to implement and optimize autonomous navigation algorithms on radiation-hardened FPGA systems. One example of radiation-hardened FPGA is the Xilinx Virtex-5QV product line.

One such example is presented in [8]: bundle adjustment (BA) is the most computationally demanding step in 3D scene reconstruction, and the authors developed a BA accelerator engine on an embedded FPGA. Experimental results confirm that this design outperformed ARM processors by 50-fold while maintaining similar power consumption. As more autonomous navigation workloads are implemented and optimized on radiation-hardened FPGAs, we look forward to enabling more autonomous navigation scenarios for robotic space explorers.

10.5 Conclusion

Autonomous space exploration robots are still in their infancy. Many challenges are yet to be solved. Progress in these areas will definitely increase the efficiency of autonomous explorers. The development of autonomous space explorers also opens up exciting possibilities including commercial use, such as exploiting mineral resources on other planets. Eventually, hopefully in the near future, we will have commercial autonomous space robotic explorers building infrastructures for human settlement on Mars.

In this chapter, we have introduced environments on Mars and explored technologies required to enable future commercial autonomous space robotic explorers. Last but not least, we have indicated that one of the urgent technical challenges for autonomous space explorers is computing power: if we have sufficient computing power onboard, we would be able to enable much more efficient robots on Mars. Together, let us build autonomous robots for the space exploration age.

References

1 Maimone, M., Biesiadecki, J., Tunstel, E. et al. (2016). Surface navigation and mobility intelligence on the Mars exploration explorers. In: *Proceedings of Intelligence for Space Robotics*, 45–69. TSI Press.

2 European Space Agency (2019). Comparing the atmospheres of Mars and Earth. http://exploration.esa.int/mars/60153-comparing-the-atmospheres-of-mars-and-earth (accessed 1 May 2019).

3 Phoenix Mars Mission (2019). Mars/Earth Comparison Table. http://phoenix.lpl.arizona.edu/mars111.php (accessed 1 May 2019).

4 Li, R., Di, K., Matthies, L.H. et al. (2004). Explorer localization and landing-site mapping technology for the 2003 Mars exploration explorer mission. *Photogrammetric Engineering & Remote Sensing* 70 (1): 77–90.

5 Roumeliotis, I.S. and Bekey, A. 3-D localization for a Mars explorer prototype. In: *Artificial Intelligence, Robotics and Automation in Space*, vol. 440, 441. European Space Agency.

6 Mars Exploration Program (2011). MARS Curiosity Rover. https://mars.jpl.nasa.gov/msl/mission/rover (accessed 1 October 2019).

7 Maimone, M., Cheng, Y., and Matthies, L. (2007). Two years of visual odometry on the mars exploration rovers. *Journal of Field Robotics* 24 (3): 169–186.

8 Qin, S., Liu, Q., Yu, B., and Liu, S. (2019). π-BA bundle adjustment acceleration on embedded FPGAs with co-observation optimization. In: *2019 IEEE 27th Annual International Symposium on Field-Programmable Custom Computing*, 100–108. IEEE.

9 Agarwal, S., Furukawa, Y., Snavely, N. et al. Building Rome in a day. *Communications of the ACM* 54 (10): 105–112.

11

Edge Computing for Autonomous Vehicles

11.1   Introduction

As indicated in Chapter 10, onboard autonomy is often constrained by processing power because multiple sensor inputs have to be evaluated in real time. This is not only true for space exploration robots on Mars but also for autonomous vehicles on Earth.

For instance, if an autonomous vehicle travels at 60 miles per hour, and thus with about 30 m of braking distance, this requires the autonomous driving system to predict potential dangers up to a few seconds before they occur. Therefore, the faster the autonomous driving edge computing system can perform these complex computations, the safer the autonomous vehicle.

To summarize, the overarching challenge of autonomous vehicle edge computing system design is to efficiently process a massive amount of data in real time, within a limited energy budget, and without sacrificing the security of the users.

In the following chapters, we review state-of-the-art approaches in building edge computing systems for autonomous vehicles. In this chapter, we focus on onboard computing systems; in Chapter 12, we focus on how vehicle-to-everything (V2X) technologies can help alleviate stress on onboard computing systems; in Chapter 13, we review security problems in edge computing systems for autonomous vehicles.

Particularly, in this chapter, we review the latest progress in the design of edge computing systems for autonomous driving applications. First, we start with benchmark suites available for evaluating edge computing system designs. Secondly, we review different approaches in designing computer architectures for autonomous driving workloads. Thirdly, we describe the designs of runtime layers for efficient mapping of incoming workloads onto heterogeneous computing units. Fourthly, we discuss the designs of middleware for binding different autonomous driving functional modules. Last, we present real-world implementations of autonomous driving edge computing systems.

Engineering Autonomous Vehicles and Robots: The DragonFly Modular-based Approach,
First Edition. Shaoshan Liu.
© 2020 John Wiley & Sons Ltd. Published 2020 by John Wiley & Sons Ltd.

11.2 Benchmarks

To improve a computing system, the most effective tool is a standard benchmark suite to represent the workloads widely used in the target applications. The same principle applies when it comes to designing and improving edge computing systems for autonomous vehicles.

Current research in this area can be divided into two categories: datasets and workloads. KITTI was the first benchmark dataset related to autonomous driving [1]. It is composed of rich vision sensor data with labels, such as monocular/stereo image data and 3D Light Detection and Ranging (LiDAR) data. According to different data types, it also provides a dedicated method to generate the ground truth and to calculate the evaluation metrics. KITTI was built for evaluating the performance of algorithms in the autonomous driving scenario, including but not limited to visual odometry, lane detection, object detection, and object tracking.

In addition to KITTI, there are some customized benchmark datasets for each algorithm, such as TUM RGB-D [2] for RGB-D simultaneous localization and mapping (SLAM), PASCAL3D [3] for 3D object detection, and the MOTChallenge benchmark [4] for multi-target tracking. These kinds of datasets serve as very good data sources for stressing edge computing systems.

Another class of related benchmark suites is designed to benchmark the performance of novel hardware architectures and software framework, which usually consists of a set of computer vision kernels and applications. The San Diego Vision Benchmark Suite (SD-VBS) [5] and MEVBench [6] are both performance benchmark suites for a mobile computer vision system. SD-VBS provides single-threaded C and MATLAB implementations of nine high-level vision applications. MEVBench is an extended benchmark based on SD-VBS. It provides single- and multi-threaded C++ implementations of 15 vision applications. However, these two benchmarks are prior works in the field, so they are not targeted toward heterogeneous platforms such as graphics processing units (GPUs) and do not contain novel workloads, such as deep learning algorithms.

SLAMBench [7] concentrates on using a complete RGB-D SLAM application to evaluate novel heterogeneous hardware. It takes KinectFusion [8] as the implementation and provides C++, OpenMP, OpenCL and CUDA versions of key function kernels for heterogeneous hardware. These efforts are a step in the right direction but we still need a comprehensive benchmark which contains diverse workloads that cover varied application scenarios of autonomous vehicles (such as MAVBench [9] for micro aerial vehicle system benchmarking) to evaluate the autonomous vehicle edge computing systems.

CAVBench is a recently released benchmark suite specially developed for evaluating the connected and autonomous vehicles (CAVs) computing system performance [10]. It summarizes four application scenarios on CAVs (autonomous driving, real-time diagnostics, in-vehicle infotainment, and third-party applications), and chooses six classic and diverse real-world on-vehicle applications as evaluation workloads (SLAM, object detection, object tracking, battery diagnostics, speech recognition, and edge video analysis).

CAVBench takes four real-world datasets as the standard input to the six workloads and generates two categories of output metrics. One metric is an application perspective metric, which includes the execution time breakdown for each application, helping developers find the performance bottleneck in the application side. Another is a system perspective metric, which is the quality of service–resource utilization curve (QoS-RU curve). The QoS-RU curve can be used to calculate the Matching Factor (MF) between the application and the computing platform on autonomous vehicles. The QoS-RU curve can be considered as a quantitative performance index of the computing platform that helps researchers and developers optimize on-vehicle applications and CAVs computing architecture. We hope to see more research in the area of benchmarking for autonomous vehicle workloads but currently, CAVBench serves as a good starting point to study edge computing systems for autonomous driving.

As autonomous driving is still a fast developing field, we hope to see continuous effort to incorporate more dynamic workloads and data to cover emerging autonomous driving usage scenarios. In addition, standardized scoring methods are required (but still missing) to rank different edge computing systems based on different optimization metrics.

11.3 Computing System Architectures

Once we have standard benchmark suites, we can start developing suitable architectures for autonomous driving workloads. Liu et al. proposed a computer architecture for autonomous vehicles which fully utilizes hybrid heterogeneous hardware [11]. In this work, the applications for autonomous driving are divided into three stages: sensing, perception, and decision-making. The authors compared the performance of different hardware running basic autonomous driving tasks and concluded that localization and perception are the bottlenecks of autonomous driving computing systems, and they also identified the need for different hardware accelerators for different workloads. Furthermore, the authors proposed and developed an autonomous driving computing architecture and software stack that is modular, secure, dynamic, high performance, and energy efficient. By fully utilizing heterogeneous computing components, such as a central processing unit (CPU), GPU, and digital signal processor (DSP), their prototype system on an ARM mobile system on chip (SoC) consumes 11 W on average and is able to drive a mobile vehicle at 5 miles per hour. In addition, the authors indicated that with more computing resources, the system would be able to process more data and would eventually satisfy the need of a production-level autonomous driving system.

Similarly, Lin et al. explored the architectural constraints and acceleration of the autonomous driving system in [12]. The authors presented and formalized the design constraints of autonomous driving systems in performance, predictability, storage, thermal, and power. To investigate the design of the autonomous driving systems, the authors developed an end-to-end autonomous driving system based on machine learning algorithmic components. Through the experiments on this system, the authors identified three computational bottlenecks, namely localization, object detection, and object tracking. To design a system which can meet all the design constraints, the authors also explored three different accelerator platforms to accelerate these computational bottlenecks. The authors demonstrated that GPU, field programmable gate array (FPGA), and ASIC-accelerated systems could effectively reduce the tail latency of these algorithms. Based on these acceleration systems, the authors further explored the trade-offs among performance, power, and scalability of the autonomous driving system. Their conclusion is that although power-hungry accelerators like GPUs can predictably deliver the computation at low latency, their high power consumption, further magnified by the cooling load to meet the thermal constraints, can significantly degrade the driving range and fuel efficiency of the vehicle. Finally, the authors indicated that computational capability remains the bottleneck that prevents us from benefiting from the higher system accuracy enabled by higher resolution cameras.

Interestingly, in their pioneering architectural exploration work, the authors discussed above both concluded that localization and perception are the computing bottlenecks and heterogeneous computing is a feasible approach to accelerate these workloads. For localization acceleration, Tang et al. proposed a heterogeneous architecture for SLAM [13]. The authors first conducted a thorough study to understand visual inertial SLAM performance and energy consumption on existing heterogeneous SoCs. The initial findings indicated that existing SoC designs are not optimized for SLAM applications, and systematic optimizations are required in the IO interface, the memory subsystem, as well as computation acceleration. Based on these findings, the authors proposed a heterogeneous SoC architecture optimized for visual inertial SLAM applications. Instead of simply adding an accelerator, the authors systematically integrated direct IO, a feature buffer, and a feature extraction accelerator. To prove the effectiveness of this design, the authors implemented the proposed architecture on a Xilinx Zynq UltraScale MPSoC and this was able to deliver over 60 frames per second (FPS) performance with average power less than 5 W. These results verify that the proposed architecture is capable of achieving performance and energy consumption optimization for visual inertial SLAM applications.

Similarly, to solve the localization computing problem, Zhang et al. proposed an algorithm- and hardware co-design methodology for Visual-Inertial Odometry (VIO) systems, in which the robot estimates its ego-motion (and a landmark-based map) from onboard camera and inertial measurement unit (IMU) data [14]. The authors argued that scaling down VIO to miniaturized platforms (without sacrificing performance) requires a paradigm shift in the design of perception algorithms, and the authors advocated a co-design approach in which algorithmic and hardware design choices are tightly coupled. In detail, the authors characterized the design space by discussing how a relevant set of design choices affects the resource-performance trade-off in VIO. Also, the authors demonstrated the result of the co-design process by providing a VIO implementation on specialized hardware showing that such implementation has the same accuracy and speed of a desktop implementation, while requiring a fraction of the power.

Besides academic research, PerceptIn has recently released a commercial production SLAM system titled DragonFly+ [15]. DragonFly+ is a FPGA-based real-time localization module with several advanced features: (i) hardware synchronizations among the four image channels as well as the IMU; (ii) a direct IO architecture to reduce off-chip memory communication; and (iii) a fully pipelined architecture to accelerate the image processing frontend. In addition, parallel and multiplexing processing techniques are employed to achieve a good balance between bandwidth and hardware resource consumption. Based on publicly available data, for processing four-way 720p images, DragonFly+ achieves 42 FPS performance while consuming only 2.3 W of power. In comparison, Nvidia Jetson

TX1 GPU SoC achieves 9 FPS at 7 W and Intel Core i7 achieves 15 FPS at 80 W. Therefore, DragonFly+ is three times more power efficient and delivers five times the computing power compared with Nvidia TX1, and is 34 times more power efficient and delivers three times the computing power compared with Intel Core i7.

For perception acceleration, most recent research has focused on the acceleration of deep convolutional neural networks (CNNs). To enable CNN accelerators to support a wide variety of different applications with sufficient flexibility and efficiency, Liu et al. proposed a novel domain-specific Instruction Set Architecture (ISA) for neural network accelerators [16]. The proposed ISA is a load-store architecture that integrates scalar, vector, matrix, logical, data transfer, and control instructions, based on a comprehensive analysis of existing neural network acceleration techniques. The authors demonstrated that the proposed ISA exhibits strong descriptive capacity over a broad range of neural network acceleration techniques, and provides higher code density than general-purpose ISAs such as x86, MIPS, and GPGPU.

Realizing that data movement is a key bottleneck for CNN computations, Chen et al. presented a dataflow to minimize the energy consumption of data movement on a spatial architecture [17]. The key is to reuse local data of filter weights and feature map pixels, or activations, in the high-dimensional convolutions, and minimize data movement of partial sum accumulations. The proposed dataflow adapts to different CNN shape configurations and reduces all types of data movement by maximally utilizing the processing engine (PE) local storage, spatial parallelism, and direct inter-PE communication. Through the CNN configurations of AlexNet, evaluation experiments show that the proposed dataflow is more energy efficient than other dataflows for both convolutional and fully connected layers.

In the near future, as more autonomous driving workloads and usage scenarios emerge, we look forward to the designs of more accelerators targeted for these workloads. Also, we expect to see more exploration studies on the cache, memory, and storage architectures for autonomous driving workloads. In addition, hardware security for autonomous driving is of utmost importance. Within a decade, the research community and the industry shall be able to come up with a "general-purpose" architecture design for autonomous driving workloads.

11.4 Runtime

With heterogeneous architectures ready for autonomous driving tasks, the next challenge is how to dispatch incoming tasks to different computing units at runtime to achieve optimal energy efficiency and performance. This can be achieved through a runtime layer. Designing runtime for heterogeneous autonomous driving systems is a whole new research area with tremendous potential as most existing runtime designs focus on either mapping one algorithm to one type of accelerator, or on scheduling for homogeneous or heterogeneous systems with a single accelerator.

Several existing designs focus on mapping one deep learning or computer vision workload to heterogeneous architectures: Hegde et al. [18] proposed a framework for easy mapping of CNN specifications to accelerators such as FPGAs, DSPs, GPUs, and Reduced

Instruction Set Computer (RISC) multi-cores. Malik et al. [19] compared the performance and energy efficiency of computer vision algorithms on on-chip FPGA accelerators and GPU accelerators.

Many studies have explored the optimization of deep learning algorithms on an embedded GPU or FPGA accelerator [20, 21]. There have also been many projects on optimizing computer vision related tasks on embedded platforms. Honegger et al. [22] proposed FPGA acceleration of embedded computer vision. Satria et al. [23] performed platform specific optimizations of face detection on an embedded GPU-based platform and reported real-time performance. Vasilyev et al. [24] evaluated computer vision algorithms on programmable architectures. Nardi et al. [25] presented a benchmark suite to evaluate dense SLAM algorithms across desktop and embedded platforms in terms of accuracy, performance, and energy consumption. However, these designs did not consider the complexity of integrating the various kind of workloads into a system, and only focus on mapping one task to different accelerators.

Other existing designs focus on scheduling for heterogeneous architectures with one accelerator that has been broadly studied for single-ISA multiprocessors, such as asymmetric multi-core architectures, i.e. big and small cores, and multi-ISA multiprocessors such as CPU with GPU. On the single-ISA multiprocessor side, much work has been done at the operating system level to map workload onto the most appropriate core type in run time. Koufaty et al. [26] identified that the period of core stalls is a good indicator to predict the core type best suited for an application. Based on the indicator, a biased schedule strategy was added to operating systems to improve system throughput. Saez et al. [27] proposed a scheduler that adds efficiency specialization and TLP (thread-level parallelism) specialization to operating systems to optimize throughput and power at the same time.

Efficient specialization maps CPU-intensive workloads onto fast cores and memory-intensive workloads onto slow cores. TLP specialization uses fast cores to accelerate sequential phases of parallel applications and uses slow cores for parallel phases to achieve energy efficiency. On the asymmetric multi-core architectures side, Jiménez et al. [28] proposed a user-level scheduler for CPU with a GPU-like system. It evaluates and records the performance of a process on each PE at the initial phase. Then, based on this history information, it maps the application on to the best suited PE. Luk et al. [29] focused on improving the latency and energy consumption of a single process. It uses dynamic compilation to characterize workloads, determines optimal mapping and generates codes for CPUs and GPUs.

Unlike existing runtime designs, recently, Liu et al. proposed PIRT (PerceptIn Runtime), the first runtime framework that is able to dynamically map various computer vision and deep learning workloads to multiple accelerators and to the cloud [30]. The authors first conducted a comprehensive study of emerging robotic applications on heterogeneous SoC architectures. Based on the results, the authors designed and implemented PIRT to utilize not only the on-chip heterogeneous computing resources but also the cloud to achieve high performance and energy efficiency. To verify its effectiveness, the authors have deployed PIRT on a production mobile robot to demonstrate that full robotic workloads, including autonomous navigation, obstacle detection, route planning, large map generation, and scene understanding, can be efficiently executed simultaneously with 11 W of power consumption.

The runtime layer connects autonomous driving software and hardware but there are several upcoming challenges in the design of runtime systems for autonomous driving. First, as the computing system becomes more heterogeneous, the runtime design becomes more complicated in order to dynamically dispatch incoming workloads. Secondly, as more edge clouds become available, the runtime system needs to be cloud-aware and able to dispatch workloads to edge clouds. Thirdly, the runtime shall provide good abstraction to hide all the low- level implementations.

11.5 Middleware

Robotic systems, such as autonomous vehicle systems, often involve multiple services, with a lot of dependencies in between. To facilitate the complex interactions between these services, to simplify software design, and to hide the complexity of low-level communication and the heterogeneity of the sensors, a middleware is required.

An early design of robotic middleware is Miro, a distributed object-oriented framework for mobile robot control, based on Common Object Request Broker Architecture (COBRA) technology [31]. The core components have been developed with the aid of Adaptive Communications Environment, an object-oriented multi-platform framework for OS-independent inter-process, network and real time communication. Miro provides generic abstract services like localization or behavior engines, which can be applied on different robot platforms. Miro supports several robotic platforms including Pioneers, the B21, some robot soccer robots, and various robotic sensors.

ORCA is an open-source component-based software engineering framework developed for mobile robotics with an associated repository of free, reusable components for building mobile robotic systems [32]. ORCA's project goals include enabling software reuse by defining a set of commonly used interfaces; simplifying software reuse by providing libraries with a high-level convenient application program interfaceI; and encouraging software reuse by maintaining a repository of components.

Urbi is open source cross-platform software used to develop applications for robotics and complex systems [33]. Urbi is based on the UObject distributed C++ component architecture. Urbi includes the urbiscript orchestration language, a parallel and event-driven script language. In this design, UObject components can be plugged into urbiscript as native objects to specify their interactions and data exchanges. UObjects can be linked to the urbiscript interpreter, or executed as autonomous processes in "remote" mode, either in another thread, another process, a machine on the local network, or a machine on a distant network.

Runtime (RT)-middleware is a common platform standard for distributed object technology based robots [34]. RT-middleware can support the construction of various networked robotic systems through the integration of various network-enabled robotic elements called RT-components. In the RT-middleware, robotic elements, such as actuators, are regarded as RT-components, and the whole robotic system is constructed by connecting these RT-components. This distributed architecture helps developers to reuse the robotic elements and boosts the reliability of the robotic system.

OpenRDK is an open source software framework for robotics for developing loosely coupled modules [35]. It provides transparent concurrency management, inter-process via sockets, and intra-process via shared memory. Modules for connecting to simulators and generic robot drivers are provided.

The above-mentioned middleware projects mostly focused on providing a software component management framework for mobile robots and they were not used in autonomous vehicles. On the other hand, the Robot Operating System (ROS) has been widely used in autonomous vehicle development [36], mainly due to the popularity of ROS robotic developers and the richness of its software packages. However, as discussed in Section 11.2, in its current state, ROS is not suitable for the production deployment of autonomous vehicles as it suffers from performance, reliability, and security issues.

The middleware layer facilitates the communication between different autonomous driving services. Here, we summarize several challenges. First, the middleware should impose minimal computing overhead and memory footprint, thus making it scalable. Secondly, as some autonomous driving services may stay in edge clouds, the middleware should enable a smooth edge client and cloud communication. Thirdly, and most importantly, the middleware should be secure and reliable to guarantee quality of service and autonomous vehicle safety.

Layer	Purpose	Proposed solutions	Research directions
Architecture	Hardware computing units to execute autonomous driving workloads	[11]–[17]	Accelerators for various autonomous driving workloads; cache and memory architecture design; non-volatile storage for critical data; hardware security
Runtime	Software layer to efficiently dispatch incoming tasks at run time to different computing units	[18]–[30]	Scheduler and dispatcher for highly heterogeneous computing systems; abstraction to hide low-level details; cloud awareness
Middleware	Software layer to enable complex interactions between autonomous driving services	[31]–[36]	Low overhead and memory footprint; edge–cloud interaction; security and reliability
Benchmark	Tools to evaluate edge computing systems	[1]–[10]	More dynamic workloads and data to cover more usage scenarios; standardized, scoring methods to rank edge computing systems

11.6 Case Studies

To simultaneously enable multiple autonomous driving services, including localization, perception, and speech recognition workloads on affordable embedded systems, Tang et al. designed and implemented Π-Edge, a complete edge computing framework for autonomous robots and vehicles [37]. The challenges of designing such a system include the following: managing different autonomous driving services and their communications with minimal overheads, fully utilizing the heterogeneous computing resources on the edge device, and offloading some of the tasks to the cloud for energy efficiency. To achieve these, first, the authors developed a runtime layer to fully utilize the heterogeneous computing resources of low-power edge computing systems; secondly, the authors developed an extremely lightweight middleware to manage multiple autonomous driving services and their communications; and thirdly, the authors developed an edge-cloud coordinator to dynamically offload tasks to the cloud to optimize client system energy consumption.

OpenVDAP is another real-world edge computing system which is a full-stack edge-based platform including a vehicle computing unit, an isolation-supported and security and privacy-preserved vehicle operation system, an edge-aware application library, as well as task offloading and scheduling strategy [38]. OpenVDAP allows CAVs to dynamically examine each task's status, computation cost and the optimal scheduling method so that each service could be finished in near real time with low overhead. OpenVDAP is featured as a two-tier architecture via a series of systematic mechanisms that enable CAVs to dynamically detect service status and identify the optimal offloading destination so that each service could be finished at the right time. In addition, OpenVDAP offers an open and free edge-aware library that contains how to access and deploy edge-computing-based vehicle applications and various commonly used artificial intelligence models, thus enabling researchers and developers to deploy, test, and validate their applications in the real environment.

References

1 Geiger, A., Lenz, P., and Urtasun, R. (2012). Are we ready for autonomous driving? The KITTI vision benchmark suite. In: *2012 IEEE Conference on Computer Vision and Pattern Recognition (CVPR)*, 3354–3361. IEEE.

2 Sturm, J., Engelhard, N., Endres, F. et al. (2012). A benchmark for the evaluation of RGB-D SLAM systems. In: *2012 IEEE/RSJ International Conference on Intelligent Robots and Systems (IROS)*, 573–580. IEEE.

3 Xiang, Y., Mottaghi, R., and Savarese, S. (2014). Beyond PASCAL: a benchmark for 3D object detection in the wild. In: *2014 IEEE Winter Conference on Applications of Computer Vision (WACV)*, 75–82. IEEE.

4 Leal-Taixé, L., Milan, A, Reid, I. et al. (2015). MOTChallenge 2015: Towards a benchmark for multi-target tracking. arXiv preprint arXiv:1504.01942.

5 Venkata, S.K., Ahn, I., Jeon, D. et al. (2009). SD-VBS: the San Diego vision benchmark suite. In: *2009 IEEE International Symposium on Workload Characterization (IISWC)*, 55–64. IEEE.

6 Clemons, J., Zhu, H., Savarese, S., and Austin, T. (2011). MEVBench: a mobile computer vision benchmarking suite. In: *2011 IEEE International Symposium on Workload Characterization (IISWC)*, 91–102. IEEE.

7 Nardi, L., Bodin, B., Zeeshan Zia, M. et al. (2015). Introducing SLAMBench, a performance and accuracy benchmarking methodology for SLAM. In: *2015 IEEE International Conference on Robotics and Automation (ICRA)*, 5783–5790. IEEE.

8 Newcombe, R.A., Izadi, S., Hilliges, O. et al. (2011). KinectFusion: real-time dense surface mapping and tracking. In: *2011 10th IEEE International Symposium on Mixed and Augmented Reality (ISMAR)*, 127–136. IEEE.

9 Boroujerdian, B., Genc, H., Krishnan, S. et al. (2018). MAVBench: micro aerial vehicle benchmarking. In: *2018 51st Annual IEEE/ACM International Symposium on Microarchitecture (MICRO)*, 894–907. IEEE.

10 Wang, Y., Liu, S., Xiaopei, W., and Shi, W. (2018). CAVBench: a benchmark suite for connected and autonomous vehicles. In: *2018 IEEE/ACM Symposium on Edge Computing (SEC)*, 30–42. IEEE.

11 Liu, S., Tang, J., Zhang, Z., and Gaudiot, J.-L. (2017). Computer architectures for autonomous driving. *Computer* 50 (8): 18–25.

12 Lin, S.-C., Zhang, Y., Hsu, C.-H. et al. (2018). The architectural implications of autonomous driving: constraints and acceleration. In: *Proceedings of the Twenty-Third International Conference on Architectural Support for Programming Languages and Operating Systems*, 751–766. ACM.

13 Tang, J., Yu, B., Liu, S. et al. (2018). π-SoC: heterogeneous SoC architecture for visual inertial SLAM applications. In: *2018 IEEE/RSJ International Conference on Intelligent Robots and Systems (IROS)*, 1–6. IEEE.

14 Zhang, Z., Suleiman, A.A.Z., Carlone, L. et al. (2017). Visual-inertial odometry on chip: An algorithm-and-hardware co-design approach. Robotics: Science and Systems, Cambridge, MA.

15 Fang, W., Zhang, Y., Bo, Y., and Liu, S. (2018). DragonFly+: FPGA-based quad-camera visual SLAM system for autonomous vehicles. In: *2018 IEEE HotChips*, 1. IEEE.

16 Liu, S., Zidong, D., Tao, J. et al. (2016). Cambricon: an instruction set architecture for neural networks. In: *ACM SIGARCH Computer Architecture News*, vol. 44, 393–405. IEEE Press.

17 Chen, Y.-H., Emer, J., and Sze, V. (2016). Eyeriss: a spatial architecture for energy-efficient dataflow for convolutional neural networks. In: *ACM SIGARCH Computer Architecture News*, vol. 44, 367–379. IEEE Press.

18 Hegde, G., Ramasamy, N., Kapre, N. et al. (2016). CaffePresso: an optimized library for deep learning on embedded accelerator-based platforms. In: *Proceedings of the International Conference on Compilers, Architectures and Synthesis for Embedded Systems (CASES)*, 14. ACM.

19 Malik, M., Farahmand, F., Otto, P. et al. (2016). Architecture exploration for energy-efficient embedded vision applications: from general purpose processor to domain specific accelerator. In: *2016 IEEE Computer Society Annual Symposium on VLSI (ISVLSI)*, 559–564. IEEE.

20 Cavigelli, L., Magno, M., and Benini, L. (2015). Accelerating real-time embedded scene labeling with convolutional networks. In: *2015 52nd ACM/EDAC/IEEE Design Automation Conference*, 108. ACM.

21 Qiu, J., Wang, J., Yao, S. et al. (2016). Going deeper with embedded FPGA platform for convolutional neural network. In: *ACM International Symposium on FPGA*, 26–35. ACM.

22 Honegger, D., Oleynikova, H., and Pollefeys, M. (2014). Real-time and low latency embedded computer vision hardware based on a combination of FPGA and mobile CPU. In: *2014 IEEE/RSJ International Conference on Intelligent Robots and Systems*, 4930–4935. IEEE.

23 Satria, M.T., Gurumani, S.T., Zheng, W. et al. (2016). Real-time system-level implementation of a telepresence robot using an embedded GPU platform. In: *2016 Design, Automation & Test in Europe Conference & Exhibition (DATE)*, 1445–1448. IEEE.

24 Vasilyev, A., Bhagdikar, N., Pedram, A. et al. (2016). Evaluating programmable architectures for imaging and vision applications. In: *2016 49th Annual IEEE/ACM International Sysmposium on Microarchitecture (MICRO)*, 38–49. ACM.

25 Nardi, L., Bodin, B., Zia, M.Z. et al. (2015). Introducing SLAMBench, a performance and accuracy benchmarking methodology for SLAM. In: *IEEE International Conference on Robotics and Automation (ICRA)*, 5783–5790. IEEE.

26 Koufaty, D., Reddy, D., and Hahn, S. (2010). Bias scheduling in heterogeneous multi-core architectures. In: *Proceedings of the 5th European Conference on Computer Systems*, 125–138. ACM.

27 Saez, J.C., Prieto, M., Fedorova, A., and Blagodurov, S. (2010). A comprehensive scheduler for asymmetric multicore systems. In: *Proceedings of the 5th European Conference on Computer Systems*, 139–152. ACM.

28 Jiménez, V.J., Vilanova, L., Gelado, I. et al. (2009). Predictive runtime code scheduling for heterogeneous architectures. In: *High Performance Embedded Architectures and Compilers. HiPEAC 2009*, 19–33. Springer.

29 Luk, C.-K., Hong, S., and Kim, H. (2009). Qilin: exploiting parallelism on heterogeneous multiprocessors with adaptive mapping. In: *Proceedings of the 42nd Annual IEEE/ACM International Symposium on Microarchitecture*, 45–55. ACM.

30 Liu, L., Liu, S, Zhang, Z. et al. (2018). PIRT: A runtime framework to enable energy-efficient real-time robotic applications on heterogeneous architectures. arXiv preprint arXiv:1802.08359.

31 Utz, H., Sablatnog, S., Enderle, S., and Kraetzschmar, G. (2002). Miro-middleware for mobile robot applications. *IEEE Transactions on Robotics and Automation* 18 (4): 493–497.

32 Brooks, A., Kaupp, T., Makarenko, A. et al. (2005). Towards component-based robotics. In: *2005 IEEE/RSJ International Conference on Intelligent Robots and Systems (IROS)*, 163–168. IEEE.

33 Baillie, J.-C. (2005). URBI: towards a universal robotic low-level programming language. In: *2005 IEEE/RSJ International Conference on Intelligent Robots and Systems (IROS)*, 820–825. IEEE.

34 Ando, N., Suehiro, T., Kitagaki, K. et al. (2005). RT-middleware: distributed component middleware for RT (robot technology). In: *2005 IEEE/RSJ International Conference on Intelligent Robots and Systems (IROS)*, 3933–3938. IEEE.

35 Calisi, D., Censi, A., Iocchi, L., and Nardi, D. (2008). Open- RDK: a modular framework for robotic software development. In: *2008 IEEE/RSJ International Conference on Intelligent Robots and Systems (IROS)*, 1872–1877. IEEE.

36 Quigley, M., Conley, K., Gerkey, B. et al. (2009). ROS: an open-source robot operating system. In: *ICRA Workshop on Open Source Software*, vol. 3, 5. IEEE.

37 Tang, J., Liu, S., Yu, B., and Shi, W. (2018). Pi-edge: A low-power edge computing system for real-time autonomous driving services. arXiv preprint arXiv:1901.04978.

38 Zhang, Q., Wang, Y., Zhang, X. et al. (2018). OpenVDAP: an open vehicular data analytics platform for CAVs. In: *2018 IEEE 38th International Conference on Distributed Computing Systems (ICDCS)*, 1310–1320. IEEE.

12

Innovations on the Vehicle-to-Everything Infrastructure

12.1   Introduction

One effective method to alleviate the stress on autonomous driving edge computing systems is vehicle-to-everything (V2X) technology. V2X communication focuses more on the communication infrastructure, while edge computing focuses more on the computing side, and how to distribute the computing workloads to the V2X infrastructure.

V2X is defined as a vehicle communication system which consists of many types of communication: vehicle-to-vehicle (V2V), vehicle-to-network (V2N), vehicle-to-pedestrian (V2P) Vehicle-to-Infrastructure (V2I), vehicle-to-device (V2D), and vehicle-to-grid (V2G). Currently, most research focuses on V2V and V2I. While conventional autonomous driving systems require costly sensors and edge computing equipment within the vehicle, V2X takes a different approach by investing in road infrastructure, thus alleviating the computing and sensing costs in vehicles.

Meanwhile, more and more autonomous driving applications have started leveraging V2X communications to make the in-vehicle edge computing system more efficient. The most representative example is cooperative autonomous driving. The cooperation of autonomous driving edge computing system with V2X technology makes it possible to build a safe and efficient autonomous driving system [1]. However, the applications of a cooperative system of V2X and autonomous driving are still open research problems.

In this chapter, we discuss the evolution of V2X technology and present several usage cases of V2X for autonomous driving: convoy driving, cooperative lane change, cooperative intersection management, and cooperative sensing.

12.2   Evolution of V2X Technology

As summarized in Table 12.1, in the development of V2X technology, many researchers have contributed solutions to specific challenges of V2X communication protocol. The Inter-Vehicle Hazard Warning (IVHW) system is one of the earliest studied to take the idea of improving vehicle safety based on communication. The project is funded by the German Ministry of Education and Research and the French government. IVHW is a

Engineering Autonomous Vehicles and Robots: The DragonFly Modular-based Approach,
First Edition. Shaoshan Liu.
© 2020 John Wiley & Sons Ltd. Published 2020 by John Wiley & Sons Ltd.

Table 12.1 Summary of V2X solutions for autonomous driving.

Research	Application scenario	Proposed solutions	Communication protocol
IVHW	Safe driving	Warning messages are transmitted as broadcast messages, and vehicle takes a local decision-making strategy	Frequency band of 869 MHz
FleetNet	Safe driving, Internet Protocol-based applications	Uses ad-hoc networking to support multi-hop inter-vehicle communications, proposes a position-based forwarding mechanism	IEEE 802.11 wireless LAN
CarTALK 2000	Cooperative driver assistance applications	Uses ad-hoc communication network to support cooperative driver assistance applications, a spatial aware routing algorithm which takes some spatial information, such as underlying road topology, into consideration	IEEE 802.11 wireless LAN
AKTIV	Safe driving	Use of wireless LAN technology as the latency required for safety-related applications is less than 500 ms	Cellular systems
WILLWARN	Warning applications	Propose a risk detection approach based on in-vehicle data. The warning message includes obstacles, road conditions, low visibility, and construction sites. A decentralized distribution algorithm to transmit the warning message to vehicles approaching the danger spot through V2V communication	IEEE 802.11 wireless LAN
NoW	Mobility and internet applications	A hybrid forwarding scheme considering both network layer and application layer is developed. Also, some security and scalability issues are discussed	IEEE 802.11 wireless LAN
SAFESPOT	Safe driving	An integrated project which aims at using roadside infrastructure to improve driving safety. Detects dangerous situations and shares the warning messages in real time	IEEE 802.11 wireless LAN
simTD	Traffic manipulation, safe driving, and Internet-based applications	Real environment deployment of the whole ITS. The system architecture of simTD can be divided into three parts: ITS vehicle station, ITS roadside station, and ITS central station.	IEEE 802.11p (Dedicated Short Range Communications)

ITS, Intelligent Transportation System.

communication system in which warning messages are transmitted as broadcast messages in the frequency band of 869 MHz [2]. IVHW takes a local decision-making strategy. After the vehicle receives the message, it will do relevant checks to decide whether the warning message is relevant and should be shown to the driver. The majority of the research effort has been on the design of relevant check algorithms. However, as IVHW takes a broadcast mechanism to share the message, there can be a huge waste in both bandwidth and computing resources.

Compared with the broadcast message in IVHW, ad-hoc networking can be a better solution to support multi-hop inter-vehicle communication [3]. FleetNet is another research project using the idea of vehicle communication [4], and it is based on ad-hoc networking. In addition, the FleetNet project also provides a communication platform for some Internet Protocol-based applications. FleetNet is implemented based on the IEEE 802.11 wireless LAN (WLAN) system [5]. For V2V communication, if two vehicles are not directly connected wirelessly, it would need some other vehicles to forward the message for them. Designing the routing and forwarding protocol can be a major challenge. In order to meet the requirements for adaptability and scalability, FleetNet proposed a position-based forwarding mechanism. The idea is to choose the next hop to forward the message based on the geographical location of the vehicle.

CarTALK 2000 is a project focusing on applying ad-hoc communication network to support cooperative driver assistance applications [6]. There can be a major challenge for ad-hoc-based routing in V2V communication because the vehicle network topology is dynamic, and the number of vehicles is frequently changing [7]. In order to solve the problem, a spatial aware routing algorithm is proposed in CarTALK 2000 which takes some spatial information, such as underlying road topology, into consideration.

Compared with FleetNet, CarTALK 2000 achieves better performance as it uses spatial information as additional input for the routing algorithm. Another similarity of CarTALK 2000 and FleetNet is that they are both based on WLAN technology. AKTIV is another project to apply cellular systems in some driving safety applications [8]. One of the reasons that the FleetNet and CarTALK 2000 projects built their system based on WLAN technology is that the latency required for safety-related applications is less than 500 ms. However, with the assumption that a Long-Term Evolution (LTE) communication system can be greatly further developed, cellular systems can be a better choice for sparse vehicle networking.

Meanwhile, some research projects have focused on warning applications based on V2V communication. Wireless Local Danger Warning (WILLWARN) proposed a risk detection approach based on in-vehicle data. The warning message includes obstacles, road conditions, low visibility, and construction sites [9]. Unlike other projects focusing on the V2X technology itself, WILLWARN focuses on enabling V2X technology in some specific scenarios such as the danger spot. Suppose some potential danger is detected in a specific location but there is no vehicle within the communication range that supports the V2X communication technology to share the warning message [10]. To share warning messages, WILLWARN proposed a decentralized distribution algorithm to transmit the warning message to vehicles approaching the danger spot through V2V communication.

The project Network on Wheels (NoW) takes the idea of FleetNet to build vehicle communication based on 802.11 WLAN and ad-hoc networking [11]. The goal of NoW is to set up a communication platform to support both mobility and Internet applications. For example, a hybrid forwarding scheme considering both the network layer and application layer is developed. Also, some security and scalability issues are discussed in NoW.

As the infrastructure also plays a very important part in V2X technology, some studies focus on building safety applications based on cooperation with infrastructure. SAFESPOT is an integrated project which is aimed at using roadside infrastructure to improve driving safety [12]. Through combining information from the on-vehicle sensors and infrastructure sensors, SAFESPOT detects dangerous situations and shares the warning messages in real time. Also, the warning forecast can be improved from milliseconds level to seconds level, thus giving the driver more time to prepare and take action. Five applications are discussed in SAFESPOT, including hazard and incident warning, speed alert, road departure prevention, cooperative intersection collision prevention, and safety margin for assistance and emergency vehicles [13].

In 2007, a non-profit organization called the Car-2-Car Communication Consortium (C2C-CC) was set up to combine all solutions from different projects to make a standard for V2X technology. Since 2010, the focus of work on V2X technology has moved from research topics to the real environment deployment of the whole ITS. One of the most popular deployed projects is simTD [1], targeted on testing the V2X applications in a real metropolitan field. In simTD, all vehicles can connect with each other through Dedicated Short Range Communications (DSRC) technology which is based on IEEE 802.11p. Meanwhile, vehicles can also communicate with roadside infrastructure using IEEE 802.11p. The system architecture of simTD can be divided into three parts: ITS vehicle station, ITS roadside station, and ITS central station. Applications for testing in simTD include traffic situation monitoring, traffic flow information and navigation, traffic management, driving assistance, local danger alert, and Internet-based applications.

Cellular vehicle-to-everything (C-V2X) is designed as a unified connectivity platform which provides low latency V2V and V2I communications [14]. It consists of two modes of communications. The first mode uses direct communication links between vehicles, infrastructure, and pedestrians. The second mode relies on network communication, which leverages cellular networks to enable vehicles to receive information from the Internet. C-V2X further extends the communication range of the vehicle and it supports a high capacity of data for information transmission for vehicles.

12.3 Cooperative Autonomous Driving

Cooperative autonomous driving can be divided into two categories: cooperative sensing and cooperative decision [15]. Cooperative sensing focuses on sharing sensing information between V2V and V2I. This data sharing can increase the sensing range of autonomous vehicles, making the system more robust. The cooperative decision enables a group of autonomous vehicles to cooperate and make decisions.

Some studies have focused on the exploration of applications for cooperative autonomous driving. In [15], four use cases including convoy driving, cooperative lane change, cooperative intersection management, and cooperative sensing are demonstrated. According to the design of AutoNet2030 [16], a convoy is formed of vehicles on multi-lanes into a group and the control of the whole group is decentralized. The safety and efficient control of the convoy requires high-frequency exchanges of each vehicle's dynamic data. As shown in Figure 12.1, a roadside edge server and a cloud server are used to coordinate and manage the vehicles and convoys to go through crossroads safely. One convoy control algorithm in [17] only exchanges dynamic information of the nearby vehicle rather than for all the vehicles within a convoy. This design makes the algorithm easy to converge.

Cooperative lane change is designed to make vehicles or convoys collaborate when changing lanes. Proper cooperative lane change not only can avoid traffic accidents but it also reduces traffic congestion [18]. MOBIL [19] is a general model whose objective is to minimize overall braking induced by lane changes. Cooperative intersection mangement is also helpful for safe driving and traffic control. The World's Smartest Intersection in Detroit [20] focuses on safety and generates data that pinpoints areas where traffic-related fatalities and injuries can be reduced. Effective cooperative intersection management is based on a coordination mechanism between vehicles to vehicles and vehicle to infrastructure.

Cooperative sensing increases the autonomous vehicle sensing range through V2X communication. Meanwhile, cooperative sensing also helps in cutting the cost of building autonomous driving. As vehicles can rely more on the sensors deployed on roadside infrastructure, the cost of on-vehicle sensors can be reduced. In the future, sensor information may become a service to the vehicle provided by the roadside infrastructure.

V2X networking infrastructure is also a very important aspect for cooperative autonomous driving. Heterogeneous Vehicular NETwork (HetVNET) [21] is an initial work on networking infrastructure to meet the communication requirements of the ITS. HetVNET integrates LTE with DSRC [22] because relying on the single wireless access network cannot provide satisfactory services in dynamic circumstances. In [23], an improved protocol stack is proposed to support multiple application scenarios of autonomous driving in

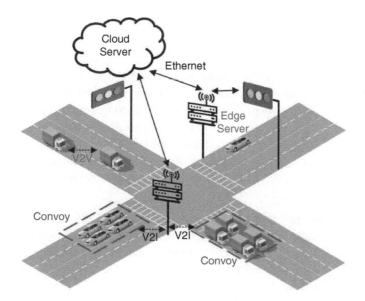

Figure 12.1 V2X communications in crossroads.

HetVNET. In the protocol, the authors redefined the control messages in HetVNET to support autonomous driving.

Similarly, the Vehicular Delay-Tolerant Network (VDTN) [24] is an innovative communication architecture which is designed for scenarios with long delays and sporadic connections. The idea is to allow messages to be forwarded in short-range WiFi connections and reach the destination asynchronously. This property enables VDTN to support services and applications even when there is no end-to-end path in current VANET. In [25] the authors discuss several cooperation strategies for VDTN. The challenge for cooperation in VDTN is how to coordinate the vehicle nodes to share the constrained bandwidth, energy resources, and storage with one another. Furthermore, an incentive mechanism which rewards or punishes vehicles for cooperative behavior is proposed.

In order to support seamless V2X communication, handover is also a very important topic for V2X networking infrastructure. Due to the dynamic changing of the networking topology and the relatively small range of the communication coverage, the handover mechanism in a cellular network is no longer suitable for VANET. Based on proactive resource allocation techniques, in [26] the authors propose a new handover model for VANET. With the help of proactive handover, cooperative services can be migrated through Roadside Units (RSUs) with the moving of the vehicle. Hence, proper designing of proactive handover and resource allocation are essential for developing reliable and efficient cooperative systems.

The development of edge computing in the automotive industry is also very inspiring. The Automotive Edge Computing Consortium (AECC) is a group formed by automotive companies to promote edge computing technologies in future automobiles (https://aecc.org). According to AECC, the service scenarios include intelligent driving, high-definition map, V2Cloud cruise assist, and some extended services such as finance and insurance. In addition, the white paper discusses the service requirements in terms of data source, volume of data generated in vehicle, target data traffic rate, response time, and required availability.

12.4 Challenges

In order to guarantee the robustness and safety of autonomous driving systems, autonomous vehicles are typically equipped with numerous sensors and computing systems, leading to extremely high costs and preventing ubiquitous deployment of autonomous vehicles. Hence, V2X is a viable solution in decreasing the costs of autonomous driving vehicles as V2X enables information sharing between vehicles and computation offloading to RSUs. There are several challenges in achieving cooperative autonomous driving. The challenges and our vision for application scenario of cooperative decision and cooperative sensing are as follows:

Cooperative decision: The challenge of cooperative decisions is handling the dynamic changing topology with a short-range coverage of V2X communications. The design of VDTN is a good way to solve this challenge. Effective proactive handover and resource allocation can be a potential solution. Also, the coming 5G wireless communication [27] provides a way to handle this challenge.

Cooperative sensing: The main challenge of cooperative sensing is sharing the information from infrastructure sensors to autonomous vehicles in real time. Another challenge is to dynamically trade-off the cost of infrastructure sensors and on-vehicle sensors. For the first challenge, edge computing technology can be used to solve the problem because edge computing enables the edge node (vehicle) and edge server (infrastructure) to conduct computation and compression to provide real-time performance. In addition, the trade-off of cost on infrastructure sensors and on-vehicle sensors will be determined by the automobile market.

References

1 Stubing, H., Bechler, M., Heussner, D. et al. (2010). simTD: a car-to-X system architecture for field operational tests [topics in automotive networking]. *IEEE Communications Magazine* 48 (5): 148–154.

2 Chevreuil, M. (2002). IVHW: an inter-vehicle hazard warning system concept within the DEUFRAKO program. *e-Safety Congress and Exhibition*, Lyon, France (16–18 September 2002). The Transportation Research Board.

3 Franz, W., Hartenstein, H., and Mauve, M. (2005). *Inter-Vehicle-Communications Based on Ad Hoc Networking Principles: The FleetNet Project*. Universitätsverlag Karlsruhe.

4 Hartenstein, H., Bochow, B., Ebner, A. et al. (2001). Position-aware ad hoc wireless networks for inter-vehicle communications: the Fleetnet project. In: *Proceedings of the 2nd ACM International Symposium on Mobile Ad Hoc Networking & Computing*, 259–262. ACM.

5 Festag, A., Fußler, H., Hartenstein, H. et al. (2004). Fleetnet: bringing car-to-car communication into the real world. *Computer* 4 (L15): 16.

6 Reichardt, D., Miglietta, M., Moretti, L. et al. (2002). CarTALK 2000: safe and comfortable driving based upon inter-vehicle-communication. In: *2002 IEEE Intelligent Vehicle Symposium*, vol. 2, 545–550. IEEE.

7 Morsink, P.L.J., Hallouzi, R., Dagli, I. et al. (2003). CarTALK 2000: development of a co-operative ADAS based on vehicle-to-vehicle communication. In: *10th World Congress and Exhibition on Intelligent Transport Systems and Services*. IEEE.

8 Yi, C., Gehlen, G., Jodlauk, G. et al. (2008). A flexible application layer protocol for automotive communications in cellular networks. In: *15th World Congress on Intelligent Transportation Systems (ITS 2008)*. ITS World Congress.

9 Schulze, M., Nocker, G., and Bohm, K. (2005). PReVENT: a European program to improve active safety. In: *Proceedings of 5th International Conference on Intelligent Transportation Systems Telecommunications*. ITST.

10 Hiller, A., Hinsberger, A., Strassberger, M., and Verburg, D. (2007). Results from the WILLWARN project. *6th European Congress and Exhibition on Intelligent Transportation Systems and Services*, Aalborg, Denmark (June 2007).

11 Festag, A., Noecker, G., Strassberger, M. et al. (2008). 'NoW–network on wheels': Project objectives, technology and achievements.

12 Toulminet, G., Boussuge, J., and Laurgeau, C. (2008). Comparative synthesis of the 3 main European projects dealing with Cooperative Systems (CVIS, SAFESPOT and COOPERS) and description of COOPERS Demonstration Site 4. In: *2008 11th International IEEE Conference on Intelligent Transportation Systems (ITSC 2008)*, 809–814. IEEE.

13 Bonnefoi, F., Bellotti, F., Scendzielorz, T., and Visintainer, F. (2007). SAFESPOT applications for infrasructurebased co-operative road safety. In: *14th World Congress and Exhibition on Intelligent Transport Systems and Services*, 1–8. ITS World Congress.

14 Papathanassiou, A. and Khoryaev, A. (2017). Cellular V2X as the essential enabler of superior global connected transportation services. *IEEE 5G Tech Focus* 1 (2): 1–2.

15 Hobert, L., Festag, A., Llatser, I. et al. (2015). Enhancements of V2X communication in support of cooperative autonomous driving. *IEEE Communications Magazine* 53 (12): 64–70.

16 De La Fortelle, A., Qian, X., Diemer, S. et al. (2014). Network of automated vehicles: the autonet 2030 vision. ITS World Congress, Detroit, USA.

17 Marjovi, A., Vasic, M., Lemaitre, J., and Martinoli, A. (2015). Distributed graph-based convoy control for networked intelligent vehicles. In: *2015 IEEE Intelligent Vehicles Symposium (IV)*, 138–143. IEEE.

18 Khan, U., Basaras, P., Schmidt-Thieme, L. et al. (2014). Analyzing cooperative lane change models for connected vehicles. In: *2014 International Conference on Connected Vehicles and Expo (ICCVE)*, 565–570. IEEE.

19 Kesting, A., Treiber, M., and Helbing, D. (2007). General lane-changing model MOBIL for car-following models. *Transportation Research Record* 1999 (1): 86–94.

20 Miovision (2018). Miovision unveils the World's Smartest Intersection in Detroit. https://miovision.com/press/miovision-unveils-the-worlds-smartest-intersection-in-detroit (accessed 1 June 2019).

21 Zheng, K., Zheng, Q., Chatzimisios, P. et al. (2015). Heterogeneous vehicular networking: a survey on architecture, challenges, and solutions. *IEEE Communications Surveys and Tutorials* 17 (4): 2377–2396.

22 Kenney, J.B. (2011). Dedicated short-range communications (DSRC) standards in the United States. *Proceedings of the IEEE* 99 (7): 1162–1182.

23 Zheng, K., Zheng, Q., Yang, H. et al. (2015). Reliable and efficient autonomous driving: the need for heterogeneous vehicular networks. *IEEE Communications Magazine* 53 (12): 72–79.

24 Isento, J.N.G., Rodrigues, J.J.P.C., Dias, J.A.F.F. et al. (2013). Vehicular delay-tolerant networks? A novel solution for vehicular communications. *IEEE Intelligent Transportation Systems Magazine* 5 (4): 10–19.

25 Dias, J.A.F.F., Rodrigues, J.J.P.C., Kumar, N., and Saleem, K. (2015). Cooperation strategies for vehicular delay-tolerant networks. *IEEE Communications Magazine* 53 (12): 88–94.

26 Ghosh, A., Paranthaman, V.V., Mapp, G. et al. (2015). Enabling seamless V2I communications: toward developing cooperative automotive applications in VANET systems. *IEEE Communications Magazine* 53 (12): 80–86.

27 Andrews, J.G., Buzzi, S., Choi, W. et al. (2014). What will 5G be? *IEEE Journal on Selected Areas in Communications* 32 (6): 1065–1082.

13

Vehicular Edge Security

13.1 Introduction

The previous chapters reviewed innovations in onboard edge computing and vehicle-to-everything (V2X) infrastructure to make autonomous driving computing more efficient in terms of performance and energy consumption. As mentioned previously, each autonomous vehicle is equipped with or supported by dozens of computing units in the edge and cloud to process the sensor data, to monitor the vehicles' status and to control the mechanical components, etc. Hence, the security threats against these computing units are of paramount concern.

Specifically, the attacks targeting autonomous vehicles could cause terrible traffic accidents, threatening both personal and public safety. In this chapter, we review recent advancements in the security of autonomous vehicles, including sensor security, operating system security, control system security, and communication security. These security problems cover different layers of the autonomous driving edge computing stack.

13.2 Sensor Security

Autonomous vehicles are equipped with various sensors (camera, Global Navigation Satellite System [GNSS], Light Detection and Ranging [LiDAR], etc.) to enable the perception of the surrounding environments. The most direct security threats against autonomous vehicles are attacks against the sensors. With this attack method, attackers can generate incorrect messages or completely block sensor data so as to interfere with autonomous driving behaviors without hacking into the computing system. According to the working principle of sensors, the attackers have many specific attack methods to interfere, blind, or spoof each of them [1].

A camera is the basic visual sensor in autonomous driving systems. Modern autonomous vehicles are usually equipped with multiple cameras with the same or different lenses [2, 3]. In general, many autonomous driving perception workloads take camera images as inputs; for example, object detection and object tracking. The attackers can place fake

Engineering Autonomous Vehicles and Robots: The DragonFly Modular-based Approach,
First Edition. Shaoshan Liu.
© 2020 John Wiley & Sons Ltd. Published 2020 by John Wiley & Sons Ltd.

traffic lights, traffic signs, and traffic objects (cars or pedestrians) to spoof autonomous vehicles and cause them to make the wrong decisions [4]. The cameras can also be interfered with by infrared, so attackers can use a high-brightness infrared laser to blind the cameras, thus preventing these cameras from providing effective images for the perception stage [4, 5].

Autonomous vehicles use GNSS and inertial navigation system (INS) sensors to update the vehicles' real-time locations. Typical attacks against GNSS sensors are jamming and spoofing. The attackers could use out-of-band or in-band signals to intentionally interfere with the function of the GNSS receiver [6]. They could also deploy a GNSS transmitter near the autonomous vehicles to deceive the GNSS receiver by replicating original signals and providing false locations [4, 6]. In addition, the INS sensors are sensitive to magnetic fields, so an extra and powerful magnetic field could effectively interfere with the INS sensors to produce incorrect orientation of the vehicles under attack.

LiDAR provides point clouds of the vehicle's surroundings to enable 3D perception of the environments. LiDAR measures the distance to a target by illuminating the target with pulsed laser light and measuring the reflected pulses. A smart surface which is absorbent or reflective can deceive LiDAR sensors to miss real obstacles in traffic [1], and a light laser pulse illuminating the LiDAR could also manipulate the data sensed by the LiDAR, deceiving the LiDAR to sense objects in incorrect positions and distances [4]. For ultrasonic sensors and radars, which are mostly used for passive perception and the last line of defense for the autonomous vehicles, Yan et al. have successfully spoofed and jammed these two kinds of sensors in the Tesla Autopilot system via the specific signal generator and transmitter [7].

13.3 Operating System Security

One widely used autonomous vehicle operating system is ROS (Robot Operating System). Attackers can target ROS nodes and/or ROS messages. In the ROS running environment, there is no authentication procedure for message passing and new node creation. Attackers can use the IP addresses and ports on the master node to create a new ROS node or hijack an existing one without further authentication [8]. If a service on the node keeps consuming system resources, for example, memory footprint or CPU utilization, it will impact the performance of other normal ROS nodes, even crashing the whole autonomous driving system. The attackers also can use the controlled ROS node to send manipulated messages to disturb other nodes running and output.

As for the attacks on ROS messages, the first security threat is message capture. Attackers can monitor and record every ROS message topic via the IP address and port on the master node. The recorded data are stored in the ROS bag file; attackers can play the ROS bag file to resend some history ROS messages, which will affect current ROS message communication [8]. The message passing mechanism of ROS is based on socket communication, so attackers can sniff the network packets to monitor and intercept the ROS messages remotely without hacking into the master node [9, 10]. The attacks on ROS messages do not need to start or hijack a ROS node; the security threat level is not lower than attack with the ROS node method.

13.4 Control System Security

In modern vehicles, many digital devices and mechanical components are controlled by Electronic Control Units (ECUs). The ECUs are connected to each other via digital buses, which form the in-vehicle network. Controller Area Network (CAN) is the primary bus protocol in the vehicle [11]. CAN is the typical bus topology; there is no master/slave node concept in the CAN bus, so any node connected to the CAN bus can send a message to any other node. Thus, the CAN network usually uses the priority to control access to the bus. The CAN network is isolated to the external network but attackers can hack the digital devices in the vehicle to attack the CAN and ECUs indirectly, which is very dangerous to the vehicle and public.

There are many attack surfaces of the CAN bus. First is the OBD-II port, which is used for vehicle status diagnostics, ECU firmware update, and even vehicle control. The OBD-II port is connected to the CAN bus, so attackers can use the OBD-II device and diagnostic software to sniff the messages on the bus or control the vehicle [12, 13]. Attackers can easily gain access to the CAN bus through OBD-II ports. Second is the media player (e.g. CD player) in the vehicle. The media player needs to receive the control message from the driver and send the status to the screen (user interface), so the media player usually has a connection to the CAN. Attackers can easily flash a malicious code to the CD; when the driver plays the CD, the malicious code can attack the CAN bus [14].

In addition, attackers can utilize the Bluetooth interface in the vehicle. Modern vehicles support Bluetooth connections to smart phones. Attackers can use smart phones to upload malicious applications via Bluetooth to take over the CAN bus, or they can sniff the vehicle status via Bluetooth. It is important to note that attackers can use this interface to attack the vehicle remotely.

Once the attacker hijacks the CAN bus, there are some security threats to the CAN network [12]. The first is broadcast attack. A CAN message is broadcast to all nodes, the attackers can capture and reverse-engineer these messages and inject new messages to induce various actions.

The second is denial of service (DoS) attack. CAN protocol is extremely vulnerable to DoS attacks because of the limited bandwidth. In addition to message flooding attacks, if one hijacked node keeps claiming highest priority in the network, it will cause all other CAN nodes to back off, so the whole CAN network will crash.

The last is no authentication fields. The CAN message does not contain the authentication fields, which means any node can send a packet to any other node without an authentication process, so the attackers can use this to control any node in the CAN network.

13.5 V2X Security

With V2X, vehicles can access the Internet to obtain real-time traffic data (e.g. real-time map and weather data) or leverage the cloud computing for autonomous driving [15], and the vehicle also can communicate with other nodes in the V2X network via some emerging technologies (e.g. Dedicated Short Range Communications [DSRC]) [16]. This V2X network creates many new application scenarios for connected and autonomous vehicles but it also causes more security problems [17–19].

The traditional Internet and ad-hoc networks suffer from many security threats, which may occur in the V2X network but with different manifestations. DoS attack and distributed denial of service (DDoS) attack are two basic attack methods on the Internet. In V2X networks, every node can be an attacker or a victim, causing various traffic problems [20]. If the infrastructure is the victim, it cannot provide real-time service for the nearby vehicles. In contrast, if the vehicle is the victim, it cannot receive the messages from the infrastructure or cloud, and the DoS attack also can interfere with the performance of other tasks on the vehicle, causing unacceptable latency of some autonomous driving applications [1].

In V2X networks, attackers can create multiple vehicles on the road with the same identity or remain anonymous, which we call Sybil attack [21]. The Sybil attack may force the vehicles running on the road to make way for the fake vehicles and prevent other vehicles driving on this road because they are deceived to think that there is a traffic jam. Information forgery is also a common attack; a vehicle can change its identity or send fabricated messages to V2X networks, thus preventing it from being detected or to shirk some of its responsibilities [22]. There are many other traditional network threats, such as replay attack and block hole attack, but the attack method is similar to the threats mentioned above.

The V2X network brings new types of network nodes, such as the infrastructure and pedestrian, so it will have some new threats that are rare in the traditional Internet. The first is about privacy. The communication between the vehicle to pedestrian and vehicle to infrastructure may be based on some short-range protocol (Bluetooth Low Energy and DSRC); if the access authentication is not strict, the privacy of both drivers and pedestrians will be exposed [23]. The second concerns the infrastructure. If the infrastructure (Roadside Unit [RSU]) has been attacked and fake traffic information is broadcast, it can influence the running state of a nearby vehicle.

13.6   Security for Edge Computing

Security is a critical topic for edge computing, so studies on security in some general scenarios may provide solutions for security problems in connected and autonomous vehicle scenarios. The related work can be divided into two categories: network in edge and running environment for edge computing.

Bhardwaj et al. proposed ShadowNet [24], which deploys the edge functions on the distributed edge infrastructure, and aggregates that information about the Internet of Things (IoT) traffic to detect an imminent IoT-DDoS. ShadowNet detects IoT-DDoS 10 times faster than existing approaches and also prevents 82% of traffic from entering the Internet infrastructure, reducing security threats. Yi et al. summarized a method that uses software-defined networking to solve edge network security problems [25], such as network monitoring and intrusion detection and network resource access control. This kind of work will help us solve the related network threats in connected and autonomous vehicle scenarios.

Ning et al. evaluated several trusted execution environments (TEEs) on heterogeneous edge platforms, such as Intel SGX, ARM TrustZone, and AMD SEV, and deployed the TEEs on an edge computing platform to efficiently improve the security with a low-performance overhead [26]. KLRA [27] is a Kernel Level Resource Auditing tool for IoT and edge operating system security. KLRA takes fine-grained events measured with low cost and reports the relevant security warning the first time the behavior of the system is abnormal with this device. This kind of work will help us solve the security problems in the operating system on connected and autonomous vehicles.

Table 13.1 summarizes the security threats and potential defense mechanisms for autonomous vehicles.

Table 13.1 Summary of security threats.

Security category	Security threats	Defense technologies
Sensors	Spoofing cameras by fake traffic objects Jamming GPS receiver by high-power false GPS transmitter Jamming IMU sensor by powerful magnetic field Jamming LiDAR by light laser pulse Jamming and spoofing ultrasonic sensors and MMW radars by specific signal generator	*Multi-sensor data fusion*: System check and correct the sensor data from multiple sources
Operating system	Hijacking ROS node to consume system resources Hijacking ROS node to send manipulated messages Sniffing ROS message to steal private data Repeating the intercepted ROS message to disturb other ROS nodes	*Linux container*: Use the container technology to throttle the resource utilization of each ROS node *Trusted execution environment*: Run the key ROS node in a trusted execution environment
Control system	Hijacking CAN bus by OBD-II port Hijacking CAN bus by media player. Hijacking CAN bus by Bluetooth Injecting manipulated messages on CAN bus DoS attack on CAN bus	*Message encryption*: Encrypt message in CAN bus
V2X	DoS and DDoS attack on vehicle and infrastructure Sybil attack by creating multiple fake vehicles in road Sniffing private data by short-range wireless protocol Broadcasting fake traffic information to nearby vehicles	*Authentication and certification*: The node access to the V2X network should be authenticated and security certificates and keys provided

References

1 Petit, J. and Shladover, S.E. (2015). Potential cyberattacks on automated vehicles. *IEEE Transactions on Intelligent Transportation Systems* 16 (2): 546–556.

2 Liu, S., Tang, J., Zhang, Z., and Gaudiot, J.-L. (2017). Computer architectures for autonomous driving. *Computer* 50 (8): 18–25.

3 Geiger, A., Lenz, P., and Urtasun, R. (2012). Are we ready for autonomous driving? The KITTI vision benchmark suite. In: *2012 IEEE Conference on Computer Vision and Pattern Recognition (CVPR)*, 3354–3361. IEEE.

4 Petit, J, Stottelaar, B., Feiri, M., and Kargl, F. (2015). Remote attacks on automated vehicles sensors: Experiments on camera and LiDAR. *Black Hat Europe 2015*, Amsterdam, the Netherlands (10–13 November 2015).

5 Truong, K.N., Patel, S.N., Summet, J.W., and Abowd, G.D. (2005). Preventing camera recording by designing a capture-resistant environment. In: *International Conference on Ubiquitous Computing*, 73–86. Springer.

6 Ioannides, R.T., Pany, T., and Gibbons, G. (2016). Known vulnerabilities of global navigation satellite systems, status, and potential mitigation techniques. *Proceedings of the IEEE* 104 (6): 1174–1194.

7 Yan, C, Xu, W., and Liu, J. (2016). Can You Trust Autonomous Vehicles: Contactless Attacks Against Sensors of Self-Driving Vehicles. DEF CON 24.

8 Jeong, S.-Y., Choi, I.-J., Kim, Y.-J. et al. (2017). A study on ROS vulnerabilities and countermeasure. In: *Proceedings of the Companion of the 2017 ACM/IEEE International Conference on Human-Robot Interaction*, 147–148. ACM.

9 Lera, F.J.R., Balsa, J., Casado, F. et al. (2016). Cybersecurity in autonomous systems: evaluating the performance of hardening ROS. *Proceedings of the Workshop of Physical Agents (WAF 2016)*, Málaga, Spain (16–17 June 2016).

10 McClean, J., Stull, C., Farrar, C., and Mascareñas, D. (2013). A preliminary cyber-physical security assessment of the robot operating system (ROS). In: *Unmanned Systems Technology XV*, vol. 8741, 874110. International Society for Optics and Photonics.

11 Johansson, K.H., Törngren, M., and Nielsen, L. (2005). Vehicle applications of controller area network. In: *Handbook of Networked and Embedded Control Systems*, 741–765. Springer.

12 Koscher, K., Czeskis, A., Roesner, F. et al. (2010). Experimental security analysis of a modern automobile. In: *2010 IEEE Symposium on Security and Privacy (SP)*, 447–462. IEEE.

13 Wang, Q. and Sawhney, S. (2014). VeCure: a practical security framework to protect the can bus of vehicles. In: *2014 International Conference on the Internet of Things (IOT)*, 13–18. IEEE.

14 Checkoway, S., McCoy, D., Kantor, B. et al. (2011). Comprehensive experimental analyses of automotive attack surfaces. In: *USENIX Security Symposium*, 77–92. USENIX.

15 Liu, S., Tang, J., Wang, C. et al. (2017). A unified cloud platform for autonomous driving. *Computer* 50 (12): 42–49.

16 Hu, J., Chen, S., Zhao, L. et al. (2017). Link level performance comparison between LTE V2X and DSRC. *Journal of Communications and Information Networks* 2 (2): 101–112.

17 Raya, M. and Hubaux, J.-P. (2007). Securing vehicular ad hoc networks. *Journal of Computer Security* 15 (1): 39–68.

18 Engoulou, R.G., Bellaïche, M., Pierre, S., and Quintero, A. (2014). VANET security surveys. *Computer Communications* 44: 1–13.

19 Yang, Y., Wei, Z., Zhang, Y. et al. (2017). V2X security: a case study of anonymous authentication. *Pervasive and Mobile Computing* 41: 259–269.

20 Malla, A.M. and Sahu, R.K. (2013). Security attacks with an effective solution for DOS attacks in VANET. *International Journal of Computer Applications* 66 (22).

21 Yu, B., Xu, C.-Z., and Xiao, B. (2013). Detecting Sybil attacks in VANETs. *Journal of Parallel and Distributed Computing* 73 (6): 746–756.

22 Petit, J., Feiri, M., and Kargl, F. (2011). Spoofed data detection in VANETs using dynamic thresholds. In: *Proceedings of the IEEE Vehicular Networking Conference (VNC)*, 25–32. IEEE Communications Society.

23 Liu, J. and Liu, J. (2018). Intelligent and connected vehicles: current situation, future directions, and challenges. *IEEE Communications Standards Magazine* 2 (3): 59–65.

24 Bhardwaj, K., Chung Miranda, J., and Gavrilovska, A. (2018). Towards IoT-DDoS prevention using edge computing. USENIX Workshop on IIot Topics in Edge Computing (HotEdge 18), Boston, MA.

25 Yi, S., Qin, Z., and Li, Q. (2015). Security and privacy issues of fog computing: a survey. In: *International Conference on Wireless Algorithms, Systems, and Applications*, 685–695. Springer.

26 Ning, Z., Liao, J., Zhang, F., and Shi, W. (2018). Preliminary study of trusted execution environments on heterogeneous edge platforms. In: *2018 IEEE/ACM Symposium on Edge Computing (SEC)*, 421–426. IEEE.

27 Li, D., Zhang, Z., Liao, W., and Zhiwei, X. (2018). KLRA: a Kernel Level Resource Auditing tool for IoT operating system security. In: *2018 IEEE/ACM Symposium on Edge Computing (SEC)*, 427–432. IEEE.

Index

Engineering Autonomous Vehicles and Robots: The DragonFly Modular-based Approach,
First Edition. Shaoshan Liu.
© 2020 John Wiley & Sons Ltd. Published 2020 by John Wiley & Sons Ltd.